DEADLY PARALLELS

D0530895

DEADLY PARALLELS

Film and the Left in Britain
1929–1939

BERT HOGENKAMP

LAWRENCE AND WISHART
LONDON

Lawrence and Wishart Limited
39 Museum Street
London WC1A 1LQ

First published 1986

Photoset in North Wales by
Derek Doyle & Associates, Mold, Clwyd.
Printed in Great Britain by
Oxford University Press

Contents

Illustrations

Preface

The present book is the result of ten years of research into the use of the film medium by the workers' movement in the period between the two world wars, in this case in Great Britain. I started this research because I was convinced of the need to return a past, their own past, to the left-wing (socialist, independent or whatever epithet is preferred) film groups of the 1970s. A past from which they could learn and draw strength. Like many of my generation, who had gained political consciousness as a result of May '68 and the students' movement, I was interested in the relation between politics and the arts, in the nature of political film making. Therefore our endeavour to retrace the roots of political culture, particularly that which existed in the 1920s and 30s. The rediscovery of the work of Willi Münzenberg – the German Communist who had revolutionised left-wing propaganda in the 1920s – was seminal in this respect. The ensuing changes in the economic and political climate have given our research work a new, less clear-cut perspective. But the same goes for the left-wing film groups, which find themselves in a struggle for survival, in which they have to deal with the state rather than with the labour movement. The coming of Channel Four has to a certain extent camouflaged this development in Great Britain: BFI grants and Channel Four subsidies have been responsible for the survival of many groups which otherwise would have had to suspend their activities, as has occurred on the Continent.

In the following study I have reconstructed the history of the workers' and left film movement in Great Britain in the 1930s from the various sources which I have examined: notices and articles in newspapers and other contemporary periodicals, records in archives, interviews with participants, and films which have survived the Blitz, wear, internal combustion or simple neglect. During my researches a remarkable number of films have turned up, making the survival rate a very high one compared to countries like Germany, France, the United States and my own Holland. I have refrained from writing a theoretical discourse. This book is not primarily aimed at an academic readership. Moreover, a highly theoretical approach seemed completely out of place when dealing with a movement which produced virtually no theory, which excelled in its pragmatism, especially compared with similar movements abroad (Germany before 1933, France and the United States). This is not to say that I have not taken care to describe the political context out of which these film groups grew and to which they responded through their work. It has been my intention to let the movement speak for itself by using, as far as possible, quotes from contemporary sources. In accordance with these, I am using the epithets *workers', socialist, left* or *progressive* – but not *independent* – in reference to the film groups mentioned in this book. In my opinion, they defined themselves not so much by their independence from commercial film production, distribution and exhibition, as rather by their dependence – voluntary, self-imposed – on the labour movement. The notion of *independence* was connected with the avant-garde movement (experimental film making) in the 1930s. After the war, when the state started subsidising the arts, independence began to acquire the meaning of 'not made for profit and therefore subsidised by the state'. Of course, the state subsidised Grierson's Empire Marketing Board and General Post Office film units in the 1930s, but none of the workers' or left film groups, not even during the short-lived 1929-31 Labour government.

A lot of emphasis is placed in this book on British-produced films. One might argue, quite justifiably, that to some of the film groups the distribution and exhibition of Soviet films was just as or even more important. After all, these were films made in the first socialist state. The interest they raised was certainly not confined to Communists or even to the working class. Contrary to myth, persisting until today, the Soviet Union did not flood Great Britain with its films. A battle had to be fought in order to get them, followed by another battle against open and hidden censorship. Soviet films were a source of inspiration for all the film groups mentioned in this book. Keeping this in mind, I have described and analysed the British-produced films, their strengths and weaknesses.

Given the costs of film making, then and now, it is not surprising that the film camera was taken up by sympathisers to the cause of labour rather than by workers themselves. I was not in position to make a sociological study of the class background of the film makers involved, but it is conspicuous that building worker Alf Garrard is the only working-class film maker I have hit upon, who actually made a film on the job. There were other juxtapositions than the working-class versus non-working-class background at work in the 1930s: amateur versus professional film makers; films preaching to the converted versus the unconverted; propaganda versus education; art versus politics. The questions they raised have remained unresolved; their relevance in our age of rapid technological development of television, video, cable and satellite cannot be doubted. If the film movement of the 1930s has made one thing perfectly clear, it is that the left cannot afford to sit down and wait. It must act now.

There is a contradictory relation between the public and the private, when one is writing a book. The present one was written during two periods of virtual isolation from the outside world in my study in Amsterdam (1983-84). But nobody is more aware than I am, that the text is the result of the assistance, support and encouragement many have given me. As such it is very much *their* book, but of course they cannot be held responsible for any mistakes I may have made in writing down the final text.

In the first place I would like to thank my mother and my colleagues at the International Telephone Exchange (Amsterdam), who had to put up with me (and my temper) during these periods of writing.

I am particularly grateful to two 'veterans' of the 1930s film movement: Ralph Bond and the late Ivor Montagu. It was the latter who introduced me – then a young student looking for films on the Spanish Civil War – to the subject of this book, when he explained to me the success of his film *Defence of Madrid*. Ivor has always been extremely helpful to me while preparing and writing this book. Sadly, he passed away before I could even show him the proofs. Through Ivor I met Ralph

Bond who, quite typically, received me at the office of the ACTT (Association of Cine- and Television Technicians), in Soho Square, London. Ralph made clear to me the trade-union dimension of left film making in the 1930s and now. He too was always ready to answer my questions.

Many people helped me by making their own research available to me: John Attfield (Bromley), Edmund Frow (Manchester), Steve Jones (Hyde), Peter Latham (London), Dave Russell (London), Trevor Ryan (Hull), Anna Shepherd (London), Victoria Wegg-Prosser (London) and others whose forgiveness I beg for not listing their names.

Terry Dennett (London) not only provided me with references and documents, he also made available some of the stills illustrating this book by enlarging single images from the frame of a number of films. Terry's enthusiasm was also very effective in keeping my spirits high.

Maarten Hin (Haarlem) also provided frame-enlargements which illustrate this book. The illustration on page 15 was reproduced by the Photography Department of the International Institute for Social History (Amsterdam).

Donald Alexander (Dundee), Charlie Mann (Wiveliscombe) and the late Frank Jackson (London) were so kind as to allow me to interview them on their film experiences in the 1930s.

Patricia Cockburn (Youghal, Eire), Idris Cox (Talywain), Norman McLaren (Montreal, Canada), A.L. Morton (Clare) and Ernie Trory (Brighton) kindly answered my letters.

For my researches I have largely relied on the extensive collections of the International Institute for Social History (Amsterdam) and the Marx Memorial Library (London). Other libraries and archives I have consulted include the British Film Institute Library (London), British Museum Newspaper Library (Colindale), John Grierson Archive (Stirling), Labour Party Library (London), Manchester Working-Class Movement Library, Manchester Studies Archive, National Museum of Labour History (London), Nederlands Filmmuseum (Amsterdam), Public Record Office (Kew), South Wales Miners' Library (Swansea), TUC Library (London) and University College Swansea. I would like to thank all the Librarians and their assistants for their kind help.

Virtually all the films mentioned in this book were viewed in

London, in the viewing cubicles of the National Film Archive, the cutting room of Metropolis Pictures or the office of ETV. I would like to thank Jeremy Boulton, Elaine Burrows, Jonathan Lewis, Elizabeth Taylor-Mead and Stanley Forman for giving me the opportunity to view the films.

Many people put me up during those ten years, when I came over from Amsterdam for research in Great Britain: Jenni, Ros and Geoffrey, Peter and Lesley, Leena and Sukhi, my WFA friends, Peter and Elizabeth, Philip and Margareth, Jeff and Eva. Thank you all for your wonderful hospitality.

I would like to thank the publishers of this book for their patience. After all, I have been behind schedule all the time ...

John Attfield was so kind as to go over the text, checking it for inconsistencies and linguistic errors.

Last but not least, I would like to thank Stanley Forman for his support for my work. He has done more than anybody else in coaxing me, without harsh words, into finishing the manuscript of this book. Through ETV Films – the company he runs together with Betty Baker – Stanley has assisted many young film makers, in a way worthy of a true heir to Kino or the Progressive Film Institute. I dedicate this book to him.

Chapter 1

Labour's Eyes

'The eyes are more exact witnesses than the ears,' began the Labour Party's circular on 'Labour Cinema Propaganda' issued in March 1920. According to the circular, the cinema had become the 'new form of political warfare [which] may have serious consequences at election times' and therefore had to be counteracted with 'effective measures'.[1] Twenty-five years after the introduction of the cinema in Great Britain, the parliamentary representatives of the labour movement came to this conclusion.[2] Why such a belated reaction?

In 1898 the Manchester, Salford and District Independent Labour Party (ILP) proudly announced its 'sixth Grand Annual Social' at St James's Hall in Manchester.[3] One of the many attractions of this 'Greatest Labour Social on Earth' was the projection of 'Living Pictures by the Cinematograph'. This – probably the first ever film show organised by a British working-class body – took place on Friday 25 February 1898. The report in *Clarion* mentioned only that 'the cinematograph purveyed a series of living pictures'.[4] Given the music hall character of this ILP social – other attractions included dance music, palmistry, skirt dancing (by one of the Pankhurst daughters!) and humorous entertainment – one can assume that the film show simply represented the introduction of an entertainment novelty without any political content. There is no indication that the films screened that evening were propagating the cause of labour.

Visual propaganda was, however, by no means unfamiliar in the British labour movement of that time. One of the direct precursors of the cinematograph, the 'magic lantern' slide, was used with great effect for that purpose. To contemporaries photography still held the 'aura of truth'. 'Socialism on the Screen' was the title of a lecture organised by the Peckham branch of the Social Democratic Federation (SDF) on 26 April 1892. Publicity in the SDF newspaper *Justice* makes clear that it was not so much the socialist future that the sixty lantern slides to be screened at the lecture would illustrate; rather they would show 'shots from the camera at the old order of things'.[5] For many years the lantern projector had also played an important part in popular entertainment – hence its epithet 'magic'.[6] Combining this tradition of popular entertainment with the 'aura of truth' generally attached to photography, 'Whiffly Puncto' toured the country 'with his celebrated magic picters'. His main act was entitled 'Merrie England', a slide show with '163 dissolving views and accompanied by music' based on Robert Blatchford's best-selling book.[7] 'Whiffly Puncto' was William Palmer, a Lancashire artist who had worked with Blatchford. A contemporary labour periodical described the 'Greatest Lantern Show on Earth'[8] as follows:

> Whiffly Puncto's lecture abounds in wit and clever points. The limelight views which accompany it are arranged with masterly consideration for the lesson he seeks to teach ... The comparisons between the reeking slums and the princely palaces are described and depicted with a fearful vividness which cannot fail to convince the most thoughtless that some more drastic remedy is required than any yet prescribed by leaders of our nation.[9]

Or in Whiffly's own words, 'Once seen, never forgotten'.[10] This motto might well have rung true for Robert Tressell, the author of *The Ragged Trousered Philanthropists*. The 'Pandorama' in Chapter 29 of this novel reads like a detailed description of Whiffly's 'Merrie England' programme, with the presenter Bert abounding the same kind of wit and the pictures displaying a similar class-based analysis of society.

In 1895 the Clarion movement made an effort to organise those professional photographers who sympathised with the Labour movement, together with the few workers who possessed their own cameras, into the Clarion Camera Club. According to its secretary J. Cruwys Richards, a Birmingham photographer:

WHIFFLY PUNCTO

IS COMING

With his Celebrated

MAGIC PICTERS,

And will give his

FAMOUS LECTURE

'Merrie England'

In

PICTON HALL,

On

Saturday, 29th February,

Illustrated by

163 DISSOLVING VIEWS

And accompanied by Music.

Accompanist - - *HARRY BESWICK*

The piano will be played by " Clarionette,'
So every *Solo* must be a *Duet.*

Admission—SIXPENCE.

N.B.—The overflow Meeting will be held outside, and will
be addressed by the Policeman on the beat. No collection

Advertisement, *Labour Chronicle*, March 1896

... in showing the glaring discrepancies between the lives of the classes and masses we may be useful. On the one hand the stately palace, a monument of artistic instinct and skill of the workers, standing in one of Britain's fairest spots, nestling, maybe, at the foot of a rugged hill, or embowered in a fertile valley; but on all four quarters of the compass, the country fresh and pure, no sign of factory, furnace, or mill, wherein the life blood of the people is being drained away. On the other hand the dwelling-place of the toilers. Pent all day in the vitiated air of the sweater's den; at night they take their rest in the foul, unwholesome slum; at all points of the compass nothing but brick and plaster, smoke and filth, degradation and despair.[11]

In his columns in the *Scout* (the monthly journal for the 'cadre' of the Clarion movement) J. Cruwys Richards paid much attention to technical matters and published an article on the making of lantern slides by F.W. Knowles, a Liverpool photographer.[12] The actual subject-matter of these lantern slides became a matter of concern in 1896, following a request by the London Fabian Society for new slides 'illustrating social and economic evil'.[13] The secretary of the Clarion Camera Club passionately appealed to members: 'it is really important work for the *Socialist Photographer*' (my italics, B.H.)[14]

This prototype of the 'Socialist Photographer' disappeared with the demise of the Clarion Camera Club, before the turn of the century. But the basic principle of juxtaposing the old and the new, the capitalist and the worker, was adopted by successors such as the Parks Press Studio, Fleet Street, London. This socialist photo agency advertised in 1907 with the slogan: 'Socialist and Labour Photographs – Pictures Illustrating Social Evils. Photographs of Every Phase of Life – From the Slum to the Palace'.[15] 'Lantern Slides Supplied', it added. This advertisement was published in *The Deadly Parallel*, a periodical which offered ample illustration of such juxtapositions:

Everywhere you go in the world's richest city, you meet life's 'deadly parallels'. Sumptuous wealth on one hand; abject poverty on the other. These terrible contrasts are presented most forcibly by London's two great classes of unemployed – the exploited poor, and the idle rich.[16]

To illustrate this point *The Deadly Parallel* published a still photograph of an 'Unemployed Workers' Parade – Embankment' next to one of an 'Unemployed Church Parade – Hyde Park'. *The Deadly Parallel*, was an illustrated monthly, edited by W.B. Northrop. Only three issues appeared, from October to December 1907. *The Deadly Parallel* advocated a radical programme of land nationalisation and Georgeite land tax schemes to relieve the plight of the poor, under the motto 'Equal opportunity for All – Privilege for None'. Lay-out and illustrations were used to convince the readers of the deadliness of the parallels quoted by the magazine.

The application of the principle of 'deadly parallels' in films produced by the labour movement was to take a long time, although the movement showed a certain awareness of the attraction that the new medium had for the workers. In February 1908, for example, the Southwark ILP and the Southwark Workers Unemployed Committee used an orchestra and a 'short cinematograph entertainment' to draw a big crowd at a meeting in the Surrey Theatre.[17] The main speaker was Ramsay MacDonald. A newspaper reported that 'the Surrey Theatre was packed'.[18] Had the workers come to hear MacDonald or to see the films?

By the outbreak of the First World War the cinematograph had ceased to be a simple music-hall attraction among many others. All over the country cinemas were built to exhibit films on a permanent basis. The emphasis changed from just showing films, to showing particular films. The feature film made its appearance. The influence of the cinema on the regular patrons of picture houses became a topic of heated debate. Film historian Rachael Low pointed out: 'The 1912 coal strikes, it seems, failed to lead to the usual violence because the strikers spent their temporary freedom at the pictures.'[19]

In 1909 a Cinematograph Act was passed by Parliament, providing for the necessary safety regulations in connection with the exhibition of films. Administration of the Act was left to the local authorities. It made no provision for the censorship of films exhibited by cinema owners granted a licence under the Act. However in 1912 the film trade itself took the initiative to set up the British Board of Film Censors (BBFC), after a public outcry against the indecency of cinematographic representations (crime, sexual perversion, etc.), had started to affect cinema attendances. Although the local authorities retained the right to exercise their own kind of film censorship (or non-censorship), the BBFC's decisions were considered to be binding by virtually all of them.

During the First World War the cinema was used on a large scale for propaganda purposes. Cameramen went to France to film the actual fighting at the front. At home the cinemas showed a great number of patriotic pictures, though it was claimed by some that simply making people forget the horrors of the war for a couple of hours was their biggest contribution to the war effort. In 1917 the Department of Information formed a Cinematograph Branch, which after the reorganisation in 1918 that changed the Department into the Ministry of Information, became a Cinematograph Department. It produced two feature films and a great number of short films for various government departments, besides handling many other films.[20] Moreover, American and German exercises in film propaganda caused a heightened sense of awareness of the medium's importance.

It is therefore not surprising that the Labour Party's 1920 circular on Labour Cinema Propaganda referred explicitly to the war:

> During the War the Cinematograph became a powerful instrument of propaganda in the hands of the Government. The experience gained in this attractive and striking method of publicity is now being used by capitalist interest in various ways to undermine and check the progress of Labour throughout the country ...[21]

The circular was the result of an inquiry into the subject of film propaganda by the party's subcommittee on Literature, Publicity and Research. According to the minutes of a meeting on 11 November 1919,

> suggestions were made for adapting Cinema films to the purpose of propaganda. Estimates were submitted for producing a film illustrating life and labour conditions in mining areas. A scheme outlined by Captain Kendall (Labour candidate for Stroud) was discussed, proposing the formation of a company to produce films which could be used by local organisation in local halls.[22]

The Executive Committee of the Labour Party discussed the proposal and decided to refer it back for further consideration by the subcommittee.[23] On 18 December 1919 a special meeting, chaired by Sidney Webb, was held

> to discuss the formation of a syndicate with the double object of producing films that could be used by the ordinary trade, but which would be more or less of propaganda character; and secondly, to produce other films for use in a portable projector which could be hired out or sold to local Labour organisations for propaganda, especially in rural constituencies.[24]

As a result of this meeting two further reports were prepared, one on film projectors (by H.D. Harben and C.W. Kendall) and another on labour propaganda films available from commercial renters (by Herbert Farjeon and Walter Peacock). Harben and Kendall had no difficulty in recommending two portable projectors. Farjeon and Peacock, however, came to the conclusion 'that the manufacturers of films have not made any films presenting directly or indirectly the Labour point of view'.[25] In February 1920 the subcommittee decided to draft a circular to be sent to local Labour parties, outlining 'a scheme to supply the local organisations with portable projectors and films for propaganda'.[26]

In March 1920 the circular was finally sent out, after a final revision by Sidney Webb. As outlined by the subcommittee, it dealt with the purchase of portable projectors and the supply by commercial renters of 'films not purely propaganda, but capable of being used to point a moral [and] films of ordinary and topical interest'. It was pointed out that films 'of a purely propaganda nature will have to be specially made and then hired out by the central organisation to whomsoever may require them'. In the meantime other films had to be used 'in the nature of stop-gaps, and later on, as matters develop, we anticipate being able to make some films ourselves, and by letting them out to the trade in the usual way cheapen the cost of supply to Labour organisations'.[27] The circular ended with an appeal to local Labour parties to act on the proposals. The response must have been very meagre. Notwithstanding the donation of a sum of £100 for the proposed syndicate, nothing further was heard of the whole scheme.[28]

Why did this 'Labour Cinema Propaganda' circular fail to get a response from the local Labour parties? For the purchase of projection equipment or the hire of films from commercial renters local parties were not dependent on the scheme proposed in the circular. What they could not get through normal channels were films of an overtly Labour propaganda character. However on this crucial point the circular was vague. It did not even mention the original idea of making 'a film illustrating life and labour conditions in mining areas'. An outright appeal for financial support towards a Labour film production company may well have aroused more enthusiasm.

Moreover, by concentrating entirely on the exhibition of films by means of portable projectors, the circular ignored other possibilities. In October 1922 the Scottish revolutionary John Maclean stood as a candidate in a Glasgow municipal election. His election address stressed the principle of municipalisation: 'We favour municipal theatres, music halls, picture houses, and other forms of amusement for the people.'[29] Maclean's idea would undoubtedly have met fierce resistance from the trade, but this did not justify the complete absence of a municipal cinema policy on the part of the Labour Party, which in other respects firmly espoused policies of municipal enterprise. The Labour press often bemoaned the influence of the BBFC. Under the 1909 Cinematograph Act local authorites – including Labour-controlled ones – were free to ignore the BBFC's decisions. They could permit the exhibition of films banned by the BBFC, or suppress films approved by it. The Labour Party never formulated a clear policy on this matter.

Shortly before the Labour Party considered the matter of film propaganda, *The Times* had carried the following note: 'A cinema in the Rhondda Valley has been bought for £8,500 by one of the colliery workman's [*sic*] committees'.[30] The identity of the committee was not given. It was very rare for a workmen's committee to spend such a large sum on the purchase of a cinema, but many had their main hall equipped with screen and projection booth. The minute book of the Ogmore Vale Workmen's Hall and Institute records a session of its Bioscope Committee on 1 May 1912, during which the selection of film programmes was discussed.[31] In the minute book of the Mardy Workmen's Institute the prices of admission of the cinema were listed as 7d. (balcony) and 5d. (body of hall), as from 27 November 1918.[32] George Baker has recalled how the Parc and Dare Workmen's Institute built its own cinema in 1913, with the workmen's contributions covering the costs.[33] Although the heyday of these South Wales miners' cinemas in the 1930s was yet to come, a number were already operating at the time when the 'Labour Cinema Propaganda' circular was sent out. Together with halls with projection equipment elsewhere in Britain, their number might have been sufficient to provide some sort of financial guarantee for the production of a Labour propaganda film. Why did the Labour Party fail to consider this unique possibility? One can only guess that a rather strict view of the separation of entertainment from propaganda was to blame. The miners went to the cinemas of their Halls and Institutes to be entertained. They were supposed to be already converted to the cause of the Labour and hence there was no need for Labour Cinema Propaganda in Workmen's Halls or Miners' Institutes.

The successful combination of entertainment and propaganda precisely characterised the Soviet films of the 1920s. Their introduction in the United Kingdom, from 1924 onwards, brought about a fundamental change: the excuse of the absence of films presenting the Labour point of view could now be countered. A crucial role in the introduction of Soviet films into Western Europe and the United States was played by the Berlin-based relief organisation Internationale Arbeiter Hilfe (Workers' International Relief). This organisation had been founded in 1921 to provide relief for the famine-stricken areas in the Soviet Union. For this purpose it mobilised the latest propaganda methods at its disposal, such as the illustrated press and the cinema. The British section, first known as WIRR (Workers' International Russian Relief), and later, after the Russian famine had come to an end, as Workers' International Relief (WIR), published its own lavishly illustrated monthly, *Soviet Russia Pictorial* (1923-24) and *Workers' International Pictorial* (1924-25).[34] As distinct from other countries, however, the British section was rather slow in making use of film propaganda. Films on the Russian famine, produced by the German WIR, were used by the German, Dutch and French sections in order to collect money and sell bonds for the First Workers' Loan to Soviet Russia.[35] For some reason the plans of the British WIR to use the cinema failed to materialise.

It had all looked very promising in August 1923, when Edgar T. Whitehead published an article on 'The Film Work of the WIRR' in *Soviet Russia Pictorial*. Whitehead summed up the contents of a number of WIRR films 'which it is hoped to shortly place before British workers'. Top of the list was the *International May Day Film* 'showing the Workers Demonstrations in all the chief capital cities of Europe'.[36] Whitehead described the British contribution:

> The London demonstration is remarkable for the thousands of policemen who accompanied the demonstration – police are seen everywhere. The film also shows fine 'close-ups' of that fine old internationalist Alex. Gossip speaking from platform four. He has taken part in more May Day Demonstrations than we care to remember. Comrades Wall and Goldsmith are also shown speaking, and Comrade Mark Starr pokes his nose in front of the camera, as large as life, just as the big sweep-round is being taken in the park.[37]

Other films mentioned in the article include the *Vorowski Film*[38] and the *Children's Film of Russia*.[39] Whitehead pointed out that

> different national committees have adopted various methods of bringing these films before the Workers in their respective countries. The French committee has purchased a motor van with cinema apparatus complete, which tours France from town to town ... In Berlin, the German National Committee has purchased a Cinema Theatre outright, situated in the heart of the working quarter of Berlin. Here are shown all the above-mentioned films, and also the best Russian art films, such as *Polikushka, Iola, The Miracle of the Soldier Ivan*, and many others.[40]

What Whitehead forgot to mention was how the British committee was going to show these films. It seems that the organisation did discuss the purchase of a van to be fitted out with film projection equipment, but the plan fell through.[41]

It is by no means certain that any of the films listed by Whitehead were ever used by the British WIR, with one exception. In the autumn of 1924 the WIR released the Russian

feature film *Polikushka*. Based on a Leo Tolstoy story and
starring the well-known actor Ivan Moskvin, this film had been
received very favourably in Western Europe. *Polikushka* was
shown at St James's Picture Palace, London, from 7 to 14
October 1924.[42] This date was no coincidence: it was the week
when the Labour Party held its annual conference in London,
and the WIR hoped that this would result in extra publicity for
the film. However, the defeat of the first Labour government in
Parliament and the preparations for the forthcoming election
completely overshadowed the premiere of the Soviet film.
Polikushka received favourable reviews in, for example, the *Daily
Herald* ('the greatest screen tragedy yet produced'[43]), but did
not attract big crowds. In his pamphlet *Erobert den Film!*
('Conquer the Film!') in 1925 WIR secretary Willi Münzenberg
qualified the effort 'agitationally [as] a fair success, financially
less satisfying'.[44] *Polikushka* was advertised as being available to
'Trade Unions and Co-operative Societies [at] special terms',
because the WIR was 'loth to leave it wholly to capitalist
exhibitors'.[45] How often it was shown by these organisations
cannot be traced.

A last attempt by the British WIR to use the cinema for
propaganda purposes has been recorded. At an unknown date
a film group was formed in Bethnal Green, London. It seems
that lack of money forced the four members of the group to
abandon their original idea of making films. Instead they
resorted to the cheaper method of putting together lantern
slide shows.[46] Given the importance attributed to film work by
the WIR, the record of the British section was a very poor one.
Still, the directives given from the WIR headquarters had been
simple and clear. Münzenberg's pamphlet *Erobert den Film*!
offers a good example.

In the first chapter Münzenberg stressed the need for the
working-class movement to come to terms with the film
medium. He tried to convince his readers with simple Marxist
logic. Recalling the reception of the anti-Soviet film *Todesreigen*
('Deathdance') in Germany, Münzenberg wrote:

> In some industrial areas the workers revolted against this
> slanderous picture and wrecked without hesitation – as in
> Leipzig – the projection equipment and burned the piece of
> slander. The revolt of the workers was justified and

understandable, but it is reminiscent of the events in the early days of capitalism, when the workers who felt themselves threatened by the machines, in their first instinctive defence destroyed the machines and burned the factories, because these ousted their manual labour. Only later the proletarians learned that it makes no sense to destroy the machines, but that it is much more important to conquer the machines and use them in such a way that the workers will benefit from them. The same goes today for the film.'[47]

In case this was not convincing enough, Münzenberg quoted leading Communists (Lenin, Zinoviev, Lunarcharsky, Voroshilov and Clara Zetkin) who had stressed the importance of the film medium for the movement. The third chapter was devoted to the production of films. After all, 'one of the major obstacles in the attempt to show socialist and revolutionary films, was, in the past, the fact that there were none.'[48] The Russian revolution had fundamentally changed this situation. 'The possibility of making revolutionary mass films is feasible through the Russian film industry. Herewith is created the first condition for the introduction and development of a proletarian film propaganda on a large scale.'[49] The second stage was treated in the next chapter: the creation of an exhibition network in various countries. Münzenberg paid special attention to the ways in which the national WIR sections had solved this problem. In the last chapter he listed the films produced by the WIR and the production schedule for 1925 of the WIR-owned Mezhrabpom Film Studio in Moscow.

Apart from the few abortive attempts mentioned above, Münzenberg's ideas on film propaganda were not followed in Great Britain. The reason is not quite clear. Münzenberg's pamphlet was never translated or even summarised in the British left press, but this accounts only partially for this failure.[50] In the end Soviet films reached Great Britain via the Berlin-based WIR organisation Prometheus Film (founded in 1925), which handled their distribution and sales in Western Europe on strictly commercial terms. After the signal success of *Battleship Potemkin* (directed by Sergei Eisenstein) demand for Soviet films increased massively. They made an enormous impression on many artists and intellectuals.[51] The British rights for *Battleship Potemkin* were acquired by the London firm

Film Booking Offices, which saw its attempts to release the film thwarted by the BBFC and the London County Council (LCC). What the *Sunday Worker* called the 'World's Greatest Film' was banned from British cinema screens.[52] A new strategy was required, and a different organisation to put it into practice.

Notes

1. 'Labour Cinema Propaganda', circular, the Labour Party, March 1920. The quotation is from Heraclitus.

2. The first public film exhibitions in Great Britain took place in 1895 and 1896. The various claims are listed in Rachael Low and Roger Manvell, *The History of the British Film, 1896-1906*, London 1948, p.113.

3. *Clarion*, 19 February 1898, p.62.

4. Ibid., 5 March 1898, p.75.

5. *Justice*, 2 April 1892, p.3.

6. See Michael Chanan, *The Dream that Kicks, The Prehistory and Early Years of Cinema in Britain*, London, 1980.

7. *Labour Chronicle*, February 1896, p.29.

8. Ibid., October 1896, p.155.

9. Ibid., March 1896, p.34.

10. Ibid., October 1896, p.155.

11. *The Scout*, June 1895, p.72.

12. Ibid., August 1895, pp.139-40.

13. Ibid., April 1896, p.144.

14. Ibid.

15. *The Deadly Parallel*, October 1907, p.8.

16. Ibid., p.1.

17. *South London Press*, 7 February 1908, p.2. For further information on the Southwark campaign against unemployment, see Dave Russell, *Southwark Trades Council. A Short History 1903-1978*, London 1978., pp.4-5.

18. *South London Press*, 7 February 1908, p.2.

19. Rachael Low, *The History of the British Film, 1906-1914*, London 1949, p.32.

20. Rachael Low, *The History of the British Film, 1914-1918*, London 1950, pp.34-8.

21. 'Labour Cinema Propaganda', loc. cit.

22. Minutes, Subcommittee on Literature, Propaganda and Research, the Labour Party, 11 November 1919, p.4.

23. Minutes, Labour Party Executive Committee, 12 November 1919, p.46.

24. Minutes, Meeting on Film Propaganda, Labour Party, 18 December 1919.

25. Report on Labour Propaganda Films, filed under: Minutes, Meeting on Film Propaganda, Labour Party, 18 December 1919.

26. Minutes, Subcommittee on Literature, Publicity and Research, Labour Party, 9 February 1920.

27. 'Labour Cinema Propaganda', loc. cit.

28. Minutes, Finance Subcommittee, Labour Party, 18 March 1920; 'Statement of accounts, year ending December 31st, 1920', in *Report of the Twenty-First Annual Conference of The Labour Party, Brighton, 1921*, London 1922, p.71.

29. John Maclean, 'Kinning Park election address', quoted in Nan Milton, *John Maclean*, London 1973, p.271.

30. *The Times*, 27 September 1919, p.3.

31. Minutes, Bioscope Committee, Ogmore Vale Workmen's Hall and Institute, 1 May 1912 (in University College Swansea).

32. Minutes, Mardy Workmens Institute, 27 November 1918 (in University College Swansea).

33. Hywel Francis, interview with George Baker, 18 July 1974, transcript, p.8 (in South Wales Miners' Library, Swansea).

34. *Soviet Russia Pictorial* and *Workers' International Pictorial* were modelled after *Sowjet-Russland im Bild* and *Hammer und Sichel*, illustrated magazines published by the German WIR. Whereas the latter was able to extend its magazine into the extremely popular *AIZ* (Arbeiter-Illustrierte-Zeitung), the British WIR could not continue its publication. In December 1929 some members of the *Sunday Worker* staff made another attempt and published *WIN* (Workers Illustrated News). Due to lack of money only one issue of *WIN* could be published. See Terry Dennett, 'The Evolution of an Illustrated Workers' Literature', in: *Photography/Politics: One*, London 1979, pp.114-5.

35. See Rolf Surmann, *Die Münzenberg-Legende. Zur Publizistik der revolutionären deutschen Arbeiterbewegung 1921-1933*, Cologne 1983, pp.59-61; Bert Hogenkamp, ' "Hier met de film". Het gebruik van het medium film door de communistische beweging in de jaren twintig en dertig', in *Cahiers over de geschiedenis van de Communistische Partij Nederland*, No.8 (April 1983), p.79; 'Filme der IAH in Frankreich', in *Not und Brot*, No.40 (1925), p.11; 'Le Cinéma du Peuple', in *Bulletin du SOI*, April 1925, p.11.

36. In Germany this film was distributed under the title *Völkermai* ('Peoples' May Day').

37. *Soviet Russia Pictorial*, No.3, August 1923, p.4.

38. This film on the funeral of the assassinated Soviet diplomat Vorovski was distributed in Germany under the title *Eines russischen Diplomaten letzte Fahrt* ('The Last Trip of a Russian Diplomat').

39. This film on child-care in the Soviet Union, featuring the WIR children's homes, was distributed in Germany under the title *Kinderheime und Kindererziehung in Sowjet-Russland* ('Children's Homes and Child Education in Soviet Russia').

40. *Soviet Russia Pictorial*, No.3, August 1923, p.5.

41. See Terry Dennett, 'England; The (Workers') Film & Photo League' in *Photography/Politics: One*, p.101.

42. *Daily Herald*, 7 October 1924, p.8.

43. Ibid., 11 October 1924, p.7.

44. Willi Münzenberg, *Erobert den Film! Winke aus der Praxis für die Praxis proletarischer Filmpropaganda*, Berlin 1925; reprinted in: Willi Lüdecke, *Der Film in Agitation und Propaganda der revolutionären deutschen Arbeiterbewegung* (1919-1933), West Berlin 1973, p.93.

45. *Workers' International Pictorial* No.7 November 1924, p.5.

46. See Terry Dennett, 'England: The (Workers') Film & Photo League, p.102.

47. Münzenberg, op.cit., p.80.

48. Ibid., p.86.

49. Ibid., p.89.

50. This happened in the United States, where the New York *Daily Worker* published a summary in its issue of 23 July 1925, p.3.

51. See Herbert Marshall (ed.), *The Battleship Potemkin*, New York 1978; Helmut Kresse, *Panzerkreuzer Potemkin, Siegeslauf eines Films*, Illustrierte historische Hefte 18, East Berlin 1979.

52. *Sunday Worker*, 27 May 1928, p.7.

Chapter 2

Workers' Film Societies

In the *Sunday Worker* of 23 September 1928 the film critic Henry Dobb (the pen-name of Aubrey Flanagan) wrote:

> Since *Potemkin* first staggered the world the Russian Cinema has continued to turn out films that are intellectually, dramatically, and cinematographically miles above any others ... With them the cinema comes to fruition. Repeated attempts to secure the showing of these in public have failed. And nothing much has been done after the first rebuffs. It is true that the Film Society hope to show *Mother* and *Bed and Sofa* during the coming season, but unless my information is incorrect these will be seen in a trimmed, bowdlerised version. And at any rate the Film Society with its minimum subscription of twenty-five shillings is not for the class for whom the Russian workers' productions were made. Kenneth Macpherson, the courageous spirit who edits *Close-Up*, has done more than any man living to champion the cause of the Russian Cinema. Now he wants to do something concrete to get these masterpieces of the cinema before the workers. Since it seems impracticable at the moment to obtain a public showing, he is forming a society which, although to avoid conflicts with censor and similar authorities it will be private, will be so arranged with subscription and entrance fee as to permit of any ordinary film fan being a member and a spectator. It is proposed to screen as many as possible of the Russian films in their entirety and with the original settings and music. Performances would be held at a time and place of arranged convenience, in London. If the venture is a success the experiment would be repeated in centres where interest is shown, Manchester, Birmingham, Cardiff, or Clydebank ...[1]

Macpherson's strategy seemed simple, but before it could be

carried out various obstacles had to be removed.

The Film Society mentioned by Dobb had been founded in 1925 with the object of showing films of artistic interest, which could not be seen in the ordinary cinemas, to members only. The idea had been derived from the existence of a similar body in the theatre world (the Stage Society, founded in 1889) and the network of 'ciné-clubs' in France. For twenty-five shillings per season the Film Society offered its members six to eight showings of films which were either considered commercially not viable by the film trade or had run into trouble with the BBFC. The film trade initially looked suspiciously at the activities of the new society, but left it alone when it discovered that no harm was being done to its interests. The Film Society had more trouble securing a permit from the London County Council (LCC), the licensing authority under the 1909 Cinematograph Act. Undoubtedly its respectable, predominantly intellectual, membership helped in getting a favourable decision (albeit by a small majority) from the LCC. This meant that the Film Society was able to show its members a film like *Battleship Potemkin*, which had been banned both by the BBFC and the LCC.[2]

There was no Act of Parliament covering the censorship of films. Two Acts had a bearing on certain aspects of the cinema: the Cinematograph Act of 1909 and the Cinematograph Films Act of 1927. The purpose of the former was to invest local authorities with the necessary power to take measures regarding safety at the exhibition of inflammable film. The latter restricted 'blind booking' (i.e. enforced booking of films before they could be seen) and decreed a quota of British films to be distributed and exhibited. As was pointed out in Chapter One, virtually all the local authorities took the decisions of the BBFC – an institution created and sponsored by the film trade, without any legal backing – as the criterion of what to allow and what not to allow. If the BBFC objected to a film, two courses were left open. Firstly one could apply for permission to the relevant county or borough council. The other possibility was offered by the use of non-inflammable film stock, for the Cinematograph Act of 1909 only covered inflammable film. In this case one had to use a building or hall without a cinematograph licence issued under the 1909 Act. In the 1920s non-inflammable stock was not current; only in

France Pathé had tried to create a market for it without much commercial success (after the legal measures which would have made its use compulsory had failed to materialise). It was only applied in 'home-movies' which used a different and smaller format – 16mm or 9.5mm – as against the commercial 35mm format. In the late 1920s the so-called small film format did not seem a practical solution to those who were anxious to show banned Soviet films to the workers. They sought to extend the privilege enjoyed by the Film Society of London to other film societies: workers' film societies.[3]

When Henry Dobb disclosed the intention of starting a workers' film society in the *Sunday Worker*, such societies were already active in other West European countries. In January 1928 in Germany an appeal was launched for the foundation of a Volksfilmverband (Popular Association for Film Art), signed by some ninety progressive artists and intellectuals. Following the example of the Volksbühne (People's Stage), the German Social-Democratic theatre movement, this association tried to 'rescue' the film for large working-class audiences:

> ... film has to become what it can and must be: a means to spread knowledge, illumination and education, notions, thoughts and ideas – a means to approach and reconcile the nations – a living, active factor in daily life as well as the spiritual and artistic life![4]

The Volksfilmverband started its activities in February 1928. The writer Heinrich Mann became chairman, and other members of the board included Käthe Kollwitz, Erwin Piscator and Rudolf Schwarzkopf, proof of the broad political support it enjoyed.[5] A magazine appeared, *Film und Volk* ('Film and People'), edited by Franz Höllering, former editor of the *AIZ*. On 29 February 1928 the first film show of the association, Pudovkin's *The End of St Petersburg*, took place in Berlin, Heinrich Mann making the opening speech. Film shows were organised in other German cities, such as Hamburg, Stuttgart and Frankfurt am Main.

In France in 1928 a group of Communists and sympathisers[6] founded Les Amis de Spartacus ('The Friends of Spartacus'), a 'society for documentary studies in order to improve cinematographic production'.[7] Its aim was 'to allow the members of the Society to appreciate and judge the censorship measures taken against Russian films like *Battleship Potemkin, Mother*, German films like *The Weavers* and many others that are an honour to the cinema ...'[8] On 15 March 1928 Les Amis de Spartacus gave its first film show, featuring Pudovkin's film *Mother*, in the Parisian cinema Casino de Grenelle which was completely sold out for the occasion. Membership increased enormously: in two months the Paris section had 8,000 members.[9] In the summer of 1928 Les Amis de Spartacus organised film shows in virtually all the Parisian suburbs (the famous 'Red Belt'). In October 1928 the Ministry of the Interior banned the exhibition of films without censorship visas at private shows for members of film societies. The chief commissioner of police intervened with the management of the Casino de Grenelle, actually forcing them to lock out Les Amis de Spartacus. The association tried to continue by showing films with a censorship visa, but members stayed away. It was disbanded early in 1929.[10] In the Netherlands the Vereeniging voor Volks Cultuur (Association for Popular Culture) was founded in January 1928 by a group of Communists. Its aim was 'to facilitate the organisation of film, cabaret and other performances, and in such a way that undesirable interference from authorities who are not kindly disposed towards us can be limited to a minimum'.[11] One of the first activities of the association was the exhibition of the banned Soviet film *Bed and Sofa* for its members.

These workers' film societies were founded as a direct response to the censorship's interference with the exhibition of Soviet films. The film society as a legal and organisational form offered the possibility to get round censorship measures; bourgeois film societies had proved that this could be done in the name of Art. The people who took the initiative of founding the workers' film societies would be the last to deny the artistic merits of the Soviet films. But class, not art, was their first concern: West European workers should be able to see films produced in the first workers' and peasants' state. It is not surprising that Communists played a crucial rôle in the foundation and day-to-day activities of the workers' film societies, given the direct link with the Soviet Union. The workers' film societies therefore inevitably reflected the evolution of the Communist movement in their respective countries. Thus in 1929 the Volksfilmverband became a member of the German Communist umbrella organisation for the arts, the Interessegemeinschaft für Arbeiterkultur, cutting off all connections with Social-Democratic or bourgeois organisations.[12] After the February 1930 Congress of the Dutch CP, the Vereeniging voor Volks Cultuur (VVVC) was given the opportunity to expand its activities to other arts than the cinema, because of the importance attached to its work by the party leadership. This led to an enormous expansion of the VVVC's activities, from agitprop theatre to worker photography and the production of VVVC-newsreels.[13] Instead of drawing superficial conclusions on the relation between Communism and the arts, as many historians have done in the past,[14] recent publications have stressed the complexity of this matter.[15] What applied to the workers' film movement in one country did not apply to the workers' theatre movement in the same country, nor to the workers' film movement in another country, and so on.

After the October Revolution the Russian cinema had gone through an extremely difficult period. Virtually all the established film producers had sided with the counter-revolution, fleeing Soviet territory with their money, equipment, film stock and skills. Consequently film production almost came to a standstill during the Civil War, with the exception of newsreels which were screened all over the country by special agitprop columns travelling in trains or on steamboats. The New Economic Policy period breathed new life into the Russian cinema. Film stock could now be imported from abroad, although still in insufficient quantities. With a whole generation of Russian film-makers, technicians and actors in exile in Paris or Berlin, young talent was offered a unique chance to experiment in an art considered by Lenin to be the most important of all.

Two film directors symbolised the success of the young Soviet cinema in the eyes of the world: Sergei Eisenstein and Vsevolod Pudovkin. Their films *Battleship Potemkin* (Eisenstein) and *Mother* (Pudovkin) became *causes célèbres*, falling foul of censorship measures in many countries. *Battleship Potemkin* (1925), presented an episode from the 1905 revolution, with sailors of the Black Sea fleet revolting against their superiors. This was considered an act of extreme subversion by many censorship bodies, including the British Board of Film

Censors. The film's strength lay in its refusal to use professional actors and in its editing: the production of meaning through the arrangement in proper sequence of seemingly unconnected film shots. In particular the sequence showing the massacre by tsarist troops of innocent civilians on the Odessa steps was a masterpiece of editing. Pudovkin too used editing techniques to the maximum effect in his film *Mother* (1926), which was based on Maxim Gorki's celebrated novel. The main character of the film is a mother (marvellously played by Vera Baranovskaya) who joins the revolutionary struggle after the arrest of her son by tsarist troops. In 1927 Pudovkin and Eisenstein made their contribution to the celebrations of the tenth anniversary of the October Revolution with respectively *The End of St Petersburg* and *October* (also known as *Ten Days that Shook the World*). Pudovkin's next film, *Storm over Asia* (1928), was an indictment of imperialism, while Eisenstein sounded the praises of agricultural co-operation in *The General Line* (1929).

Not only Soviet films with overtly revolutionary themes were beset by censorship problems. An obvious example was *Bed and Sofa* (1927), a film directed by Abram Room. It was set in contemporary Moscow, examining the relationship between a woman and two men who are forced to share one apartment due to the housing shortage. With its references to women's emancipation, abortion and 'free love', *Bed and Sofa* was considered highly immoral and subversive. Not only in Moscow, but in other parts of the Soviet Union too, film production flourished. Of the Ukrainian films eventually two were to be seen in Great Britain: Grigori Stabavoi's revolutionary drama *Two Days* (1927) and Alexander Dovzhenko's poetic *Earth* (1930). Grigori Kozintsev and Leonid Trauberg worked in Leningrad and made among others *CBD*, the Club of the Big Deed (1927), on the Decembrist revolt of 1825, and *New Babylon* (1929), on the Paris Commune of 1871. Dziga Vertov was undoubtedly the most influential documentary film maker, although his work was rarely seen outside the Soviet Union at the time, with the exception of his virtuoso *The Man with the Movie Camera* (1929), a dazzling experiment in film editing.

The introduction of sound by the end of the 1920s brought the Soviet cinema to a temporary standstill. There was no money to buy foreign sound equipment and it took Soviet scientists some time to develop a sound system of their own. Additional sound tracks were made for some silent films. *The Blue Express* (1929), a silent film directed by Ilya Trauberg, became the first 'sound film' to be screened in Great Britain. The film's action took place on an express train in China, presenting a microcosm of Chinese society with its class differences through the train with its different compartments, its passengers and personnel. The first real Soviet sound feature was, however, Nikolai Ekk's *The Road to Life* (1931), the story of the integration of the 'wild children', *bezprizorni*, into Soviet society.

Berlin was the distribution centre for Soviet films. Prometheus Film, a company set up by the Workers' International Relief, had been able to exploit the signal success of *Battleship Potemkin*. It was in an excellent position to do so, as it had direct access to Mezhrabpom productions, which included all the Pudovkin films. The WIR owned the Mezhrabpom studios in Moscow. Prometheus Film was less successful with its German-Soviet co-productions. Transactions with Prometheus Film could range from the purchase of one Soviet film to exclusive deals giving the right to distribute all Soviet film productions for a certain period in a certain territory. Non-commercial transactions, for example with political organisations, were handled by a subsidiary, Weltfilm.

At its Sixth Congress (July to September 1928) the Communist International (Comintern) decided on a radical change in policy. It concluded that a period of relative stabilisation of capitalism – the 'second period' (the 'first' being the era of revolutionary upheavals from 1918 to 1923) – had come to an end, and the 'third period' was about to begin, in which the capitalist system would undergo a severe, virtually insoluble, crisis. It was only through the Communist parties that the proletariat would be able to defend itself against the forthcoming capitalist onslaught. Thus all political alliances must be broken off; henceforward it must be 'Class against Class'. As a result of this 'left turn' two major themes were singled out by the Comintern and the national Communist parties. The Soviet Union was threatened by an imperialist war prepared by the major capitalist powers; therefore the workers must be rallied to the defence of the Soviet Union. The treacherous role of social democracy had to be exposed at all costs: although pretending to defend the interests of the working class, social democracy in the end wanted only to uphold the capitalist system; it gave the workers false illusions about the feasibility of parliamentary democracy. In that respect social democracy was worse than fascism; the Comintern jargon labelled social democrats as 'social fascists'.

The sectarianism engendered by the 'Class against Class' policy caused serious damage to the working-class movement, above all in Germany but also in Britain and elsewhere. Despite 'favourable' conditions (economic crisis, high unemployment) the Communist Party of Great Britain made no headway, losing many members and suffering setbacks in its trade union and other work.[16] Nevertheless, as has recently been pointed out, the 'Class Against Class' policy had a profound influence on the political culture of the time, a fact generally obscured by those historians who have condemned the policy outright.[17] In fact 'Class Against Class' provided the political justification for the development of a new form of proletarian culture. For years theoreticians had discussed the possibilities of a proletarian culture under capitalism. The new Comintern policy made this not just a possibility, but a necessity. The proletariat had to fight on three fronts, the political, the economic and the cultural. One of the characteristics of this new proletarian culture was its search for new forms and its concern for new media, fostered by the wish to be as distinct as possible from existing, social democratic, cultural traditions. One of these new media was the cinema.

It took a year to put Kenneth Macpherson's idea – of founding a workers' film society in order to show films like *Battleship Potemkin* and *Mother* to the British workers – into practice. One gets the impression that the greatest problem consisted in finding an organisation that would actually sponsor the enterprise. The British WIR had made an heroic effort in providing relief for the locked-out miners after the General Strike, which must have sapped its energies quite considerably. The Friends of the Soviet Union – an organisation that certainly had an interest in showing Soviet movies – set up its own circuit, showing the film *A Journey to Soviet Russia* after the customs authorities had released it.[18] In the end some members of the Minority Movement (the

Communist-led trade union organisation[19]) took the initiative by founding a Federation of Workers' Film Societies on 28 October 1929.[20] The constitution of the new federation was published in *The Worker*, the weekly paper of the Minority Movement. The Federation of Workers' Film Societies (FOWFS) set out the following aims:

a) To encourage the formation of local workers' film societies.
b) To make arrangements for the supply of films or apparatus required by such societies.
c) To advise local workers' film societies on the best methods of carrying on their work, and to secure legal advice or assistance in cases affecting the Federation or its members.
d) To encourage the production of films of value to the working-class.
e) To co-operate with any organisations either in Britain, Ireland or abroad, having similar objects.
f) To issue publications and to engage in any other activities in furtherance of the above objects or tending to facilitiate the exhibition and production of films of value to the working-class.[21]

These aims do not particularly show the trade union background of the enterprise. Still it is not surprising that the MM stood at the base of the new federation. After the Comintern's 'left turn' the Red International of Labour Unions (RILU), to which the MM was affiliated, had propagated the development of cultural activities. It published a monthly bulletin, *Trade Union Propaganda and Cultural Work*, with directives, reports of conferences and a survey of the cultural activities of Communist trade unions in various countries.[22] In the few years of its existence the FOWFS kept up its special relationship with the MM.

To set up a Federation of Workers' Film Societies would have made little sense unless there were societies to join it. Ralph Bond, one of its founding members, published an appeal for the formation of a London Workers' Film Society (LWFS) in the *Sunday Worker*.[23] ' "The response to the appeal of the London Workers' Film Society for members has surpassed all expectations," said a member of the Council yesterday.'[24] The LWFS Council booked the Gaiety Cinema, Tottenham Court Road, for Sunday 17 November 1929 to show two Soviet films, the short *Snapshots of Soviet Russia* and the feature *Two Days*. The LCC intervened and informed the proprietor of that cinema that he must not allow the performance to be given on that date. The Council of the Society has, however, made arrangements for its performance to be given in the Co-op Hall, Tooting, on Monday 18 November at 8 p.m.[25]

It was the first of a number of skirmishes between the LWFS and the LCC. A second LWFS show was announced, again at the Tooting Co-op Hall, on 16 December 1929.[26] It featured the German film *Hunger in Waldenburg* (later known as *The Shadow of the Mine*). This film had been produced jointly by the Volksfilmverband and Weltfilm, with Phil (or Piel) Jutzi as director. In a mixture of documentary and fiction *Hunger in Waldenburg* shows how a young weaver (played by Holmes Zimmermann) gives up his trade to try and find a job in one of the pits. He has no luck, faces starvation and ends up killing the rent-collector in an effort to help his landlady, a miner's widow. Jutzi had recut the original specially for the British version.[27]

With *Two Days* and *Hunger in Waldenburg* the LWFS presented two British premieres to its members. Because the commercial renters had no suitable films in their libraries, with a few exceptions, the FOWFS had to make new films available for exhibition by its member societies. In view of this the Atlas Film Company, the production and distribution company of the FOWFS, opened relations with the German firm Weltfilm. In late 1929 Ralph Bond, the driving force behind the FOWFS and the LWFS, paid a vist to the Weltfilm headquarters in Berlin and was able to bring back a number of films. He left copies of the constitutions of the FOWFS and the LWFS, and these were published in the February 1930 issue of *Film und Volk*, the organ of the Volksfilmverband.[28] Weltfilm had been founded in 1927. It worked along strictly non-commercial lines – as opposed to its parent-organisation Prometheus Film – providing political organisations with films which could be used for propaganda purposes. Its film list covered a wide range of themes and included Soviet films, documentaries produced by German working-class organisations, and also capitalist feature films with a progressive tendency. Apart from its Berlin headquarters, Weltfilm had branches in half a dozen German cities and agencies in many foreign countries.[29] Its support to Atlas Film was precious, given the latter's weak financial position.[30]

The FOWFS started the new year 1930 on a note of
optimism. The first two performances of the LWFS had met
with a reasonable success – the first show had been attended by
some 500 people.

> Both before and after London's first performance, the
> Federation had been receiving letters from enthusiasts in many
> provincial towns, and from workers in the mining areas of
> South Wales and other coalfield districts. The Federation is now
> busily engaged in assisting these workers to organise local
> societies on a similar basis to the London Society.[31]

Ralph Bond described how the LWFS

> again applied to the LCC, this time for a permit to show
> *Potemkin* on one specified occasion to its members. The LCC
> replied saying that the Council had decided that under no
> circumstances could *Potemkin* be shown in any Cinema licensed
> by them under the 1909 Act. Back went a letter pointing out
> that *Potemkin* had been exhibited by the Film Society as recently
> as November 10th, 1929 in premises licensed by the LCC
> under the 1909 Act. Would the LCC please explain?[32]

The LCC adhered to its ban on *Battleship Potemkin*, but at least
gave in on the matter of allowing the LWFS to organise Sunday
shows in a West End Cinema. On Sunday 2 February 1930 the
LWFS showed its third programme of the season at the New
Scala Theatre. It composed a Soviet comedy, *The Girl with the
Hatbox*, and a remarkable documentary on China, filmed in
1927, entitled *Shanghai Document*.[33]

On 28 January 1930 the LWFS held its first general meeting.
According to the report in the *Daily Worker* (which had first
appeared on 1 January 1930 and covered the activities of the
FOWFS extensively), 'there was an excellent attendance'. A
rapid increase in membership was reported; the establishment
of 'local societies in the South-Western and Eastern districts of
London' was even considered. A constitution and set of rules
were adopted and an Executive Committee of ten elected. 'The
meeting endorsed the Council's recommendation that every
effort should be made to develop the Society on the basis of
members and groups of members in the factories.'[34] Was this

simply contemporary Communist rhetoric or a reminder of the trade union background of the FOWFS? The Council's recommendation at least had the merit of focusing on the question of the composition of the LWFS audience, which was later to become a point of debate.

The Labour Party was highly suspicious of the activities of the workers' film societies and on 26 February 1930 its Executive Committee decided 'that enquiries be made as to whether this Society [the LWFS, B.H.] is Communistic in character'.[35] Although the results of the enquiry were never published the outcome must have been affirmative, since the Labour Party ignored the workers' film societies.[36] However, no less than four Labour Cabinet Ministers – J.R. Clynes, George Lansbury, Sir Charles Trevelyan and F.O. Roberts – had been among the founding members of a 'competitor' to the FOWFS, the Masses Stage and Film Guild, founded in the autumn of 1929. It was an initiative of the Arts Guild of the Independent Labour Party, which co-ordinated the activities of the various ILP arts groups (mainly amateur theatre). With this new venture the Arts Guild hoped to breathe new life into its activities and to set exemplary standards. The Masses Stage and Film Guild (MSFG) sought to stage the best plays (Upton Sinclair's *Singing Jailbirds* was the first play announced), with the best actors and actresses (among its supporters were a number of theatre people such as Sybil Thorndike).[37] Film seemed a matter of secondary importance, and it would probably not have been included at all if it had not been for the campaign waged by 'Benn', the film critic of the ILP weekly *New Leader*. In a series of articles – 'How Labour Can Use the Films', 'A Workers' Film Society?' and 'Why Not A Socialist News Reel?' – 'Benn' (whose identity is unknown) outlined realistically what a workers' film movement in Great Britain might achieve.[38] In the end his ideas were better understood by the FOWFS than by the MSFG, his 'own' organisation. The MSFG produced no newsreels and was dependent on Atlas Film, the FOWFS production and distribution company, for the supply of films.

In February and March 1930 the MSFG hit the headlines. It had applied to the LCC for permission to show Pudovkin's film *Mother* at the Regal Cinema, London. This Soviet film had been banned by the BBFC, but the LCC had given the Film

Society permission to show it in October 1928. The LCC refused. The ILP MP Fenner Brockway stated in *The Times*:

> We cannot escape the conclusion that the LCC is prepared to allow the select intellectuals to see the film, but is not willing to permit the working classes to see it. Despite the opposition of the LCC we are determined to show the film, and we shall organize a very big and influential protest against the action of the LCC.[39]

Fenner Brockway, who was chairman of the MSFG, also announced a meeting on the question of film censorship at the House of Commons. At this meeting on 24 February he had to report another defeat. The MSFG had made an application to show *Mother* 'in a theatre over which the Lord Chamberlain had control. The Lord Chamberlain has informed the Guild that he cannot in any circumstances allow the film to be shown.'[40] At short notice the MSFG organised an alternative programme for its members at the New Scala on Sunday 2 March. It comprised *Two Days, Snapshots of Russia* and Ivor Montagu's *Daydreams*.[41] It was obviously assumed that the audience would be different from the one at the first programme of the LWFS, where both *Two Days* and *Snapshots of Russia* had been shown.

A protest against the ban on *Mother* was signed by such notables as J.M. Keynes, Julian Huxley, Sybil Thorndike, Bertrand Russell and George Bernard Shaw.[42] The MSFG decided to press the matter further with the LCC. It applied to the Theatres and Music Halls Committee for permission to show at the Regal Cinema, Marble Arch, on Sunday 23 March and Sunday 27 April 1930 any of the following films: *Mother, Battleship Potemkin, Storm over Asia, New Babylon, October* and *The General Line*. The first four had been refused a certificate by the BBFC; the last two had not yet been submitted. *The Times* quoted the report drawn up by the Theatres and Music Halls Committee:

> We have caused inquiry to be made of the Board of Film Censors whether in its opinion those films are provocative or likely to cause a breach of the peace if shown (a) publicly or (b) privately, for example, to members of the guild and their guests. The board's opinion is definitely in the affirmative on

both (a) and (b). The board further expresses the view that there is little difference between a public exhibition and an exhibition to which the public may obtain admission on payment of 1s.[43]

The Theatres and Music Halls Committee fully adopted the BBFC's views and advised the LCC to reject the MSFG application, which it duly did. It had all come down to the interpretation of 'public' and 'private'. The low membership fee and admission prices of the MSFG (and the LWFS) – making its activities accessible to the purses of the workers – meant that its activities were practically 'public'. There was a distinct smell of class bias.

The MSFG campaign put the suppression of Soviet films under the spotlight. It brought unexpected dividends in West Ham – a Labour-controlled borough – where the council decided on 25 March 1930,

> to allow the Russian film *Mother* ... to be exhibited at licensed premises. The Mayor (Alderman Hollins) said the Council had hitherto been guided in such matters by the Board of Film Censors, but the Council had full authority to deal as it desired with the film in question. Alderman Scoulding (chairman of the Works Committee which recommended exhibition), said his committee had fully considered the question, and did not think there was a justifiable reason for disallowing any film to be exhibited in order to satisfy a few fanatics.[44]

In consequence the Stratford Palladium cinema in West Ham gained quite a reputation as a sanctuary for Soviet films, exhibiting them indiscriminately whether the BBFC had banned them or not. The 'few fanatics', of course, tried to put a stop to this. The Forest Gate Ratepayers' Association appealed to the Home Office to urge the Borough Council to exercise its veto. The Home Office answered that it was 'unable to take action on the lines suggested'.[45] West Ham did not, however, become the Poplar of the cinema, though a few other Labour-controlled councils followed its example.[46]

The LWFS scored a big hit with the exhibition of the Soviet documentary film *Turksib*. The film dealt with the construction of the railway from Turkestan to Siberia. It was conspicuous for its powerful images and the rhythm of its editing. Its director Victor Turin had come to London to work on the

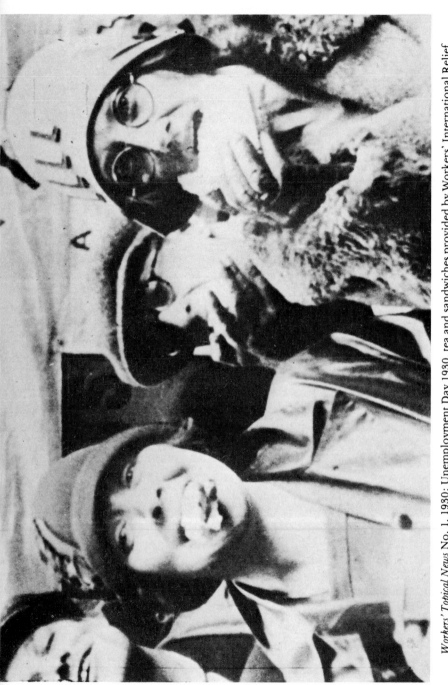

Workers' Topical News No. 1, 1930; Unemployment Day 1930, tea and sandwiches provided by Workers' International Relief.

Workers' Topical News No. 2, 1930; the Scottish contingent on the 1930 Hunger March

English version with John Grierson, at that time head of the
Empire Marketing Board Film Unit and a champion of the
cause of documentary film making. Turin introduced *Turksib*
to the LWFS audience. The BBFC had found nothing objec-
tionable in the film, and passed it for universal exhibition.
This opened a new perspective for the Atlas Film Company. It
could try to get *Turksib* shown in ordinary cinemas. At the
premiere of *Turksib* on 6 March 1930 the Atlas Film Company
also screened the first issue of its newsreel, *Workers' Topical
News*.[47]

Newreels undoubtedly played an important part in shaping
the opinions of large sections of the populations on political
and social problems. That is why they came in for a lot of
criticism. Afraid of losing their privilege of not having to
submit their films (issued twice weekly) to the BBFC, the
newsreel companies tried to avoid controversy as much as
possible and concentrated instead on 'safe' topics as sport,
fashion and royalty. With the coming of the sound film, the
newsreel found its definitive form: a balanced presentation of
four or five items, underlined by 'the voice of God' – the
omniscient commentator. In his column in *New Leader* 'Benn'
had criticised the newsreel: 'Always militarism, jingoism,
sabre-rattling or sport – never internationalism, peace,
scientific advance or any matters likely to raise the intellectual
and moral standards of the people.' According to 'Benn' the
best solution was to produce a socialist newsreel: 'There is
room here for a Workers' Film Society to photograph events of
interest to the workers.' He summed up some events which
could be filmed:

> industrial and political demonstrations; the social causes
> leading up to strikes; co-operative activities; the effects of the
> miners' eight-hour day on the miners and their families; the
> contrast of nine-in-a-room in workers' homes with one-in-
> nine-rooms in the homes of the upper class, etcetera.

It looked very similar to the list drawn up for photographers of
the Clarion Camera Club. 'Benn' concluded that such a
socialist newsreel, 'if done internationally ... would act as a
real educational weapon on behalf of Socialism.'[48] One of the
aims of the FOWFS was 'to encourage the production of films
of value to the working-class'.[49] The production of its own

newsreel seemed a logical step. The costs would be relatively low. The showing of a newsreel would enhance the attraction of the workers' film society programmes.

Workers' Topical News No.1 was completely devoted to a demonstration organised by the National Unemployed Workers' Movement on the occasion of Unemployment Day 1930, on 6 March at Tower Hill, London. During five minutes images of the mass of demonstrators, the food kitchen of the WIR and the speakers were shown. It is conspicuous that a shot of Tom Mann, seen in a characteristic pose, is not provided with a caption (the newsreel was silent). Obviously the maker of the film, Ralph Bond, did not consider this necessary as Tom Mann well enough known to the working-class audience at which the newsreel was aimed. The second issue of *Workers' Topical News* (premiered on 4 May 1930 in a LWFS programme that featured *CBD*, directed by the Russians Kozintsev and Trauberg, and *Berlin*, by the German Walter Ruttmann) showed two events: the 1930 Hunger March and May Day in London. Shots of the Hunger Marchers *en route* are mixed with shots of their rest period: eating, having a haircut, having their shoes mended or playing a game of football. Wal Hannington, the leader of the March, is shown visiting one of the contingents. The newsreel shows groups of demonstrators marching on May Day. Apart from the usual banners, they carry anti-MacDonald slogans. The number of policemen seems out of proportion with the number of demonstrators. The film ends with some shots in Hyde Park: Charlotte Despard and Shapurji Saklatvala, the former Communist MP, are shown in close-up, as symbols for the Irish and Indian freedom struggles. Saklatvala, like Tom Mann, is not captioned. These descriptions give some indication of the function of *Workers' Topical News*. It provided a visual record of important events in the revolutionary workers' movement, but, above all, it gave the audience an opportunity to see 'us' instead of 'them' on the screen. Mann and Saklatvala were 'ours'.

The international exchange of socialist newsreel footage, outlined by 'Benn', was never realised. Still it is useful to make some comparisons between *Workers' Topical News* and similar workers' newsreels made abroad. Especially so since it is known that a letter from Ralph Bond to Sam Brody in the

USA helped to inspire the idea of making workers' newsreels in
that country. Brody wrote an article in the New York *Daily
Worker*, 'For Workers' Films', in which he assimilated Bond's
suggestions. This led to the foundation of the Workers' Film
and Photo League, an organisation that produced at least a
dozen *Workers' Newsreels* in 1931 and 1932.[50] The sister
organisations of the FOWFS, the German Volksfilmverband
and the Dutch VVVC, produced workers' newsreels too:
Zeitbericht-Zeitgesicht (one issue, 1928, banned by the censor)
and *VVVC-Journaal* (five issues, 1930-31). *Zeitbericht-Zeitgesicht*
('News of the Times – Face of the Times') exclusively and the
VVVC-Journaal to a great extent used existing newsreel footage.
They were based on the principle that, in film, news was a
construction of images and that the meaning of those images
depended on the editor's view of reality.[51] *Workers' Topical News*
had more in common with the American *Workers' Newsreels*, the
Prokino-News (produced in 1930 by the Japanese League for the
Proletarian Cinema) or the five films made by Huma-Films in
France (1932).[52] These newsreels started from the assumption
that there was a reality which was not shown by the commercial
newsreels, because its rendering on the cinema screens would
hurt the interests of the ruling classes. The task of the
cameraman was therefore simply to record these events and
show them to the workers. Often this was not an easy job: the
camera was heavy and had to be reloaded frequently; film
stock was expensive and consequently there was never enough
of it; the police were never very happy with the presence of
newsreel cameramen, even less with cameramen filming for
workers' newsreels.

Workers' Topical News added more variety to the LWFS
programmes. Looking back at that period, Ralph Bond wrote:
'We rapidly acquired the "art" of showmanship, and realised
that our programmes needed to be leavened with variety and
humour.'[53] This meant the inclusion of short comedies
(Chaplin, Charlie Chase, Laurel and Hardy) and cultural films
into the programme. A film of that last category, entitled
Autumn Mists, shown by the LWFS on 25 May 1930 in a
programme that featured the Soviet documentary *Men of the
Woods*, came in for criticism from a spectator. P.J. Poole sent a
letter to the *Daily Worker* in which he condemned *Autumn Mists*
as a 'tripy film [which] has nothing to do with à workers' film

society'. He referred to the reaction of the audience in a West End cinema, where he had first seen the film. 'So amused were the audience that at the finish most were really tired from the entertainment they had obtained by clapping at the incidents in the film, which depicts a leaf gently fluttering on to water and smoothly floating away.' Poole had noticed no protest at the LWFS show, apart from 'two young workers who rose from the front and walked out; evidently they could not restrain their feelings any longer'. He concluded:

> Surely, comrades, we can leave such sentimental, meaningless rubbish to the bourgeois intelligentsia, and if we haven't anything better to show the minority of workers who do attend the shows of the LWFS, then let us have talks on film work.[54]

Surprising was not so much Poole's anti-intellectualism, but his outspoken concern for the problem of film reception by working-class audiences.[55] Although his conclusion was muddled (did workers form a minority in the LWFS audience or could the LWFS only reach a minority?), Poole had raised a point which seems to have escaped the attention of the LWFS. The society had thought about recruitment ('to develop the Society on the basis of members and groups of members in the factories'[56]), but not about the problems this posed in terms of film reception and audience education. The LWFS kept silent on the matter. Its last performance of the 1929-30 season was attended by a bumper audience of 'nearly 2,000 members and guests'.[57] Eisenstein's *The General Line* was the main attraction. *Spartakiade*, a film on the International Workers' Sports Festival in Moscow, was also shown. The British Workers' Sports Federation had had a print of this film for almost a year, but it needed help from the FOWFS/Atlas Film people to get it shown.[58]

There was no need for the LWFS, the FOWFS or the MSFG to round up their first season with the publication of an annual report. The Conservative Central Office was kind enough to publish one in June 1930, entitled *Soviet Film Propaganda*. Ralph Bond (using his pen-name Arthur West) wrote of the report that it 'is full of inaccuracies, consists in the main of the dates and places of the exhibitions of Russian films in this country, ranging from private performances of the Workers' Film Societies to the public exhibitions in the ordinary commercial cinemas'. He also pointed out that the authors of the report had relied for descriptions of the films heavily on 'quotations from the reviews that have appeared in the columns of the *Daily Worker*'.[59] In an article in *Close-Up* (also quoted by the authors of the report) Bond singled out some of the most obvious errors in order to discredit the report. He wrote: '*Turksib* was apparently made by a man called Torin, of whom we have never heard.'[60] In its issue of 12 March 1930 the *Daily Worker* had in fact carried a report of a talk given by 'Victor Torin' at the premiere of *Turksib*. The typographical error had been copied off-hand by the Conservative Central Office writers! According to their report the Soviet film *Men of the Woods* was shown by the Workers' Film Society in May 1928, whereas there was no Workers' Film Society at that date and the film itself 'did not arrive in London until months after'.[61] As Bond put it: 'I merely mention these little points in case the REPORT is given a second edition. Even our comic literature should be accurate.'[62] However inaccurate (and comic) *Soviet Film Propaganda* may have been, its aim was obvious enough: the suppression of the exhibition of Soviet films in Great Britain. This purpose was indicated by the use of the word 'propaganda' in the title of the report. As film critic P.L. Mannock wrote in the *Daily Herald*:

> There seems to be some fantastic fear that some impressionable British spectator or *Turksib* or *The General Line* might be prompted to set fire to the House of Lords or throw stones at the windows of Windsor Castle.[63]

The BBFC, not particularly renowned for its Bolshevism, had granted both films a U certificate!

Since the LCC had prohibited the MSFG to exhibit *Mother* in a private show for members, a Parliamentary Film Committee had been looking at the question of film censorship. It brought pressure to bear on both the Labour Government and the LCC. Once it had become clear that Home Secretary J.R. Clynes had no intention of changing the existing censorship regulations – neither acceding to the demands of left-wing MPs (Ellen Wilkinson, Fenner Brockway, *et al.*) to make film censorship more democratic, nor yielding to pressure from the Conservative Central Office to ban all Soviet films – the Parliamentary Film Committee approached the LCC with the request to show more flexibility regarding the activities of film societies. As a result of a visit by 'an all-party deputation of Members of Parliament' to the Theatres and Music Halls Committee of the LCC in May 1930, the committee recommended 'that permission for the exhibition of uncensored films shall be administered on a more equal basis'.[64] However, this drawing up of a new set of regulations for film societies took the LCC so much time that at the beginning of the new 1930-31 season neither the Film Society nor the LWFS and the MSFG knew where they stood. Referring to the new situation created by the film societies with regard to its Sunday cinematograph exhibition policy (normally all profits of Sunday cinema performances had to be donated to charities), the LCC expressed the wish to exercise stricter control over the films shown by the societies and over the way it applied the rules for private societies (membership, guests, etc.), and it reserved the right to inspect all books.[65] The MSFG complained that the 'series of regulations governing the conduct of these societies ... has, to some extent, crippled the work of the Guild'.[66] A similar complaint was heard from the LWFS that 'the new regulations of the London County Council put obstacles in the way of publicity on the part of the society, and members have to conform to stricter "red tape" in the method of subscription'.[67] But the new regulations at least had the advantage of allowing both workers' film societies to plan their activities in the long term, without having to wait for a last-minute sanction (or refusal) from the LCC. It was hoped that this 'normalisation' would be followed by other local authorities in the United Kingdom. In one part of the UK, however, there was no further need for 'normalisation'. The Ulster Unionist government had given its police force special powers to search premises for subversive films, Soviet films being a special target. To protect its interests the film trade chose the lesser of two evils and opted for a ban on Soviet films in Ulster.[68]

The foundation of the Federation of Workers' Film Societies in the autumn of 1929 had created the conditions for a network of local workers' film societies all over Great Britain. The FOWFS headquarters in London was to provide advice and know-how towards setting up a workers' film society, dealing with licensing authorities and obtaining suitable films.

The Federation's own film company Atlas Films dealt effectively with the supply of films. All that was needed were local working-class organisations or trade union branches to start a film society and keep it running. By the summer of 1930 two further workers' film societies had become active, in Cardiff and in Liverpool. Little is known about the Cardiff workers' film society, apart from its appeal to the workers 'in the adjoining mining valleys' to join.[69] Thanks to an article by Michael Rose Roberts in the American film magazine *Experimental Cinema*, much more is known about the Merseyside Workers' Film Society. In late 1929 or early 1930

> a conference of socialist teachers decided to show, during the course of their meeting at Birkenhead, a film called *A Journey to Soviet Russia*. The film was banned on some pretext by the local authorities and it was never shown. But the teachers called their friends and neighbours and out of their protest grew the Merseyside Workers' Film Society ... The adventures of the early days are worth recalling. After two shows an avalanche descended – the films had been *Two Days* and *Turk-Sib*. The hall – a theatre run by the University Settlement – refused permission for further performances; the press conducted a campaign against what they called the subversive character of the society, and the secretary was forced to resign by his employers. Then came a show in a cinema closed for a few days while talkies were installed, and then an application to magistrates for Sunday performances – refused, of course. Permission to use a hall belonging to the city was sought and refused, but at last fortune, in the shape of the local Co-operative Society, smiled and produced the uncomfortable but fire proof hall in which present shows are given.[70]

Notwithstanding these inconveniences, performances of the Merseyside Workers' Film Society attracted crowds of over 500, according to reports in the *Daily Worker*.[71] As a result of this *Turksib* (shown April 1930 at the society's second performance) was given a run in one of Liverpool's commercial cinemas.

The ILP Arts Guild, the sponsor of the Masses Stage and Film Guild, devoted considerable time of its 1930 annual conference in Birmingham to discussing 'the possibility of showing Russian films in various parts of the country by private organisations. Much interest in the subject was evoked, and it was agreed to send a detailed statement on the question to each branch'.[72] It seemed that the local ILP organisations lacked the punch necessary to convert the Guild's advice into a proper film organisation. Take the example of Newcastle.

> A Branch of the Masses Stage and Film Guild is being formed in Newcastle, for the purpose of exhibiting films that have failed to pass the censor. A conference of organisations and individuals likely to be interested in this project is shortly to be convened by the Newcastle Central Branch of the Independent Labour Party, which, however, is only concerned with the movement to the extent of calling the conference.[73]

No wonder the ILP Arts Guild complained in next year's report (1931) of 'the political apathy existing everywhere', adding, quite correctly, that 'the very real difficulties relating to hiring of halls, local laws, etc., has considerably retarded development.'[74] The Swansea ILP branch, for example, which tried to organise a showing of *Mother* in September 1930, found the Watch Committee's opposition too high a hurdle.[75]

The first annual conference of the FOWFS, held in London on 14 September 1930, was characterised by a note of optimism. Workers' film societies had been established in Bradford, Edinburgh, Glasgow and Salford, to join forces with the already existing societies in London, Cardiff and Liverpool. It was 'decided to launch a production fund for the purpose of producing short films based upon the lives of the workers in this country'.[76] This idea had been previously expressed by Arthur West in a *Daily Worker* article on the reactionary character of the newsreels. West stressed the importance of combating these 'most effective weapons for imperialist propaganda in the cinemas' by producing workers' newsreels. He mentioned the two issues of *Workers' Topical News*, hoping

> that all the workers' film societies will combine to extend these first efforts. I see no reason why the Workers' Film Movement should confine itself to the mere recording of actual events. There are hundreds of subjects, based on the actual lives of the workers waiting to be filmed, subjects which could be recorded on one or two thousand feet of film without the necessity for 'actors' or expensive studio sets and elaborate technical equipment.[77]

The production fund had to provide financial support, because even the kind of austerity film making that West proposed required more than just a few pennies. Financial considerations may have determined the character of Atlas's next film production. Instead of a short film based upon the life of a British worker, a compilation film with the title *Glimpses of Modern Russia* was made by Ralph Bond. This silent one-reel film, showing the progress in industry and agriculture in the Soviet Union as the result of Lenin's leadership and, after his death, of the carrying out of his principles (with Stalin conspicuously absent ...), 'was constructed from material available in this country'.[78] It must therefore have been relatively cheap to make. Once more the LWFS had the privilege of having the premiere of a 'Workers' Film Movement Production' (as a caption in *Glimpses of Modern Russia* indicated), at the opening night of the 1930-31 season on 26 October 1930.

Compared with the previous season, the workers' film societies outside London were more active. Their activities did not attract the attention of the national press in the way the LWFS or the London-based MSFG did. Worker correspondents sent in reports on the activities of their local workers' film society to the *Daily Worker*, but these were often too summarised to provide more than a few basic facts. Harassment and interference by local authorities was a recurring theme in these reports. Consequently each exhibition, public or private, of a Soviet film was greeted as a victory. One further gets the impression that the existence of a local workers' film society necessarily resulted in the public exhibition of Soviet pictures in local commercial cinemas. This had been the case in Liverpool and the same happened in Cardiff, Glasgow and Salford.[79] In Glasgow, however, the Atlas Film Company itself, not one of the local exhibitors, hired the City Hall on 5, 6 and 7 November 1930 to show *Mother* and the Borough Hall, Kinning Park for three days later in the month to show *The End of St Petersburg*.[80] The latter had already been screened in Glasgow by the Friends of the Soviet Union in the summer of 1930. This performance had served as a rallying point for the foundation of a Glasgow Workers' Film Society. The worker correspondent who wrote a report on this film show – under the title 'My first Soviet film' – gave a frank opinion on the importance of screening Soviet films ('to rouse the workers') and of a Glasgow Workers' Film Society ('The sooner this society gets to work in Glasgow, the sooner will Glasgow waken from its "mid-Left" slumber.').[81] In retrospect these assertions seem unfounded, but they have the merit of raising some crucial questions on the way the workers' film societies operated. The crux of the matter was of course the relationship between art and politics. What was the particular role of the Soviet cinema in this respect? What was the place of a workers' film society within the labour movement? Lack of sources makes it difficult to answer these questions as far as the workers' film societies outside London are concerned. Fortunately the Manchester Studies project has unearthed a great number of documents and newspaper clippings on the Salford (later Manchester and Salford) Workers' Film Society, and two surviving members of the society were interviewed as part of the project.[82] This material enables us to tackle the above questions through the Salford and Manchester experience.

The Salford Workers' Film Society was founded by a group of trade unionists, most of whom were also active politically (in the CPGB or Labour Party). They were members of the Salford Social Democratic Land and Builders' Society Ltd, which was 'formed in 1903 for the purpose of purchasing premises for Socialist activities. It acquired 69 Liverpool Street, Salford in 1903 and still owns the building and cottage adjoining. The capital is divided into 5/- shares.'[83] Tom Cavanagh, toolmaker, delegate to the Manchester and Salford Trades Council and Communist, had hit upon the idea of using the Builders' Society, in which he and his friends owned shares, as a venue for cultural activities, especially film shows. For this purpose the rules of the Builders' Society had to be amended, at a Special General Meeting held on 20 May 1930, as follows:

> The Society may erect or purchase any buildings for the exhibition of cinematograph films, plays, dramatic and musical performances, particularly those of interest to the Working Class, or may hire a building for any such purposes and may co-operate with any organisation either in Great Britain, Ireland or abroad, in such purposes. The Society may also form subsidiary organisations to further or/and carry out the foregoing objects.[84]

Such a subsidiary organisation became the Salford Workers' Film Society. Although it had been represented at the first annual conference of the FOWFS in September 1930, it was actually only founded on 15 October 1930. This meeting was attended by fifteen members. A committee was elected, which not only reflected its close links with the Builders' Society, but also the political and trade union background of those involved. The Manchester and Salford Trades Council was represented by secretary Tom Cavanagh, the Lancashire and Cheshire Federation of Trades Councils by co-opted member Jack Brewin. Chairman Charlie Rutter, membership secretary Alf Williams, Cavanagh and the members Tom Savage and Jack Williams were Communists. Brewin was an ex-Communist who played a prominent role in the Salford Labour Party.[85] Trade unionism seems to have been more of a motive force in the society's activities than party politics. A worker correspondent even complained that 'the Managing Committee have not yet thought fit to announce or advertise their activities to the *Daily Worker*, the only paper that logically the Workers' Film Society membership can look to for effective support.'[86] A few weeks later the Communist daily carried a front-page advertisement for the next Salford Workers' Film Society performance.[87] Four months later, in July 1931, another complaint was heard from a worker correspondent in the *Daily Worker* that the society 'refuses to put on screen advertisements for the *Daily Worker*' during its performances.[88] The society was obviously reluctant to label itself as Communist, notwithstanding the majority of CP members on the Management Committee. Of its links with the trade union movement, on the contrary, the society never made a secret. The 5,000 circulars it had ordered for its first performance were mainly destined for trade union branches.[89] The 'request of the South East Lancashire Labour College Council [for] an interchange of delegates between that Body and the Film Society Committee' was especially mentioned in the society's annual report.[90]

The programmes shown by the Salford Workers' Film Society were identical to those organised by other workers' film societies. The first performance, on Saturday 15 November 1930, featured the Soviet film *Two Days*, preceded by a Laurel and Hardy comedy, *Water and Waves* ('a short film made by the German Workers' Film Movement'), an educational film on the Thames and a Soviet short on the Five Year Plan, *The First Time in History*.[91] Soviet features dominated subsequent performances: *Turksib* (13 December 1930), *Giant Harvest* (24 January 1931), *The Roof of the World* and *Earth* (28 February), *The End of St Petersburg* (28 March), *The General Line* (18 April), *The Girl with the Hat Box* and *CBD* (16 May) and *Storm over Asia* (27 June). Apart from the last film, the Salford Workers' Film Society showed all its programmes of the 1930-31 season in the Prince's Cinema on Liverpool Street, opposite the Socialist Club that was owned by the Builders' Society. The club was used as an office. On the day of the film show, one could enroll as a member of the society in the club, cross the road and enter the Prince's Cinema to attend a private film screening.

The founders of the society had a clear purpose: to use film as a means of political education.[92] They aimed at a working-class audience, or more precisely a trade union audience. Recruitment was essentially through trade union channels, apart from articles. in the local press. The society refused to take sides in the political struggle between the Labour Party and the CPGB. It did not attract the support it had expected. In November 1930 Tom Cavanagh had ordered 1,000 membership cards from the printers; by the end of the season membership amounted to 350.[93] Financially the society could not have done 'without the backing of the parent organisation as the income from the Film Society was barely sufficient to pay expenses'.[94] Fortunately the rules of the Builders' Society had been changed to that effect.[95] What had gone wrong? Obviously the recruitment of members among the trade unionists had failed to give the expected results. The exhibition of Soviet films did not automatically attract Salford's working-class population. Still, the indispensability of the Soviet films for the society was not questioned. On the contrary, the society decided to defy the decision of the Salford Watch Committee and show the uncensored film *Storm over Asia* to its members. Whereas until then Soviet films had acted as a veil to cover the political differences within the left (for example, between the Labour Party and the CBPG, or between the TUC and the Minority Movement), the exhibition of *Storm over Asia* had a precise political purpose: to win the right of 'Free Sight' in Salford.

The Salford Workers' Film Society had made several

applications to the local Watch Committee for permission to show uncensored films privately to its members. This permission was repeatedly refused. The society decided to force the matter over a single film, *Storm over Asia*, scheduled to be shown on 16 May 1931. The film had been made in 1928 by Pudovkin for the Mezhrabpom Film Company. Its central theme was the struggle against colonial oppression and in certain episodes the British were placed in an unfavourable light; this was sufficient for the BBFC to ban the film. The Salford Watch Committee shared the same opinion after viewing the film at the request of the Salford Workers' Film Society. A 'Storm over Salford' was the result. The Labour minority in the City Council pleaded in vain for the film. During the council debate the Tory Alderman J. Bratherton silenced his opponents who kept referring to the artistic qualities of the film with a profound statement: 'From start to finish, *Storm over Asia* is Bolshevik propaganda. The morning we spent watching that film was wasted. It was pure rubbish.'[96] By thirty to sixteen votes the decision of the Watch Committee was confirmed by the Salford City Council. The society submitted the film to the Watch Committee of neighbouring Manchester. This committee did not object to the exhibition of *Storm over Asia* by the society. A cinema was found, the Futurist, where the film was shown on 27 June 1931. The Salford Workers' Film Society decided to change its name to Manchester and Salford Workers' Film Society (MSWFG). 300 new members joined under a special scheme to see *Storm over Asia*. For the first time the society made a profit.[97]

One of the society's activities must have been virtually unknown to the membership.

> In February [1931] the Society undertook a commission for the Federation of Workers' Film Societies to obtain a film of the Textile Dispute then in a critical stage in the Burnley district. Equipment and technical advice was generously loaned and given us by a member of the Society, and two members were dispatched to the Area. Unfortunately owing to wretched weather conditions and lack of resources only a small part of the film taken had any value.[98]

This part was included in *Workers' Topical News* No.3.[99] Jack Brewin was one of the two members of the society sent to the Burnley district. Alf Williams recalled that Brewin returned with a reel of film, which was shown in the Socialist Club. It showed pictures of demonstrations and processions. Williams' recollection of this exhibition were rather vague, apart from an accident with the film projector, which set fire to a frame of the film.[100] The fact that the footage shot by Brewin and his colleague was not shown in one of the regular performances, where all the members could see it, can only be partially explained by the inferior quality of the film. If there had been a mass movement among trade unions in the North-West support the striking textile workers in Lancashire, the film would have been welcomed, even if was amateurish. It was only the Minority Movement that supported the Lancashire strikers wholeheartedly. It would be interesting to know how, given its trade union and Communist background, the Management Committee of the Salford Workers' Film Society felt about the Minority Movement. There is no evidence that the society supported it. One remark in the *Daily Worker* even suggests that the society tried to distance itself from the movement.[101]

The LWFS, on the contrary, expressed its willingness to accept criticism from the MM. As we have seen, members of the MM had played an important part in the foundation of the FOWFS and the LWFS. These close links resulted in the spring of 1931 in the production of a special film for the Charter Campaign – entitled *1931*. It was the first example of a film specially produced to support a campaign of a working-class organisation. The film itself seems to have been lost, so we have to rely on contemporary sources for a description of it. The Workers' Charter Campaign had been started in the autumn of 1930 by the Minority Movement, with support from the Communist Party. It was modelled on the Chartist agitation of the nineteenth century and consisted of a programme of direct demands concerning labour conditions and unemployment benefit. The climax was the Charter Convention in London on 12 April 1931.[102]. A couple of days after the Convention the LWFS held a special members' meeting which included a 'discussion on new Charter Film'.[103] Previewing the film for the LWFS performance on 3 May, 'Arthur West' (Ralph Bond) wrote:

> *Nineteen thirty-one*, as the film is called, is a documentary film, i.e., a film of actual life taken under natural conditions. There are no individual actors, not a single scene has been taken inside a studio, and most of it has been shot in the open air with a hand camera.[104]

Leo Wood, film critic of the MM weekly *The Worker*, gave a more tangible description of the film:

> Here is a film made without any actors or studio sets, simply setting out to show in terse flashes what 1931 means to the workers. Rationalisation, speed-up, and lowered standards in factory, mine and workshop; poverty in the home; unemployment while the band comments, 'Land of Hope and Glory'; vile housing conditions and filthy back-alleys for recreation for the children. Contrasted with these are apt settings showing the luxury, idleness and pomp of the employing class, and the sight of these lounge lizards enjoying all the good things of life while the workers slave at their grinding, ill-paid jobs is most excellent propaganda for the necessity to fight the encroachments of the boss-class. Workers' Charter demonstrations form the climax to the film and point the moral. Just one criticism of *1931*. The scenes of *work* are good, but there is not sufficient actual commentary on *working conditions*.[105]

A different description was given by Bond himself in an article for the American magazine *Experimental Cinema*.

> *1931* shows how the dockers, the railwaymen, the miners, the textile and steel workers are exploited under the rationalisation attacks of the employers. The imperialist character of British capitalism is emphasised with shots of slave labour in China and the suppression of native revolts by troops and warships. Shots of unemployed workers at the Labour Exchanges, and the slums where the workers live are contrasted with the luxury pursuits and wealth of the bourgeoisie. The struggles of the colonial workers are cross-cut with those of the British workers and there is a symbolical sequence urging solidarity with the Soviet Union. Various shots of British workers in action, strikes, marches and demonstrations build up in a rising tempo to the fade-out title, a map of Britain, with the words 'THEIR OWN' superimposed.[106]

1931 clearly was a film based on 'deadly parallels'.

However, by the time it was released the Workers' Charter Campaign had lost its momentum. For other reasons, too, the full integration of the film into the Charter campaign proved difficult. To achieve any real impact, it would have been necessary to take the film to the workers, instead of making the workers come to the film. Although *1931* was shown by several workers' film societies, the movement was not yet ripe for

extensive tours with portable projection equipment. The LWFS
for example had only one portable projector, the MSWFS
none.[107] An interesting experiment was made by the Bethnal
Green Charter Committee. It combined the screening of *1931*
with the performance of 'Rationalisation' by a South-East
Workers' Theatre Movement group.[108]

The making of *1931* induced Ralph Bond to make an
assessment of the films produced by the Workers' Film
Movement. He pointed out that financial difficulties should
not be used as an excuse to prevent

> production work of our own, however crude and fragmentary it
> may be in the first stages. We must learn to master, in a
> practical way, the elements of film production so that when we
> have the resources after the revolution we shall know how to
> make use of them.

Bond outlined a minimum production programme, consisting
of workers' newsreels, montage films and documentaries. In
other words, *Workers' Topical News* Nos. 1, 2 and 3, *Glimpses of
Modern Russia* and *1931*. The production of films based on the
lives of British workers, to which the FOWFS had pledged itself
in September 1930, was not mentioned. One can only guess at
the reasons for this. Lack of money? The exigencies of the
revolutionary struggle? Bond particularly paid attention to the
(low) costs of the Workers' Film Movement productions. *1931*
had been made for less than £50. Commercially speaking it
had been a lower-than-low-budget film. It must, however,
have been a strain on the FOWFS budget: at a meeting in May
1931 it had been decided that every workers' film society would
pay 6d. per member per year to the Federation. If all this
money was used for film production, the making of *1931*
would have required the contribution of 2,000 members!

According to Bond the decision to make *1931* had been
taken by 'delegates from the various Workers' Film Societies'.
Bond left no room for doubt that he considered the
documentary the most suitable film form for the Workers' Film
Movement. He even apologized for certain sequences in *1931*.

> Difficulties of securing interior scenes of factory and workshop
> conditions necessitated the borrowing of certain sequences
> from other films, but a very considerable proportion of the film
> we shot ourselves with a portable hand camera. The film is

entirely documentary; we employed no actors and no studio settings.

Bond concluded his assessment with the following: 'As an experiment, *1931* is valuable, not only for its propaganda content, but because it has taught us that workers' production is possible even with the most limited resources.'[109]

Soviet films dominated the 1931-32 season of workers' film societies affiliated to the FOWFS. New societies started in Birmingham, Nottingham and Sheffield, but the Glasgow Workers' Film Society could no longer continue its performances.[110] Conspicuously absent was the LWFS which had set the example for the movement from November 1929 onwards. The supply of suitable films had run out. The LWFS had closed its second season with the showing of *The Blue Express*, one of the first Soviet sound films. The transition to sound had virtually brought the Soviet film industry to a standstill, resulting in a gap in supply which affected the Workers' Film Movement in Britain and other countries. Sound film and the costs it involved had also led to a severe crisis in the production of proletarian films in Germany. The WIR film company Prometheus went bankrupt. Its sister company Weltfilm survived but was in no position to help Atlas Films, which was also in financial difficulties. In December 1931 Atlas was fined £10 and £5 costs for not acquiring 10 per cent of British films under the Cinematograph Films Act. It transpired that the company had made a loss of £500 on its previous year's working.[111] Its initial capital had been only £1,000. Ralph Bond, the motor behind Atlas, the FOWFS and LWFS, had left to work for John Grierson. Bond's departure also created a gap on the film production front. Without his perseverance and organisational skill the Atlas productions would never have been made.

In the absence of new films, the FOWFS produced its own film magazine, *Workers' Cinema*. The first issue appeared in November 1931, the second and last in January 1932.

David Bennett who had succeeded Ralph Bond as film critic of the *Daily Worker* welcomed the magazine, but criticised its highbrow tone which would

leave the people to whom it is addressed in a state of complete mystification. This defect, however, will probably be remedied as soon as numbers of worker correspondents up and down the country begin to do their job of sending in news of film activities and items relating to boss-class film dope put over at their local cinemas.[112]

A call for worker film correspondents was published in the first issue of *Workers' Cinema*.[113] The idea of worker film criticism had been put into practice with reasonable success by the German magazine *Arbeiterbühne und Film* and in a slightly different way, as 'Spectators' Criticism', by the French Communist daily *L'Humanité*.[114] In Germany and France the Communist press could rely on extensive networks of worker correspondents, from whose ranks the worker film critics were usually recruited. In Britain the idea of worker correspondents had never secured a foothold, despite attempts first by *Workers' Life* and later by the *Daily Worker* to propagate it and build up such networks. This was a serious handicap for *Workers' Cinema*: it could not fall back on an organised body of trained worker correspondents and did not exist long enough for the idea of worker film criticism to find acceptance.

How did these changes affect the local workers' film societies? We shall again single out the Salford Workers' Film Society. After it had been forced into exile from Salford over *Storm over Asia*, the society decided to stay in Manchester as the Manchester and Salford Workers' Film Society (MSWFS). For the 1931-32 season it published a special leaflet announcing the exhibition of Soviet classics like *The Blue Express, Battleship Potemkin, New Babylon, Bed and Sofa* and *The Ghost that Never Returns*. The BBFC had done its bit in building up their reputation by banning most of them. The MSWFS started the season with a Soviet film that has since become a classic although not well known at the time – Dziga Vertov's *The Man with the Movie Camera* – accompanied by *1931* and *Men of the Woods*.[115]

For its second performance the society had programmed *The Blue Express*. Being banned by the BBFC, this film had to be previewed by the Manchester Watch Committee, as did *New Babylon*, another banned Soviet film that the MSWFS planned to show.

The Watch Committee, however, refused to allow the Society to

exhibit either of the two films, no reason being given. A
substitute programme was hastily selected and a performance
given on the date intended [21 November 1931, B.H.]. Just
before the performance was due to commence the Inspector of
Police cornered the secretary of the society and demanded to
know whether the films selected were 'Communist propaganda'. He then attempted to stop the show by quoting
regulations that only applied to public exhibitions; but the
performance was held before an audience numbering 400. This
police interference was obviously designed to intimidate the
Society and the owner of the cinema, but the Society will find
ways and means of carrying on ...[116]

The case ended in the Manchester City Police Court, where the
company that owned the Futurist Cinema was fined the sum of
40s. for showing films that had not previously been
trade-shown in Manchester. It was clearly meant to deter the
Manchester cinema owners from letting their cinemas to the
MSWFS. After all, the replacement programme had consisted
of films that had been passed by the BBFC (*Refuge, Jewish
Colonisation in the Soviet Union, Touring the Caucasus* and *Cut It
Out!*). None of them, apart from *Refuge*, had been exhibited
and therefore trade-shown in Manchester. The MSWFS
decided to suspend its activities for the time being. It was time
for reflection. Tom Cavanagh proposed the purchase of a
portable projector, with which the society could show films on
reduced format, printed on non-inflammable stock, in places
where licences from the Watch Committee were not required.
He appealed for the establishment of a special fund to cover
the costs, but no immediate action was taken.[117]

The period of reflection ended in March 1932, when the
MSWFS announced the resumption of its activities. It handed
the Manchester press a list of films it intended to show during
the rest of the year. The list included G.W. Pabst's anti-war
film *Westfront 1918*, his homage to miners' international
solidarity *Kameradschaft*, René Clair's French comedies *The
Italian Straw Hat* and *Paris Qui Dort*, Robert Wiene's
expressionist classic *The Cabinet of Dr Caligari* and King Vidor's
Hallelujah with its all-black cast. The only film left over from
the original schedule from the 1931-32 season was Eisenstein's
Battleship Potemkin (still banned by the BBFC). The reasons
behind this change in programming were more complex than

simply finding a solution to satisfy the Watch Committee. Indeed, the Management Committee of the MSWFS took seriously the objection by the Manchester authorities to the practice of members bringing along 'guests' to the society's performances. The decision was made to admit henceforth only members. Obviously, the committee had done some thinking about the membership of the society. It was clear that it had largely failed to reach the working-class, trade union membership it had been looking for. Alf Williams remembered that the committee came to the conclusion that useful political work could also be done among the predominantly 'intellectual' MSWFS audience – a situation none of them had imagined when they started the society.[118] To attract and consolidate a membership of this more 'intellectual' kind a change of emphasis was required from *workers'* film society to workers' *film* society. This process was speeded up by the changes within the FOWFS, the financial difficulties of Atlas Films and the lack of new Soviet films.

The 'new line' of the MSWFS was displayed in a leaflet, 'The Cinema and Its Application to Social Questions'. This described the past history of the society, especially its battles with the authorities over the principle of 'Free Sight'. The leaflet sought to avoid the impression that Soviet films were all the society cared about and described its aims as follows:

> The Society ... is determined to bring before its members films of outstanding artistic merit and profound educational and social import, which, by their very nature, are unlikely to be shown commercially in this Country. The Society proposes to draw films of this character from all available sources, old and new, amateur and commercial, national and international, and thus contribute to the formation of an informed audience, which would be fully aware of the power and possibilities of the Cinema. It must be clear to every thinking man and woman, that the Cinema as at present commercially exploited tends habitually to present a non-social and unreal picture, completely out of sympathy with the ideas and movements existing within the present social order.[119]

The leaflet made no reference to the FOWFS although the MSWFS was still affiliated to it – indeed sales of the Federation's magazine *Workers' Cinema* ('a broadsheet [that] is

full of enthusiasm') at MSWFS performances are recorded in
the *Manchester Guardian*.[120]

It is not clear whether the new line resulted in a different
relationship with the parent body, the Salford Social
Democratic Land and Builders' Society. It seems likely that the
committee at least aimed at financial independence from it.
The Management Committee was renamed the Executive
Committee. New members were added: a Films Secretary (J.D.
Sinclair), a Publicity Secretary (C.B. Beardsworth) and a
Technical Adviser (Peter A. Le Neve Foster). A novelty was an
Advisory Council, headed by trade union veteran A.A. Purcell
and including four councillors (always useful in case the society
got into trouble with the authorities), Professor Maurice Dobb,
Emile Burns (a founding member of the FOWFS and LWFS)
and others. It seems that the changes had the desired effect: by
the end of 1932 the society had a membership of 750 after a
successful run of performances in the Majestic and Scala
cinemas.[121]

Were the changes that the MSWFS underwent limited to
Manchester and Salford? Or was there a general trend among
the workers' film societies in Britain to go for the 'better type'
of pictures from the Continent? Lack of source material makes
it impossible to answer this question. However, one can point
to the case of Glasgow, where various workers' film societies
fought a protracted battle with the authorities over the right to
show Soviet films. The first had been the Glasgow Workers'
Film Society, a member of the FOWFS. It organised four
performances during the 1930-31 season, showing among
others *The Girl with the Hat Box, Battleship Potemkin, Giant Harvest*
and *Earth*, before suspending its activities. Little is known
about the first season of the New Art Cinema Movement, a
venture of the Friends of the Soviet Union. When it started its
second season in December 1932, the *Daily Worker* summed up
its purpose: 'Soviet films ... are the Socialist answer to
capitalist propaganda on the screen.'[122] Its opening performance for the new season comprised *Two Days* and *Men of the
Woods*. It clashed with the second performance of the newly
formed Film Section of the Scottish USSR Society, featuring
Trauberg's sound film *Alone* and *Battleship Potemkin*.[123] The next
performances of the two societies on 25 December 1932
clashed again: the New Art Cinema Movement showed *The Five*

Year Plan (with which the Scottish USSR Society had opened on 13 November 1932) and the Scottish USSR Society *The Ghost that Never Returns*.[124] Early in 1933 the Glasgow Corporation interfered, alleging that the societies had failed to observe the strict regulations concerning private societies. Protests did not help and the film shows were banned.[125] In the autumn of 1934 a new society was formed, the Workers' Film Society (West of Scotland). It showed Nikolai Ekk's highly praised sound film on homeless children *The Road to Life, The Blue Express* and *Storm over Asia*. Interestingly, the programme also included two Continental films, the German *War is Hell* and the French satirical comedy *The Virtuous Isidore*.[126] Like its predecessors, the Workers' Film Society (West of Scotland) was short-lived.

The changes in the Manchester and Salford Workers' Film Society might be interpreted as a retreat from proletarian principles, while Glasgow might be seen as embodying those principles in its successive struggles with the Corporation over the exhibition of Soviet films. This would be a naïve approach, offering no answer to the questions posed earlier: what was the role of Soviet films and what was the position of the workers' film societies in relation to the local Labour movement? It is clear that the Soviet films acted as the workers' film society movement's indispensable 'capital'. They shaped the image of the societies, towards the membership, the press, and last but not least, the authorities. The Soviet films were appreciated for a complex of political and artistic reasons which it is not easy to disentangle. How the viewing of Soviet films affected the audience's cinematographic perception in general cannot be ascertained. A few years ago the West German historian Dieter Langewiesche advanced the thesis that the working-class movement failed to integrate institutionally the new mass media (radio, cinema and, although he was not directly referring to it, television), as it had done previously with virtually all existing forms of art and culture.[127] The Workers' Film Movement was an attempt at such institutional integration. Nationally and locally it was a difficult process. By the end of 1931 the Workers' Film Movement had made headway in a number of industrial cities; often, however, the local workers' film societies found the odds against them and disappeared after one season. The FOWFS did not publish membership figures, but growth must have been disappointing given the fact that a workers' film society working under reasonably favourable conditions, like the Salford one, had only 350 members after its first season. One must also doubt whether the particular form chosen by the Workers' Film Movement for its activities – the private film society – was the most suitable. Would it not have been better to show films in places where workers usually met, instead of trying to attract them to town-centre cinemas? The LWFS seemed to have been the only society that purchased portable projection equipment and made its services available to working-class organisations in the London region.

A last, important, question has been left unanswered: what was the influence of the policies of the British (and international) Communist movement on the workers' film society movement? Internationally, the policy of founding workers' film societies in response to interference in the exhibition of Soviet films was rendered out of date. The French Les Amis de Spartacus had been disbanded in 1929, the German Volksfilmverband was inactive by 1931 (with the exception of one or two local sections) and the Dutch VVVC was transformed into the Friends of the Soviet Union in March 1931. In 1931 the German magazine *Arbeiterbühne und Film* published the first appeal for an 'agitprop cinema', written by Heinz Lüdecke, the film critic of the KPD daily *Die Rote Fahne*, and Korea Senda.[128] However the small-film format indispensable for an 'agitprop cinema' met with powerful resistance within the Communist movement. *L'Humanité* film critic Léon Moussinac twice put his reputation at stake by opposing the use of 'sub-standard' (small-format) film by the French Communist movement.[129] Because of the peculiarity of the 1909 Cinematograph Act, the situation in the United Kingdom was more clear-cut than elsewhere. The use of 'sub-standard' film meant exemption from the 1909 Cinematograph Act, because the Act only applied to inflammable film, the so-called nitrate stock. The 'sub-standard' format only made use of acetate stock, which technically was non-inflammable. In other words, adoption of non-inflammable film could solve a number of problems that the Workers' Film Movement was faced with.[130] It was just a matter of who would do it and when.

Notes

1. *Sunday Worker*, 22 September 1928, p.9.
2. Ibid., 27 May 1928, p.7.
3. This paragraph is based on Ivor Montagu, *The Political Censorship of Films*, London 1929.
4. Gertraude Kühn, Karl Tümmler, Walter Wimmer (eds.), *Film und revolutionäre Arbeiterbewegung in Deutschland 1918-1932, Dokumente und Materialien zur Entwicklung der Filmpolitik der revolutionären Arbeiterbewegung und zu den Anfängen einer sozialistischen Filmkunst in Deutschland*, East Berlin 1975, Vol.II, p.237.
5. In an article on 'The Proletarian Cinema and the Weimar Republic' in the *Historical Journal of Film, Radio and Television* David Welch advanced the thesis that the Volksfilmverband was an SPD creation (*HJFRT*, Vol.I, No.1, March 1981, p.9). As I have pointed out in my comment on Welch's article, no German researcher has substantiated his claim. The most recent West German publication on this subject, by Hans-Michael Bock, in the catalogue *Vorwärts- und nicht vergessen* (1982), confirms this point of view. See Bert Hogenkamp, 'The Proletarian Cinema and the Weimar Republic: a comment' in *HJFRT*, Vol.II, No.2, 1982, pp.177-9.
6. See Léon Moussinac, 'Les Amis de Spartacus' in *Cinéma 74*, July-August 1974. pp.73-4.
7. *L'Humanité*, 4 March 1928, p.4; 5 March 1928, p.2.
8. Ibid., 4 March 1928, p.4.
9. Ibid., 12 May 1928, p.4.
10. It is generally thought that Les Amis de Spartacus were banned by the Ministry of the Interior in October 1928. See Bert Hogenkamp, 'Le Mouvement Ouvrier et le Cinéma' in *La Revue du Cinéma*, No.366, November 1981, pp.125-35, here p.125.
11. *De Tribune*, 28 January 1928, p.5.
12. See Hartmann Wunderer, *Arbeitervereine und Arbeiterparteien, Kultur- und Massenorganisationen in der Arbeiterbewegung (1890-1933)*, Frankfurt am Main, 1982, pp.165-8.
13. See Bert Hogenkamp, 'Workers' Newsreels in the 1920s and 1930s', in *Our History*, No.68. [1977], pp.6-11; Flip Bool and Jeroen de Vries (eds), *De Arbeidersfotografen, Camera en crisis in de jaren '30*, Amsterdam 1982; Bert Hogenkamp, ' "Hier met de film". Het gebruik van het medium film door de communistische beweging in de jaren twintig en dertig', in *Cahiers over de geschiedenis van de CPN*, No.8, April 1983, pp.86-92.
14. Basing their conclusions generally on biographical statements of artists and writers who had broken with 'the God that failed', the historians seldom used the available primary source material. The results were in keeping with their methods; see, for example, David Caute, *The Fellow-Travellers. A Postscript to the Enlightenment*, New York 1973.
15. With his study on the French Communist Party and its attitude towards literature, J.-P. Bernard set a model for forthcoming researchers (J.-P.

Bernard, *Le Parti Communiste Français et la question littéraire (1921-1939)*
Grenoble 1972). A further step was made by Richard Stourac in a
comparative study, 'Revolutionary Workers' Theatre in the Soviet Union,
Germany and Britain (1918-1936)', a Ph.D. thesis distributed in a roneotyped
format, May 1978. Studies on film and the labour movement, based on the
research of primary and secondary sources, will be mentioned below.

16. See Noreen Branson, *History of the Communist Party of Great Britain
1927-1941*, London 1985; Henry Pelling, *The British Communist Party. A
Historical Profile*, London 1975; Michael Woodhouse and Brian Pearce, *Essays
on the History of Communism in Britain*, London 1975; Hugo Dewar, *Communist
Politics in Britain: the CPGB from its Origins to the Second World War*, London
1976.

17. Alun Howkins, 'Class Against Class: The Political Culture of the
Communist Party of Great Britain, 1930-35', in Frank Gloversmith (ed.),
Class, Culture and Social Change. A New View of the 1930's, Brighton 1980,
pp.240-57.

18. See Montagu, op.cit., p.5; the film was also shown under the title *Soviet
Russia Today*, cf. *Sunday Worker*, 21 October 1928, p.9; *Workers' Life*, No.95, 16
November 1928, p.5.

19. See Roderick Martin, *Communism and the British Trade Unions 1924-1933. A
study of the National Minority Movement*, Oxford 1969.

20. *The Worker*, 22 November 1929, p.7; see also Ralph Bond, 'Workers'
Films: Past and Future', in *Labour Monthly*, January 1976, pp.27-30, especially
p.27; Ralph Bond, 'Cinema in the Thirties: Documentary Film and the
Labour Movement' in Jon Clark, Margot Heinemann, David Margolies and
Carole Snee (eds.), *Culture and Crisis in Britain in the 30s*, London 1979,
pp.241-56, especially p.247.

21. *The Worker*, 22 November 1929, p.7.

22. *Trade Union Propaganda and Cultural Work* (1928-29) was published by the
Agitprop Department of the RILU. This department was headed by H.
Diament who became a leading functionary in the Moscow-based
International Union of Revolutionary Theatre in the 1930's. *Trade Union
Propaganda and Cultural Work* contained directives, articles of a theoretical
nature and reports from various countries. It paid much attention to the
worker correspondent movement, to workers' theatre and workers'
education. There are scant references to the cinema, usually in the national
reports, but there is certainly no blueprint for a workers' film society
movement.

23. *Sunday Worker*, 13 October 1929, p.4. The exact date of the foundation of
the London Workers' Film Society is unknown. It might well have been
founded before 28 October 1929, in other words before the FOWFS, but it
was meant to be part of a national network from the start.

24. *Sunday Worker*, 27 October 1929, p.2.

25. Ibid., 10 November 1929, p.1.

26. Ibid., 1 December 1929, p.2.

27. Only fragments of the original version have survived, while the British
version is still extant. In the latter the staged scenes regularly alternate with
the documentary sequences. It seems that in the original version the
documentary material was used at the start, to introduce the story of the
young weaver.

28. *Film und Volk*, No.2, February 1930, p.39.

29. See Rolf Surmann, *Die Münzenberg-Legende. Zur Publizistik der revolutionären deutschen Arbeiterbewegung 1921-1933*, Cologne 1983, p.119.

30. Atlas Films started with an initial capital of £1000 (*Daily Worker*, 21 December 1931, p.6).

31. Ralph Bond, 'First Steps Towards A Workers' Film Movement', in *Close-Up*, January 1930, pp.66-9, here p.68.

32. Ralph Bond, 'Acts under the Acts', in *Close-Up*, April 1930, pp.278-83, here pp.278-9.

33. *Daily Herald*, 3 February 1930, p.5; *Daily Worker*, 4 February 1930, p.10.

34. *Daily Worker*, 4 February 1930, p.10.

35. Minutes, Executive Committee, Labour Party, 26 February 1930, p.69.

36. *The Daily Herald* published some reports on the activities of the LWFS from November 1929 to March 1930, but switched to the Masses Stage and Film Guild after that date.

37. *New Leader*, 15 November 1929, p.14; see also Harold Scott, 'The ILP and Play Production', in: *Socialist Review*, November 1929, pp.43-5.

38. 'Benn' articles in *New Leader*: 'How Labour Can Use the Films', 26 April 1929, p.2; 'A Workers' Film Society?', 3 May 1929, p.16; 'Why Not A Socialist News Reel?', 31 May 1929, p.2.

39. *The Times*, 22 February 1930, p.7.

40. *The Times*, 25 February 1930, p.12.

41. *New Leader*, 28 February 1930, p.15.

42. Ibid., 7 March 1930, p.4.

43. *The Times*, 10 March 1930, p.11.

44. *Daily Herald*, 26 March 1930, p.2.

45. Public Record Office, London, Home Office 45/14276.

46. In 1922 a group of Labour councillors in the London borough of Poplar were jailed because they had openly defied the government's decrees regarding relief scales and had distributed funds in a more liberal way to the Poplar unemployed. The imprisonment of George Lansbury and his colleagues led to a national campaign for their release and for a reform of the relief system. See Noreen Branson, *Poplarism 1919-1925*, London 1979.

47. *Daily Worker*, 10 March 1930, p.10.

48. *New Leader*, 31 May 1929, p.2.

49. *The Worker*, 22 November 1929, p.7.

50. See William Alexander, *Film on the Left. American Documentary Film from 1931 to 1942*, Princeton 1981, p.5 (for Bond's letter to Sam Brody), pp.3-64 (for the history of the (Workers') Film and Photo League); a less personal, historically more developed account of the League can be found in Russell Campbell, *Cinema Strikes Back: Radical Filmmaking in the United States, 1930-1942*, Ann Arbor 1982.

51. See Hogenkamp, 'Workers' Newsreels in the 1920s and 1930s', pp.4-11.

52. Ibid., pp.14-6; *L'Humanité*, 2 September 1932, p.4; 23 September 1932, p.4; 30 September 1932, p.5; 28 October 1932, p.4.

53. Ralph Bond, 'Workers' Films: Past and Future', in *Labour Monthly*, January 1976, p.28.

54. *Daily Worker*, 28 May 1930, p.5. P.J. Poole, the author of the letter, may well have been Philip Poole, the secretary of the Workers' Theatre Movement and member of the Hackney agitprop group Red Radio.

55. The historian certainly would like to know more about the composition of the LWFS audience (working-class or not?; male or female?; how many were members of the CPGB, the Labour Party, a trade-union, the Friends of the Soviet Union?; how many had a dual membership of the LWFS and the Film Society?; etc.). Unfortunately there are no figures available, and these questions have to remain unresolved.

56. *Daily Worker*, 4 February 1930, p.10.

57. Ibid., 16 June 1930, p.5.

58. *Sunday Worker*, 4 August 1929, p.9.

59. *Daily Worker*, 20 June 1930, p.5.

60. Ralph Bond, 'Dirty Work', in *Close Up*, August 1930, pp. 98-100, here p.99.

61. Ibid.

62. Ibid.

63. *Daily Herald*, 27 June 1930, p.6.

64. Ibid., 27 May 1930, p.2.

65. *Kinematograph Weekly*, 23 October 1930, p.23.

66. *Independent Labour Party. Report of the Annual Conference, held at Scarborough, April, 1931*, p.23.

67. *North Hackney Citizen*, No.8, December 1930, p.2.

68. *Daily Worker*, 26 May 1930, p.5.

69. Ibid., 25 February 1930, p.7.

70. *Experimental Cinema*, Vol.I, No.4 (1932), p.28.

71. *Daily Worker*, 3 May 1930, p.5; 10 September 1930, p.4.

72. *New Leader*, 6 June 1930, p.15.

73. *Kinematograph Weekly*, 19 June 1930, p.22.

74. *Independent Labour Party. Report of the Annual Conference, held at Scarborough, April, 1931*, p.23.

75. *Kinematograph Weekly*, 18 September 1930, p.33.

76. *Daily Worker*, 23 September 1930, p.4.

77. Ibid., 18 August 1930, p.5.

78. Ibid., 27 October 1930, p.3.

79. Ibid., 13 October 1930, p.3.

80. *Forward*, 1 November 1930, p.15; 15 November 1930, p.15.

81. *Daily Worker*, 19 August 1930, p.5.

82. The author would like to thank Seona Robertson for making available copies of the documents, newspaper clippings and taped interviews with Reg Cordwell and Alf Williams. Additional material was kindly provided by Edmund Frow of The Working Class Movement Library, Manchester. See also Audrey Linkman and Bill Williams, 'Recovering the People's Past: the archive rescue programme of Manchester Studies', in *History Workshop Journal*, No.8, Autumn 1979, pp.111-26.

83. Manchester and Salford Workers' Film Society, Report, Season 1930-31 (in Manchester Studies archive, referred to hereafter as MSa). Further information on the Salford Social-Democratic Land and Builders' Society Ltd. can be found in Ruth and Edmund Frow, *The Communist Party in Manchester 1920-1926*, Manchester n.d., pp.79-80.

84. Agenda, Special General Meeting, Salford Social Democratic Land and Builders Society Ltd., 20 May 1930 (in MSa).

85. See biography section in Ruth and Edmund Frow, op.cit., pp.48-73.

86. *Daily Worker*, 6 March 1931, p.4.

87. Ibid., 25 March 1931, p.1.

88. Ibid., 4 July 1931, p.4.

89. Invoice from Egerton Printing Co. to Mr (Tom) Cavanagh, Salford, 21 November 1930, (in The Working Class Movement Library, referred to hereafter as TWCML); Manchester and Salford Workers' Film Society, Report, 1930-31 Season (in MSa).

90. Manchester and Salford Workers' Film Society, Report, 1930-31 Season (in MSa).

91. Programme leaflet, Salford Workers' Film Society, 15 November 1930 (in MSa).

92. Alf Williams, interviewed by Seona Robertson, ca. 1978 (in MSa).

93. Invoice from Egerton Printing Co. to Mr (Tom) Cavanagh, Salford, 21 November 1930 (in TWCML); Manchester and Salford Workers' Film Society, Report, 1930-31 Season (in MSa).

94. Manchester and Salford Workers' Film Society, Report, 1930-31 Season (in MSa).

95. See note 84 above.

96. Newspaper clipping on debate over *Storm over Asia* in Salford City Council (in MSa).

97. Manchester and Salford Workers' Film Society, Report, 1930-31 Season (in MSa).

98. Ibid.

99. *Daily Worker*, 2 March 1931, p.4.

100. Alf Williams interview, loc. cit.

101. 'But what sort of a "workers'" film society is it which ... refuses to put on the screen advertisements for the *Daily Worker* and the Charter Gala?' asked A.P. in the *Daily Worker*, 4 July 1931, p.4.

102. See Martin, op.cit., pp.157-63.

103. *Daily Worker*, 15 April 1931, p.3.

104. Ibid., 22 April 1931, p.4.

105. *The Worker*, 9 May 1931, p.7.

106. *Experimental Cinema*, Vol.I, No.4 (1932), p.42.

107. *The Worker*, 23 May 1931, p.7; Manchester and Salford Workers' Film Society, Report, 1930-31 Season (in MSa).

108. *Daily Worker*, 2 June 1931, p.3.

109. Ralph Bond, 'The Production of Working Class Films', in *Experimental Cinema*, Vol.I, No.4 (1932), p.42. It seems very likely that Bond put the same forward in his lecture 'The Theory and Practice of Workers' Cinema' which he delivered at the weekend film schools of the Merseyside Workers' Film Society (20 June 1931) and the LWFS (25 and 26 July 1931); *Daily Worker*, 24 June 1931, p.4.; 7 July 1931, p.4.; 30 July 1931, p.4.

110. *Daily Worker*, 8 June 1931, p.4.; 7 October 1931, p.4.; 11 November 1931, p.6; 7 December 1931, p.6; 29 December 1931, p.6; 23 January 1931, p.5; Douglas Allen, 'Workers' Films: Scotland's Hidden Film Culture', in Colin McArthur, *Scotch Reels, Scotland in Cinema and Television*, London 1982, pp.93-9, here p.94.

111. *Daily Worker*, 21 December 1931, p.6.

112. Ibid., 30 November 1931, p.6.

113. 'Worker Film Fans! – Will you become a correspondent for *Workers'*

Cinema? We want your ideas, your views, your criticisms of the films you see. Write to us. Make it short and snappy! Join the army of worker film critics and extend the circulation of your paper.' This appeal was accompanied by a lengthy article, entitled 'The Film is a Weapon', outlining the tasks set by *Workers' Cinema*. The only known copy of *Workers' Cinema* No.1, November 1931, is kept in the John Grierson archive, University of Stirling. As yet no copies of No.2 have been traced.

114. See Reiner Frey, 'Geschichten von jenen, die versuchten die laufenden Bilder wieder einzufangen – die Anfänge der Zuschauerfilmkritik in Deutschland, das Beispiel Arbeiterbühne und Film (1930/31)', in *Filmfaust*, No. 19, June 1980, pp.8-16; Brigitte Hervo, 'Zuschauerfilmkritik Anfang der 30-er Jahre in Frankreich', in *Filmfaust*, No.20, November 1980, pp.35-45.

115. *Daily Worker*, 19 October 1931, p.4.

116. Ibid., 30 November 1931, p.6.

117. Various newspaper clippings, late 1931, early 1932 (in MSa).

118. Alf Williams interview, loc.cit.

119. Manchester and Salford Workers' Film Society, The Cinema and Its Application to Social Questions (in MSa).

120. Newspaper clipping, *Manchester Guardian*, 4 April 1932 (in MSa).

121. Newspaper clipping, 10 April 1933 (in MSa).

122. *Daily Worker*, 14 December 1932, p.6.

123. *Forward*, 3 December 1932, p.15.

124. Ibid., 24 December 1932, p.16; 19 November 1932, p.15.

125. Ibid., 7 January 1933, p.16; Douglas Allen, loc.cit., p.94.

126. Ibid., 6 October 1934, p.12; 24 November 1934, p.12; 15 December 1934, p.12; 5 January 1935, p.12.

127. Dieter Langewiesche, 'Politik – Gesellschaft – Kultur: Zur Problematik von Arbeiterkultur und kulturellen Arbeiterorganisationen in Deutschland nach dem I. Weltkrieg', paper delivered at the 17th Linz Conference, Internationale Tagung der Historiker der Arbeiterbewegung, 8 to 12 September 1981, pp.19-21.

128. Korea Senda, Heinz Lüdecke, 'Agitpropisierung des proletarischen Films', in *Arbeiterbühne und Film*, May 1931, pp.8-11.

129. *L'Humanité*, 8 September 1928, p.4; 7 October 1928, p.4; 23 September 1932, p.4; 30 September 1932, p.5; 28 October 1932, p.4.

130. It is not clear how far the Movement was aware of the possibilities offered by 'sub-standard' film. *Workers' Cinema* No.1 contained an article on 'The 16mm field', in which only the simplicity of operating a 16mm projector, the saving in costs and the prospective availability of Soviet films on 16mm through the German company Weltfilm were mentioned. (*Daily Worker*, 30 November 1931, p.6), but even the MSWFS which contemplated the acquisition of a 'sub-standard' film projector through Tom Cavanagh, stuck to the ordinary picture palace with its 35mm projection.

Chapter 3

The Battle Over Potemkin

In a book published in 1930, *The New Spirit of the Cinema*, the theatre and film critic Huntly Carter attacked the 'right, centre and left coalition' that was 'seeking to promote the consumption of Russian cultural commodities by English workers'.[1] He accused the 'coalition' (i.e. the Film Society, the MSFG and the FOWFS) of concentrating on a fight against the film censor whereas 'spiritually, subconsciously, instinctively, and scientifically speaking, the censor does not exist [because] he is powerless to control the mind of the audience or to suppress its reading of the function of the Cinema.'[2] Carter had been the author of works on Soviet theatre and cinema and had built up a reputation as a promoter of Soviet art, and his writings in the *Sunday Worker* in the mid-1920s had inspired the Workers' Theatre Movement in its early days, so it is not clear why he was now taking a different line. However, his views gave rise to an important debate in the left press, in which Ralph Bond in particular defended the policies of the Workers' Film Movement.

In an article in *Plebs*, the monthly journal of the National Council of Labour Colleges, Carter pointed out that the profits of the film industry were largely paid out of the pockets of the workers.

What have the workers had during 1930 from the commercial folk to satisfy their real cinema hunger? Much useful stuff poached from their own grounds. Commercial-made epics, embodying the national spirit, engineering achievements, great industrial enterprises, world-wide business transactions resting on the workers' backs, railroad, aerial, covered-wagon films showing that pioneering, conquest and construction are mainly the workers' job. What have they got from the semi-commercial folk?

Here Carter made fun of the

> aesthetes busy talking through their Freudian 'Clothes Up'
> sheets about technique, 'montage' and the 'cinema mind', and
> obscuring the socialism in films and loudly despising all films
> that need no technical tricks to make their socialist message
> clear. And on the other, the communist intellectuals who are
> chiefly concerned with marketing foreign goods, and forming
> consumers' associations on a subscription basis ... What have
> the workers had from these fundamentally-opposed schools of
> cinema thought?

Implying 'nothing much', Carter listed

> Russian, German, French fare, with a mixture of Hollywood
> fare that is slightly 'different' in pictures into which the
> commercial producer has introduced a touch of the 'unusual'
> in a moment of dementia, and thus queered their money value.

He had some scathing remarks for '*Mother, St Petersburg*, and
the rest of the stuff meant for a population in a shockingly
backward state', which he considered unfit for the British
workers, 'an insult to their intelligence'. Strangely enough,
Carter took one of the Soviet films, *Turksib*, as a model for the
British Labour film: 'It may be trusted to stir the British
workers into activity. What this country needs is the planning
and centralisation of the Labour cinema world, and a British
Labour Five Years' Cinema Plan.'[3]

Ralph Bond felt that Carter had injured the reputation of
the Workers' Film Movement and sent a lengthy reply to *Plebs*.
He pointed out that, contrary to Carter's statement, Soviet
films were understood and appreciated by the British workers.

> Perhaps Mr Carter has never mingled with a working-class
> audience during an exhibition of *St Petersburg*; perhaps he has
> never heard their applause and seen with what passionate
> interest they follow the events leading to the Russian
> Revolution; how they see in the sufferings and struggles of
> Russian peasants and the Russian workmen of this film the
> counterpart of their own sufferings and struggles.

Bond agreed with Carter that 'it is not sufficient to witness and applaud the films made in other countries'. He reproached Carter for overlooking the efforts, 'puny efforts, perhaps', made by the Workers' Film Movement.

> It is significant that Mr Carter offers no concrete suggestions as to the methods of or the character of workers' film production in Britain. Perhaps, after all, this is not surprising. If he cannot understand the significance of the Soviet film, it is scarcely to be expected that he can approach the problem here in England.

In the end, it all came down to the absence of a Marxist viewpoint. It was no use 'to initiate "new spirits" and "new religions" ', it only mattered 'to aid and encourage the workers in their fights against capitalism'.[4]

The editors of *Plebs* gave Carter the opportunity to deny the charges made by Bond, which he did in a vitriolic reply. He accused Bond of not bothering 'about definitions and distinctions' with regard to the word 'workers'. To prove his scientific thinking and his Marxist credentials, Carter sought to expose the unsuitability of Eisenstein's *The General Line*

> for consumption by British Labour. It is inconceivably old-fashioned. It is a mess of primitive magic and ritual, of religion (in the sense of god-making), of superstitution [sic], of faith in and fear of tribal gods and faith in and fear of the new god of machinery. Take the ceremony of the marriage of the Bull, wherein the bull is deified and worshipped as the God of fertility as in early Greek days. The cow to be fertilised is beribboned and garlanded like a virgin about to be given in marriage. The Bull is led forth swelling visibly till it seems ready to burst with carnal desire. The excited peasants are dolled up in their holiday best like a lot of harlots shrieking with delight at the sight of the marriage being consummated, as it is in the original Soviet film. Is British Labour so unintelligent that it requires this mixture of primitive ignorance and idolatory to stir it to economic action?[5]

History defeated Carter's reasoning. For some reason he chose to attack the one Soviet film that did achieve a big British audience. In 1931 the Royal Arsenal Co-operative Society obtained a print of *The General Line*,[6] which was used extensively by the co-operative movement and by the end of 1934 had been seen by 40,000 people in and around London.[7] The very reason for which Carter declared the film unfit for British

labour audiences may have ensured its success among the
co-operators – its unorthodox (in Carter's words 'primitive')
appeal to co-operation.

To illustrate his point about 'definitions and distinctions'
regarding 'workers', Carter described his observation of a
performance by the London Workers' Film Society.

> On the last occasion but one I mingled with the LWFS audience
> at a large theatre, and I took the trouble to note its
> composition. So far as I could judge it consisted of 50 per cent
> East End Jews, mostly Russian, and 50 per cent foreigners –
> 'high-hats', reformist bourgeoisie, teachers, 'unusual picture'
> fans, and a thin sprinkling of genuine labour-class folk.[8]

The nature of the LWFS audience was also questioned in a
more pertinent – and non-racist – way by a critic in the
Minority Movement weekly the *Worker*. Writing about a film
show at the Freedom Labour Club in Peckham on 4 May 1931,
he broached the subject of portable projector screenings
'enabling Russian and other class-conscious films to be shown
to small gatherings of workers'. He felt the LWFS film shows
were too expensive (transport into Central London, plus
entrance fee) and therefore 'out of reach of the majority of
those workers that we particularly desire to influence. Films
must be taken into every working-class district and exhibited at
far less cost to each individual.' He complained that the
charges for film hire were too high.

> If such exhibitions are to become popular they must be
> organised in such way that they pay for themselves at a price
> comparable with that at the local cinemas. The average worker
> cannot help making a comparison between the comfortable
> local cinema, with its orchestra and latest talkies and his
> meeting room with its benches, the absence of music and the
> baby cinema camera, halting four times in one picture while
> reels are changed. Only the enthusiastic will consider he is
> getting value for his money, and it is the non-converted we
> want to influence.[9]

In his reply Ralph Bond pointed out that this was a wrong
comparison:

> It is quite clear that the portable shows cannot rival the local
> cinemas, and are not intended to, except in relation to the type
> of films shown. In so far as hundreds of cinemas boycott

working-class films, the fact of these films being shown in the trade unions will, for most workers, be sufficient compensation for the lack of plush seats, mural decorations, super organs, and beautifully-attired usherettes. Now as to prices for portable projector shows. The inclusive fee for the projector, an operator and a 90-minute programme of films is three guineas. About 120 members paying 6d. each will cover this cost. And an energetic branch, with the added attraction of a film show, should not find it difficult to get a satisfactory attendance.[10]

Quite correctly Bond made a distinction between the working-class habit of paying a regular visit to the local cinema and the specific character of a film show in a trade union hall. The latter could be successful if two basic requirements were met: the film had to be of a clear working-class character and the organisers of the exhibition had to put in a little extra work. This 'debate' between the *Worker* critic and Ralph Bond epitomised the major problems that the labour movement had to overcome if it were going to use films as a means of propaganda.

At the end of Chapter Two it was pointed out that the use of 'sub-standard' small format film offered a means of avoiding the censorship provided for in the 1909 Cinematograph Act. But it also meant more than this: to take advantage of small format film it was necessary to create a new and separate exhibition circuit, offering the possibility of an alternative to the dominant commercial cinema. Just as the Workers' Theatre Movement abandoned the 'curtain stage' theatre for a 'propertyless' theatre on the streets, the Workers' Film Movement was forced to abandon the picture palaces and bring the cinema directly to the workers. Of course such a cinema could never be entirely 'propertyless'. It needed the minimum assets of film and projection equipment – both costly investments. After the demise of the FOWFS in 1932 there was no organisation to take care of the financial, technical and organisational details of such a 'sub-standard' agitprop cinema. The major impetus for the development of agitprop cinema came from members of the Workers' Theatre Movement (WTM).

The Workers' Theatre Movement had been founded in 1926. During the first stage of its existence it had tried to build up a repertoire of revolutionary stage plays to be performed by affiliated groups. One of these, the Hackney People's Players, had a hit with *The Ragged Trousered Philanthropists*, adopted for the stage by Tom Thomas. After 1929 the WTM gradually changed in character. It grew closer to the CPGB and succeeded in mastering the forms of agitprop theatre which had been developed in Germany, a country with a rich tradition of workers' theatre, and in Soviet Russia. Agitprop theatre became *the* theatrical mode of the 'Class against Class' period. Abandonment of the curtain stage; short sketches of a topical character with a clear political message, varied with revue-type songs; a bare minimum of theatrical props; performances on street corners or at meetings in workers' halls; those were the main characteristics. It was essentially amateur theatre, even if it became a full time but unpaid occupation for some unemployed members. There were groups in Scotland, Lancashire and some other places, but London was the real base of the WTM. The WTM published its own printed periodical *Red Stage*, later *New Red Stage* (1931-32), which was succeeded by the roneotyped *WTM Bulletin* (1932-33) after money had run out. The WTM organised competitions between groups, national conferences and tours through Scotland and South Wales and other areas. It was affiliated to the International Workers' Drama Union (IWDU), later International Union of Revolutionary Theatre (IURT), which had its headquarters in Moscow. In 1932 the WTM National Organiser Tom Thomas was elected on the IURT praesidium. Thomas was also a member of the editorial board of *International Theatre*, a IWDU/IURT quarterly, published in Russian, German, French and English. It contained articles of a theoretical nature, directives and reports on the activities of the national workers' theatre movements. In many ways the IWDU/IURT was the showpiece of the workers' culture the Communist movement was striving for, and the WTM was proud to be a member of this well-organised international body.[11]

The WTM was interested in the cinema, as part of the entertainment industry that was controlled by 'the bosses' as dope for the workers. In a sketch written by Tom Thomas in 1932, 'Their Theatre and Ours', this feeling was succinctly summed up: 'All this sort of stuff that is put across to you on stage and film has only one purpose. To take your attention away from the drudgery of your existence, and above all, away from any thought of struggling against your rotten conditions.'[12] The WTM opened the columns of its *(New) Red Stage* for film reviews, after the early demise of *Workers Cinema*. Under the head 'Their Films – and Ours', Ralph Bond, Ivor Montagu, *Daily Worker* film critic Dave Bennett and others wrote about Soviet ('our films') and other films. But film criticism was not considered a domain for 'specialists'. Tom Thomas, for example, did not hesitate to criticise openly the Soviet film *The Peasant Woman of Riazan* (directed by Olga Preobrazhenskaya) in a letter to the *Daily Worker*. According to Thomas, this film was 'a drama of the old type, excellently photographed and acted, but completely bourgeois in the ideas it conveys to the audience.'[13] Undoubtedly Thomas was convinced that his knowledge of the differences between bourgeois and proletarian drama gave him the tools to tackle the film medium as well. Arthur Stainthorpe from Middlesbrough felt that the WTM had a task 'to keep a visual record of demonstrations, etc.' He appealed to start 'a fund for the purchasing of a good miniature movie-camera and projector'. The editors of *Red Stage* agreed with Stainthorpe:

> Our comrade's letter is excellent and should provide a rallying ground for the making and showing of our own films. We invite the opinions and concrete assistance of readers. Let us know whether you would be willing to help, whether financially or from the technical end, to get movements going all over the country with the object of making films either from original scenarios or of working class demonstrations, struggle, etc.[14]

They listed a number of initiatives (in London, Manchester and Liverpool) in this direction. Surprisingly, the recording on film of WTM sketches was not mentioned at all; probably because the movement did not see its work as art (which had to be recorded for the future), but as agitation and propaganda within a political struggle.

Charlie Mann, son of the trade union veteran Tom Mann, was one of the WTM members with a particular interest in the cinema. As editor of *(New) Red Stage* and member of the Rebel Players, a London agitprop group, Mann was very active in the movement. The Rebel Players and the Yiddish Proltet group were rewarded with a trip to the Soviet Union, after winning a competition, as the British delegation at the International Workers' Theatre Olympiad, held in Moscow in May 1933. This event had enormous consequences for the workers' theatre movements in the capitalist countries, which eventually would lead to a return to the curtain stage.[15] Charlie Mann, however, was particularly enthused by a side event of the Olympiad, a conference organised by the Cinema Bureau of the IURT. Among the speakers were *L'Humanité* film critic Léon Moussinac and the Hungarian film theoretician in exile Béla Balázs. Mann was impressed by their film analyses, but a lecture that really inspired him treated 'the possibilities of the use of film for the type of thing we were doing in the Workers' Theatre Movement'.[16] This must have been the report by the German exile Hans Rodenburg on the importance of the 'sub-standard' film. In the American journal *New Theatre* Rodenberg's intervention was summarised as follows:

> Com. Rodenburg spoke on the importance of the small stripe [i.e. sub-standard, B.H.] film and its history. This type of film is very useful for the revolutionary film movement, since it can be shown in any hall, before any organisation. It is also more economical than the large size film and is within the reach of workers' organisations. Soviet pictures can be recopied for small stripe films and then be shown to an audience who otherwise would never see them. A workers' weekly could be built up and shown without being censored. (closed meetings and affairs). The revolutionary film organisation should produce its own films with the aid of the Workers Theatre.[17]

As an example of mutual co-operation, the French film *Prix et profits* ('Prices and Profits'), better known as *La Pomme de Terre* ('The Potato'), was shown. This film had been made by Yves Allégret, with assistance from the agitprop group Octobre, among whom were future celebrities such as Jacques and Pierre Prévert.[18] The conclusion of the conference was that 'the theatre section of the IURT in each country was to be held responsible for the building up of a revolutionary film movement,' if such a movement did not already exist.[19] An important role was reserved for the Cinema Bureau of the IURT in co-ordinating activities in the various countries. One gets the feeling that its task was not only to replace Weltfilm, which had become the victim of the Nazi regime in Germany, but was in the first place ideological.[20]

While Charlie Mann was away the ground was prepared. On 4 May 1933 the *Daily Worker* published an article, 'Propaganda in Pictures'.

> A new weapon in the hands of all working-class organisations is now available. A comrade who has been to Russia and satisfied himself about the conditions there, is able to offer to any organisation in London the loan of a Baby Cine, together with a man to operate it, and a two hours' film programme for a matter of shillings, according to the size of the meeting. The first film to be available is called *Soviet Russia, Past and Present* ...[21]

The first to react to this was Harry Edwards. He welcomed the initiative, but

> that is not all, comrade. What about using the multitudinous talent that our movement contains to produce films of working-class life here? Illustrating and punctuating our arguments in this manner. Now to business. I have equipment, technical knowledge, but no artistic ability. The movement has the people ... Now, comrades of the Editorial Board, bring us together.[22]

This 'bringing together' had to wait for Charlie Mann's return from Moscow. In the meantime another *Daily Worker* reader, Robert Eddy, supported Harry Edwards' ideas: 'The matter is certainly worth a good discussion. Here in this district we may be poverty-stricken as regards equipment, but we certainly are rich in material to work upon, particularly the cotton industry.'[23] A few days later *Soviet Russia, Past and Present* was screened to representatives of working-class organisations in London. It was announced that 9.5mm and 16mm prints of the film would be available shortly.[24]

Charlie Mann was left to pick up the threads and put the 'Propaganda in Pictures' idea into practice. He has recalled that Harry Edwards's 16mm projector was a great help. The new film section of the WTM held its first public screenings on the streets of London, in line with the WTM agitprop practice. The *Daily Worker* reported:

> With the aid of a car loaned by a comrade a section of the film, *Soviet Russia, Past and Present*, was actually exhibited to audiences outside their very homes in this densely populated

area [the East End of London, B.H.]. The apparatus used was a small projector of the box type containing its own screen, and power was obtained through a generator connected directly with the accumulator of the car. The effect was quite presentable, but owing to slow running a large amount of flicker was noticeable.[25]

According to Charlie Mann, these film screenings

stopped the crowds in the streets. It was a winner as far as arresting attention and getting people to look at stuff, people who wouldn't normally come to a left-wing performance. This to me is all important. Of course, as soon as you got a crowd, the police came in, accusing us of causing obstruction and so on.[26]

Mann recalled another occasion where the film medium was used in line with the WTM practice:

It was in Shoreditch Town Hall which held about two thousand people. It was packed, a workers' theatre demonstration of material. And I prepared something. So I had a sketch going on stage. I had, which was a developing technique at that time, voices from the audience, specially placed, which came into the run of the play, but I also had a film projector up in the gallery, which was showing film behind the sketch on stage, very large, pictures of the Hunger Marchers and so on, giving the background of the sketch.[27]

The German dramatist Erwin Piscator had experimented with this mixture of film and theatre, but it must have been a startling experience to British audiences.[28] But the Shoreditch event turned out to be a singular one and the open air screenings (Charlie Mann: 'We grew away from that.') could not be maintained for lack of support, which left the WTM Film Section with no other option but to become an independent unit.

In the *Daily Worker* of 9 December 1933, a small notice appeared in the 'What's on' column: 'Kino – London Production Group meets at 3.30 p.m. Today, at 33, Ormond Yard WC1. Bring your ideas!'[29] Kino was the Russian word for cinema. In the years that followed Kino was to become the most important distributor of left-wing films on 16mm in the United Kingdom. A couple of years later, the Co-op Sunday paper *Reynolds News* attributed to Kino 'a backyard start':

... Kino started in the backyard of an old garage in Bloomsbury. There Charlie Mann, son of the veteran Tom Mann, along with several enthusiasts, first used a toy projector to give an experimental exhibition of the Russian film *Potemkin*.[30]

The premises of the WTM were at Great Ormond Yard, so there was nothing unusual in Kino having an office there. More important was Kino's first film: Eisenstein's *Battleship Potemkin*. Kino advertised it as a 'non-flam film [which] can be shown by local organisations'.[31] Charlie Mann explained: 'Our method was to try and get a local organisation to book us to give a film show, more than doing it on our own initiative.'[32] The result was a long battle with the LCC, which had never revised its decision, taken in 1928, to ban *Battleship Potemkin*.

With its 16mm film projector Kino had the mobility to serve those halls which were not equipped with projection apparatus and therefore not licensed under the Cinematograph Act. The St Pancras branch of the Friends of the Soviet Union (FSU) was the first to test the LCC. On 11 December 1933 it hired the Itrose Hall, Mornington Crescent, which was licensed for music and dancing.

A few hours before the banned film *Potemkin* was due to be shown ... the owner of the hall was informed by the LCC that the performance could not take place. The reason given was that 14 days' notice had to be given for the film to be shown ...[33]

About two hundred people turned up in vain. The LCC used its licensing authority for music and dancing to stave off the film show, threatening the owner of Itrose Hall with legal proceedings if he did not comply.[34] A few weeks later a different variant was applied. When the Jubilee Street (East London) Cell of the CPGB organised a private show of *Potemkin* in King's Hall, the LCC sent a letter to the proprietor in which it was pointed out that his premises were not licensed under the 1909 Cinematograph Act and that the film show on 5 January 1934 had to be cancelled. The screening did not take place.[35] Two–nil to the LCC.

But the next move was Kino's. So far the argument had been about licences, not about the inflammability or non-inflammability of the 16mm print of *Potemkin*. For an

exhibition of *Potemkin* in Hampstead by the FSU the LCC sent
the Chief Officer of the Fire Brigade around, as the show could
not be banned in any other way. He

> inspected the premises and ascertained that admission was only
> obtainable by means of a membership card of the Friends of
> the Soviet Union and that money was not being taken. The
> exhibition was held and a sample of the film obtained and
> tested by the application of a lighted match to a portion of the
> film held vertically as well as horizontally. The film merely
> melted away under the action of the heat and did not sustain
> flame when held in either position after the match was
> withdrawn. The Home Office and Police were informed of the
> result of the test.[36]

In other words, the LCC had no right to prohibit the
Hampstead FSU from showing the film. On Sunday 7 January
1934 it was shown four times 'to crowded audiences'.[37] It was
Kino's first victory. It promptly decided to go on to the
offensive. Kino's organising secretary, C. Williams, wrote to
the LCC questioning the legality of its action in preventing the
exhibition at the King's Hall on 5 January 1934. Williams
pointed out that the print of *Potemkin* was non-inflammable.
The LCC consulted a solicitor and replied

> that in the case of any film which has not been granted a
> certificate by the British Board of Film Censors and which the
> Council itself under the discretionary powers conferred upon it
> has decided not to permit to be shown, the Council has always
> regarded it as being justifiable in the public interest to take
> every step possible to prevent the exhibition of such films unless
> circumstances clearly showed that it was precluded from so
> doing.

It pointed out that it had no knowledge of the non-
inflammability of *Potemkin* as this had not been made 'public',
i.e. specifically stated in 'the newspaper advertisement upon
which the Council acted'.[38] Kino was unable to force the issue
of the LCC's abuse of its authority regarding the King's Hall
exhibition.

The LCC had no intention of letting the exhibition of
Battleship Potemkin pass. The FSU had booked the Co-operative
Hall in Plumstead on 15 February 1934 to show *Potemkin*. At the

last moment the LCC sent a telegram to the owners of the hall, the Royal Arsenal Co-operative Society (RACS), warning them 'that they run the risk of prosecution'.[39] The trick worked. 'The RACS committee gave in to the LCC's bluff without even investigating the legal position.'[40] The FSU branch was angry, but could do no more than convert the evening into a protest meeting. According to the *Daily Worker*, the LCC ban on *Potemkin* had 'been broken nearly 20 times in the Greater London area' by mid-February 1934.[41] Charlie Mann recalled:

> In the end we were getting some many bookings with only this one copy of *Potemkin* ... We had three projectors that could run three shows at once in various parts of London. And I had the job, when the first reel was done at the first one, of running it down to the next. I did a shuttle service with one copy between three different halls, probably miles apart, in my old Morris two-seater.[42]

Kino therefore decided to release another film, Eisenstein's *The General Line* (a film with a BBFC certificate), and to order extra prints of *Battleship Potemkin*.

> These were ordered from the film printers in the usual way. Delivery not being made on the date promised inquiries to the printers produced the reply that 'the matter is held up owing to a Government circular having been received which cautions us against the reproduction of Russian propaganda films.[43]

The Home Office had followed the battle over *Potemkin* between the LCC and Kino with great interest. In December 1933 it contemplated 'two possible ways of dealing with "non-flam" subversive films'.[44] The first way, via the BBFC had the disadvantage of not being effective for all halls. The second way, to amend the law, would be long and cumbersome. Nevertheless, the Home Office decided on 30 December 1933 to start the 'preparation of a Bill to amend the Cinematograph Act, 1909, so as to remove doubts on the question whether a slow-burning film is to be regarded as an inflammable film for the purposes of the Act'.[45] The LCC had let the Home Office down when it had allowed the FSU to carry on the exhibition of *Potemkin* in Hampstead. The Chief Constable of Cardiff was much more in line with the Home Office's ideas:

... he has tested 16mm film and found that it did burn,
although only slowly. In the circumstances, 'he had informed
all concerned that he could not accept notices in relation to the
exhibition of films at clubs (registered or unregistered),
institutes and recreation centres, as, in his opinion, the Act
applied to all kinds of films including those previously
regarded as non-inflammable.'[46]

In other words, he interpreted the Act as if it had already been
amended. It seems that the Cardiff example was followed in
other towns and districts, scaring prospective exhibitors of
Potemkin.

In the autumn of 1934 the matter came to a head. Kino had
been touring the United kingdom with *Potemkin*. On 23
October 1934 the Miners' Hall, Boldon Colliery, Durham, had
booked the film and the services of Kino's projectionist Ivan
Seruya. The hall had been used for 'sub-standard' film shows
previously. In fact one had been held only the week before.
There was an audience of between 150 and 200 people,
increasing later to 300 or 400. They had to pay an entrance fee
of 2d. Apart from *Potemkin*, the programme included Kino's
own production *Hunger March*. The usual methods to stop the
exhibition having failed, the commanding police officer
decided to prosecute those responsible for the screening, the
trustees of the Hall and the projectionist.[47] The case was not
heard until January 1935. In the meantime, various organisations had campaigned against the Home Office's intention to
extend the 1909 Cinematograph Act to 'sub-standard' film
stock. In its zeal to suppress the exhibition of banned Soviet
films, the Home Office had failed to realise the consequences
of its move. Not only Kino, but numerous other political and
religious organisations used 'sub-standard' film as an integral
part of their activities. The General Post Office Film Unit, a
government-sponsored body, distributed many of its films on
the disputed 16mm format. Moreover, teachers had discovered
how useful the film medium could be for educational
purposes. When the Home Office made public the Bill to
amend the 1909 Act, the educational world reacted most
vociferously. The Bill was seen as a 'threat to the teaching
film'.[48] The original purpose of the Cinematograph Act had
been to enforce safety measures, not to censor the images
shown. As there were no fire risks with 'sub-standard' stock,

the educational world regarded the Bill as an attempt to interfere with its teaching methods. The Home Office had reckoned without opposition from this quarter. It decided that 'it would be better at the present not to proceed with the Bill'.[49] This was four days before the screening of *Potemkin* at Boldon Colliery.

Kino's contacts with the educational world were limited to the National Council of Labour Colleges, which had informed its members about the availability of 'sub-standard' films for workers' education in the September 1933 issue of *Plebs*. The Council protested against the plan to bring 'sub-standard' film under the 1909 Cinematograph Act, but it blamed the film trade, particularly the Cinematograph Exhibitors' Association, for the move rather than the Home Office.[50]

The support of the National Council for Civil Liberties (NCCL) was more decisive. The NCCL had been founded early in 1934, 'to assist in the maintenance of the hard-won rights of citizens – especially freedom of speech, press and assembly – from all infringement by executive or judicial authority'.[51] It campaigned against the Incitement to Disaffection Bill, succeeding in modifying it substantially before it became an Act. Kino's struggle for 'free sight' met with ready support from the NCCL. The key person was Ivor Montagu, an expert on film censorship who not only knew many of the NCCL people personally, but had also been an important adviser on film matters for the inexperienced Kino group (Charlie Mann recalled that he was the only one of a number of professional people 'who was really of any use').[52] In June 1934 NCCL secretary Ronald Kidd wrote to the LCC, complaining about the way LCC clerks abused their authority to suppress the exhibition of the 'sub-standard' print of *Potemkin*.[53] Once the Home Office had announced its intention to bring 'sub-standard' films under the 1909 Act, the NCCL started fighting the Bill. The *Manchester Guardian* offered its columns as a platform. Both Ivor Montagu and Ronald Kidd took advantage of this, explaining the reasons for their opposition and the correspondence in the paper, with a comment and some documents, was reprinted by the NCCL as a pamphlet entitled *'Non-Flam' Films*. With its concern for civil liberties the NCCL provided the link between the educational world, whose opposition to the Bill was generally based on pragmatic grounds, and the left, whose ideas about film censorship were divided, except for its aversion to the existing situation. By the end of 1934, it seemed that the opponents of the Bill had public opinion on their side.

Crucial was the result of the prosecution against the trustees of the Miners' Hall, Boldon Colliery, and Kino's projectionist Ivan Seruya – usually referred to as 'the Jarrow case'. At the hearing of the case, the prosecution enjoyed the services of Lieutenant-Colonel Simmons, fire expert at the Home Office, while the accused were defended by Mr W.H. Thompson, an NCCL lawyer. Lieutenant-Colonel Simmons stated that he had come to the conclusion that the type of 'sub-standard' film, of which the print of *Potemkin* had been made, was inflammable. Thompson asked him if he considered this type of film dangerous, but Simmons was not prepared to answer this question. As Ivor Montagu pointed out in retrospect,

> the law has not defined 'inflammability'. So-called non-inflammable film does, when heated and if the heat be great enough, undergo a chemical change. In so doing, the part heated shrivels away for an instant before the change ceases. If conditions be hot enough and dry enough, even a sort of momentary and disappearing flame accompanies the shrivelling. But precisely the same is true of anything that will combine at all with oxygen. *Precisely the same is true of steel.* But nobody in their right sense would call steel or other metals 'inflammable'. Kino's defending lawyer had no difficulty in showing that, by the definition claimed by the Home Office 'expert', all sorts of material like toughened woods would be inflammable, *although their use is insisted on in various Home Office regulations against fire for the very reason that they won't burn.*[54]

The Jarrow Bench dismissed the charges and awarded Mr Thompson 25 guineas costs, and the trustees seven guineas costs.[55]

It was generally felt that the police had been acting on behalf of the Home Office, for whom the Jarrow Bench's decision was therefore seen as a defeat. The Home Office hastened to declare 'that it in no way initiated the unsuccessful prosecution at Jarrow, which was a local police affair'.[56] This may have been true, but the bearing of the Jarrow Bench's decision was certainly more than a local one. The presence of Lieutenant-Colonel Simmons was witness to that. The Jarrow police announced their intention to appeal against the Bench's decision. There is no proof, but one can assume that the Home Office dissuaded them from lodging an appeal, realising that it would almost necessarily result in another defeat, causing even more damage to its prestige.

The consequences of the Jarrow case were more drastic than the Home Office had initially been willing to admit. It was forced to drop the Bill to bring the 'non-flam' film under the 1909 Cinematograph Act. If it still wanted to suppress the exhibition of banned films on 'sub-standard' stock, it would have to develop entirely new legislation. This the Home Office hesitated to do. *Potemkin* and other banned films could now be shown without interference from police or authorities, provided the hall used for the occasion was an unlicensed one. Some county councils brooded on other means to curb what they considered as red propaganda on the screen. The Surrey County Council, for example, did not recognise the difference between 'flam' and 'non-flam' film.[57] It is doubtful whether the Surrey County Council would have been able to uphold this decision, if challenged in court.

The Jarrow case with its favourable result finally secured Kino's right of existence, which had been hanging in the balance. From the Film Section of the WTM, Kino had developed into a proper 'Workers' Film Organisation'. In the spring of 1934 the acquisition of new feature films stagnated. Kino needed '30 guarantees of bookings (with a deposit of 5s.) from local organisations in London and Home Counties' in order to pay for a 16mm print of Eisenstein's film about the Russian revolution, *October*.[58] As the film was not released until November 1935, one can only conclude that the appeal failed. There were other difficulties as well: the Cinema Bureau of the IURT never functioned properly. Kino

> experienced little difficulty in getting audiences but very great difficulty in obtaining the films, in finding money for showing rights and the cost of the copies, and in carrying out the distribution and the shows with entirely voluntary help.[59]

In the summer of 1934 Kino mainly concentrated on producing its own newsreels (see Chapter Five). In November 1934 it managed to import two Soviet films from a Paris organisation, Ciné Mondiale, *Son of a Soldier* and *Little Screw*.

The first was premiered at St James' Club Theatre in London on 23 and 24 November 1934.[60] The cartoon film *Little Screw* had its first showing, together with Kozintsev's and Trauberg's film on the Paris Commune *New Babylon*, in January 1935.[61] According to *Daily Worker* film critic Peter Porcupine (a pen-name of Jean Ross, the model for Christopher Isherwood's Sally Bowles and at the time married to Claud Cockburn[62]) Kino

> had a good deal of bad luck this winter. No sooner had the Kino comrades tidied up their office, sorted out the files, had a telephone installed and generally got all set to distribute films in a highly efficient way than the whole place caught fire.[63]

Moreover, the prosecution at Jarrow meant that Kino had to withdraw *Potemkin* and *Hunger March* from distribution until the court had reached a decision. After the Jarrow case Kino was able to develop itself into an organisation 'run on business lines'.[64] In order to do this it had already 'sacrificed' its production department, which had merged, together with the Workers' Camera Club, into the Workers' Film and Photo League in November 1934.[65]

Notes

1. Huntly Carter, *The New Spirit in the Cinema*, London 1930, pp.284-5.
2. Ibid., p.291.
3. Huntly Carter, 'Where are the British Labour Films?', in *Plebs*, June 1931, pp.132-4, here pp.133-4.
4. Ibid., August 1931, p.186.
5. Ibid., October 1931, pp.238-9.
6. John Attfield, *With Light of Knowledge. A Hundred Years of Education in the Royal Arsenal Co-operative Society, 1877-1977*, London 1981, pp.54-5; a review of *The General Line* appeared in *Comradeship*, April 1931.
7. Joseph Reeves, 'A Co-op Success. *General Line* shown to 40,000 People', in *Kino News*, Winter 1935, p.1.
8. *Plebs*, October 1931, pp.238-9, here p.238.
9. *The Worker*, 16 May 1931, p.7.
10. Ibid., 23 May 1931, p.7.
11. See Richard Stourac, 'Revolutionary Workers' Theatre in the Soviet Union, Germany and Britain (1918-1936)', Ph.D. thesis Bristol, 1978, pp.325-415; *History Workshop Journal*, No.4, Autumn 1977, pp.102-42; Reiner Lehberger, 'Internationale Verbindungen und Beeinflussungen des sozialis-

tischen Theaters im England der dreissiger Jahre', in *Gulliver, Deutsch-englische Jahrbücher* 4, West Berlin 1978, pp.67-79.

12. Tom Thomas, 'Their Theatre and Ours' (1932), in *History Workshop Journal*, No.4, Autumn 1977, pp.137-42, here p.141.

13. *Daily Worker*, 28 March 1931, p.5.

14. *Red Stage*, No.5, April-May 1932, p.6.

15. See Stourac, op.cit.; *History Workshop Journal*, No.4, Autumn 1977, pp.102-142.

16. Charlie Mann, interview with the author, Somerset, 22 January 1979.

17. *New Theatre*, September/October 1933, pp.24-5, here p.24.

18. See Michel Fauré, *Le Groupe Octobre*, Paris 1977, pp.146-7.

19. *New Theatre*, September-October 1933, pp.24-5, here p.24.

20. The IURT Cinema Bureau did not handle any films or even offer services in providing the film sections of the national workers' theatre movements with films. Its most important feat was the publication in *International Theatre*, No.4, 1933, of a text by Béla Balázs on the foundation of a Cinema International. See *Ecran 79*, No.86, 15 December 1979, pp.38-40.

21. *Daily Worker*, 4 May 1933, p.6.

22. Ibid., 9 May 1933, p.6.

23. Ibid., 12 May 1933, p.4.

24. Ibid., 17 May 1933, p.6.

25. Ibid., 3 August 1933, p.4.

26. Charlie Mann interview.

27. Ibid.

28. See Stourac, op.cit., p.410; Erwin Piscator, *Das Politische Theater* [1929], Reinbeck bei Hamburg 1979.

29. *Daily Worker*, 9 December 1933, p.4.

30. *Reynolds News*, 3 October 1937, p.9.

31. *Daily Worker*, 15 December 1933, p.4.

32. Charlie Mann interview.

33. *Daily Worker*, 13 December 1933, p.2.

34. Public Record Office, London, Home Office 45/17067, Appendix B.

35. *Daily Worker*, 9 January 1934, p.4; Public Record Office, London, Home Office 45/17067, Appendix B.

36. Public Record Office, London, Home Office 45/17067, Appendix B.

37. *Daily Worker*, 9 January 1934, p.4.

38. Public Record Office, London, Home Office 45/17067, Appendix B.

39. Ibid.

40. *Daily Worker*, 19 February 1934, p.4.

41. Ibid.

42. Charlie Mann interview.

43. *Daily Worker*, 19 February 1934, p.4.

44. Public Record Office, London, Home Office 45/17067.

45. Ibid.

46. *Daily Worker*, 20 February 1934, p.4.

47. Public Record Office, London, Home Office 45/17068, 45/21109.

48. *The Schoolmaster*, 11 October 1934.

49. Ibid.

50. *Plebs*, November 1934, pp.255-6.

51. Quoted by Noreen Branson and Margot Heinemann, *Britain in the*

Nineteen Thirties, St. Albans 1973, pp.311-2.

52. Charlie Mann interview.

53. Public Record Office, London, Home Office 45/17067, Appendix C.

54. Ivor Montagu, 'Film Censorship', in *Kino News*, Winter 1935, p.2.

55. *Daily Herald*, 23 January 1935, p.2.

56. Ibid., 24 January 1935, p.10.

57. Public Record Office, London, Home Office 45/21108.

58. *Daily Worker*, 20 March 1934, p.4.

59. *First Annual Report, April 1936*, Kino Films (1935) Ltd., p.2, in Film and Photo League Archive (referred to hereafter as FPLa), which is currently held by the National Film Archive, London.

60. *New Leader*, 23 November 1934, p.6.

61. *Daily Worker*, 16 January 1935, p.4.; 22 January 1935, p.4; *The New Leader*, 25 January 1935, p.6.

62. A.L. Morton, letter to the author, 19 September 1980; Patricia Cockburn, letter to the author, 12 November 1980.

63. *Daily Worker*, 22 January 1935, p.4.

64. *First Annual Report, April 1936*, Kino Films (1935) Ltd., p.2 (see note 59).

65. *Daily Worker*, 27 November 1934, p.4.

Chapter 4

The Socialist Film Council

The economic crisis of the 1930s opened the eyes of a number of professional film makers, who developed a commitment to the socialist cause and offered their services to the working-class movement. Such professional people, coming from outside the workers' movement, were often met with initial suspicion, but in many cases they were able to overcome this and gain acceptance as equal comrades. One such – the documentary film maker Paul Rotha – sought to convince the leadership of the Labour Party that film was an indispensable tool in its propaganda armoury. As a professional, Rotha was shocked to find that socialist film propaganda was being run by *amateurs*. In a letter to his friend Eric Knight, Rotha wrote:

> A wealthy young man of the dilettante kind who once wrote a book called *This Film Business* has recently started a production group using 16mm. His intentions are admirable and his honesty not to be doubted. He has money of his own from oil, it is said, an Oxford background and a 'sympathy for the working-classes'. He is seriously trying to make films with a Socialist purpose, and has so far made two – *The Road to Hell* and *What the Newsreels Do Not Show* [sic]. I have seen both and declare them amateur and immature. What he has actually produced can only be called 'wheel montage' which does nobody any good. He used a few friends with cultured accents to speak dialogue for factory workers. It reminds me of what was once called the fashionable habit of slumming. In other words, they stink.[1]

The young man in question was Rudolph Messel, the founder – along with Terence Greenidge and Raymond and Daisy Postgate – of the Socialist Film Council (SFC). The 'cultured accents' heard by Rotha were not there, since the two films he mentioned were silent. Still, he had a point. Compared to other groups who produced more films or had a longer lifespan, the SFC has probably received too much attention from historians. But it was important in that it was the first left-wing film group to exploit the possibilities offered by non-inflammable, small format, 16mm film.

Rudolph Messel was the film critic of *New Clarion*, a Labour weekly, and Greenidge was film critic of *Socialist Review*. This monthly journal had been the theoretical review of the Independent Labour Party, but it became politically unattached after the ILP disaffiliated from the Labour Party in 1932. The Labour Party was going through a difficult period following the MacDonald 'betrayal' and the disastrous General Election of 1931. Soon after the ILP disaffiliated, a new partner offered itself. 'The Labour Party had lost one gadfly to find another: the Socialist League.'[2] The Socialist League united various ex-ILPers and other socialists; Stafford Cripps, Charles Trevelyan, William Mellor, H.N. Brailsford and Harold Laski were among its leading members. The League aimed to turn the Labour Party leftwards, without forcing a break from its pragmatic tradition.

In 1934, George R. Mitchison – a member of the Socialist League – published a book called *The First Workers' Government* (with an introduction by Stafford Cripps). This was a mixture of science fiction and political treatise, offering a blueprint for a future Labour government. Interestingly, Mitchison made room for the Socialist Film Council in his plans. It was to be absorbed by the Publications Committee of the First Workers' Government. Mitchison described the SFC as 'a small body which has done excellent work in the preparation and circulation of propaganda films'.[3] This starts to make sense when it is recalled that the Socialist Film Council was initially named the Socialist League Film Committee.[4]

Rudolph Messel published an appeal to Clarion Cameramen in his weekly column in *New Clarion* in March 1933. Reviewing a new American film, *Once in a Lifetime*, which satirised the Hollywood production system without ever really questioning its purpose, Messel reached the following conclusion:

The capitalist wants his films to be seen, his ideas absorbed, and no protest to be made about the quality of the ideas in question, to achieve which he produces films like *Once in a Lifetime*. And if that's foolishness, all I can say is that I wish we had a few fools at Transport House! It is, however, well known that there are no fools at Transport House, and so 'what's to do about it ... ?' For something must be done. Something must be done to counter the continual stream of anti-Socialist propaganda which goes into the cinemas every week. There is only one effective thing which we can do, and that is to produce our own films; and I suggest that we should do it.

Messel then revealed that he and Raymond Postgate had a film in mind, but for it to be of value to the Movement as a whole, 'we must have the co-operation of all Socialists who are in any way interested in movie-making.' He therefore asked any readers in the possession of a 16mm film projector to get in touch with either Mrs Postgate or himself. But that was not all.

It would also be interesting to know whether any of my readers are in possession of small-size cameras, and whether they would be willing to co-operate with us in securing shots of local conditions which could be collected and then distributed to Labour parties under the title of *What the News Reel Does Not Show*. And also, would the camera-owners be willing to stand the cost of the film which they themselves send in? Supposing that by means of this appeal we locate eight- ciné-camera owners, and that each owner sends us 100 feet of films showing just how bad certain things are in his particular locality, we should then find ourselves in a position to make an interest [*sic*] film of definitely Socialist character and of about thirty minutes in duration.[5]

Messel did not yet betray the subject of the film he was going to make with Raymond Postgate, a Labour historian who had been particularly active in workers' education.[6]

A few weeks later, in April 1933, Messel reported that the appeal had been successful and that eight 16mm projectors had been located. He appealed once more for co-operation under the motto: 'We can produce the films; can you produce the means of showing them?' He then revealed the subjects of three films that his group was preparing. 'There will be one dealing with the Means Test, another devoted to showing the foulness of slums, and a third which will deal with the war

danger as it threatens every one of us to-day.' Messel
emphasised the use of sound.

> Our own talkies! Talkies dealing with the realities of the
> moment, as opposed to talkies that just talk and consistently
> ignore every reality, from poverty to prostitution. Talkies that
> will show our side of the case, talkies that will show ordinary
> men and women, and show them in pictures just how
> hopelessly they are duped at the moment.[7]

Messel's enthusiasm (reinforced by the headline 'Talkies for
Socialists!') was a bit misleading. He had to admit that the
group's first film would only be a talkie if money permitted it.
One also wonders whether he had thought of the consequences
for the exhibition of the film. Were, for example, the available
projectors equipped with a sound system?

Messel created a degree of free publicity for the group's first
film. 'Shooting in George Lansbury's Kitchen' ran one of the
headlines in *New Clarion*.[8] This event was decidedly less
sensational if one knew that the film's star, Daisy Postgate,
happened to be George Lansbury's daughter! True to the fan
magazines of the period Messel baptised her and the other
leading star, Terence Greenidge, 'the people's favourites'. And
this is how Messel recalled Daisy Postgate's intervention, when
a London park-keeper tried to prevent the film crew from
finishing a sequence in the park:

> The actors waited, and then the leading lady stepped forward.
> Deftly, she engaged the angry man in conversation. He forgot
> all about permits, about us and about the film camera which
> was desecrating his lovely park, and talked away happily to the
> leading lady. We finished the sequence and then departed
> quietly, and I hope politely. Unless the park-keeper in question
> happens to be a *New Clarion* reader, he will never know how
> completely he was vamped![9]

Not only the Postgates and Terence Greenidge were acting in
the film, entitled *The Road to Hell*, but also the well-known
novelist Naomi Mitchison.

> Naomi is playing the part of a working-class mother, a woman
> fairly comfortably placed until her husband, as a result of an
> accident, loses his job. From then everything goes wrong, and
> as the film progresses we see the home being gradually robbed

of furniture, pictures, and all articles which might fetch something at the pawnshop. Finally the woman has to face the public assistance committee. She has to tell them her story and she has to stand by and listen while they discuss her case and then refuse her any form of relief. It is a part calling for something more than ordinary acting ability, and that 'something more' Naomi Mitchison ... has brought to it.[10]

With the 'feature film' nearing completion, Messel once more turned his attention to the newsreel that was to accompany it. Readers of *New Clarion* had been sending in material, which left the group 'in possession of some four hundred feet of film (twenty minutes showing time) showing events of interest to Socialists, happening all over the country'. Messel mentioned 'shots of the various May Day demonstrations' in particular. He singled out footage sent by Mrs Pritchard, London, of 'German working-class houses, which should prove extremely interesting to workers in this country'. Messel explained:

> These pictures show just how much a Socialist Municipal Council can do in improving working-class conditions. They demonstrate the magnificent achievements of the German Socialists, and emphasise the fact that if such things can be done in Germany and Austria, both 'bankrupt' countries, how much more can be done here.[11]

To write about 'the magnificent achievements of the German Socialists' in May 1933 undoubtedly testified to a certain political naïvety. Of course, the subject of municipal socialism was being debated within the Labour Party, with the German and Austrian experiences serving as a point of reference, but there was also a debate going on about the danger of fascism and Nazism for the working-class movement. In the end *What the News Reel Does Not Show* did not incorporate Mrs Pritchard's pictures of German working-class houses. Instead it showed a long sequence of construction under the Five Year Plan in the Soviet Union, 'some telling shots of London slums ... and the May Day celebrations in various British towns'.[12]

At the end of the July 1933 a special premiere screening of *The Road to Hell* was held under the group's newly-adopted name as the Socialist Film Council of which George Lansbury became president. He was among 'an audience of about 100, which included no professional film critics' attending the first show of *The Road to Hell*.[13] The lack of professional film critics was more than made up by the number of documentary film makers with a ready pen. Paul Rotha did not publish his criticism until 1973, but both John Grierson and Basil Wright did not hesitate to disclose their opinion on the film shortly after the screening. Neither Grierson nor Wright were bothered by the 'amateur and immature' character of the SFC productions. Grierson wrote of *The Road to Hell* that '... in every technical respect the film was well enough made'.[14] Wright said of the same film that 'It is well constructed, well acted, well cut, well lit, and well directed. It has economy of movement and largesse of effect.'[15]

However, both had severe criticism of the politics of the film. Wright wrote that

> It alleges to be propaganda against the Means Test. If it is propaganda for anything it is propaganda for the worst type of defeatism. If the working classes of England behave as the particular family in this film does under the pressure of bad government and worse administration, there is no hope for anyone ...[16]

Grierson considered the film

> queer from an ideological point of view. The father of a family is knocked down by a limousine driven by a gallivanting young gent in a top hat (Messel) and thereby loses his job. There are a dozen fundamental causes (or is it only four?) of unemployment: by which something like a million fathers of families have been knocked down. But Messel has to choose just that fortuitous one. Conclusion, presumably, that we can cure unemployment by removing the gents in top hats who knock down people with their limousines.

Grierson listed a number of further ideological deficiencies; for example, when the mother has to plead the cause of her family at the Public Assistance Committee.

> There, political layman as I am, I was bothered again. The PAC were painted very unsympathetically, and with obvious good reason. But I always understood there was a Labour representative on the PAC, and I did not see him stand up and

make a fundamental noise about things. Was this a tactful omission, or had the Labour representative retired, or what? No justification even of the lavatories!

Grierson's conclusion: 'Promise of action, organisation of action, the film does not begin to suggest.'[17]

Although the two surviving prints of *The Road to Hell* are both incomplete, they testify indeed to a surprising naïvety. It seems that Messel and company were caught between the rationale of making a film to be used by the labour movement and the desire of putting into practice the most attractive devices of the commercial cinema of those days. Grierson had noted this latter tendency and criticised it: 'Note first the title. Like much that follows it, its silly sensationalism echoes preoccupations far other than political. What need here of box-office scramblings ...?'[18] The SFC had refused to work within the documentary strand of film making, the dominant one in Great Britain outside the commercial film industry. It had determinedly opted for a fiction film, with a clear-cut story (giving the audience the possibility to identify with 'the goodies' and to hate the villains), with 'stars' (even if they were amateurs) and with dramatic highlights (car accident, mother pleading at the PAC, artist son committing suicide, etc.), with the unspoken assumption that these were what the audience wanted. Maybe the 'amateurism' was more to blame for the political weaknesses of *The Road to Hell* than Basil Wright and John Grierson were willing to admit. As Raymond Postgate put it:

> ... *The Road to Hell* is a melodrama of the Means Test. It tells the story of how a family is ground down by the operation of the Test, and how that Test is the source of suicide and crime. It does not claim to be more than a plain melodramatic story, without any very deep psychological refinements.[19]

What the News Reel Does Not Show and *The Road to Hell* were distributed by the SPC on non-inflammable 16mm stock, which meant that their exhibition did not fall under the 1909 Cinematograph Act. The SFC aimed at a distribution among constituency Labour parties, trade unions, Co-operative Guilds and Labour Colleges.[20] It is not known how the earlier scheme of locating owners of 16mm film projectors fitted into the actual distribution of the films. At the 1933 the Labour Party conference in Hastings the SFC organised a special screening of its films for the delegates.[21]

In the meantime work on the next film continued. Whereas *The Road to Hell* had been a lower-than-low-budget film, costing only £66, the anti-war film in preparation was going to be a 'talkie' and therefore required a serious investment.[22] Rudolph Messel who again directed the film, provided the lion's share of the £1,500 that the film would cost.[23] This time there was no press coverage in *New Clarion*, which disappeared in May 1934. The same principles were applied: a fiction story, written by an SFC-member (Postgate), and the use of amateurs recruited from the SFC's own ranks and among friends as actors. Outside technical assistance was called in this time to make up for the lack of 'talkie' know-how. While Naomi Mitchison was the surprising 'star' in *The Road to Hell*, builders' leader George Hicks acted in the new film. Undoubtedly Postgate, who had worked with Hicks at the National Council of Labour Colleges and written *The Builders' History* (1923), was responsible for his appearance. The title of the film was *Blow, Bugles, Blow*. A representative of the cinema trade paper *Kine Weekly* saw it at the 1934 Labour Party conference and praised it as 'an excellent example of the economically produced propaganda picture', singling out Hicks's performance: 'a richly unctuous and remarkably good portrayal of a war-mongering Press Lord that suggests that some of our professional 'heavies' had better look to their laurels'.[24]

Blow, Bugles, Blow tells the story of two middle-class couples (man and wife, brother and sister) preventing an impending war between England and France by liaising between the trade union movements of both countries and triggering off a general strike. A young newspaper editor revolts when he is confronted with his boss's support for Cabinet war plans against France. Supported by his wife he starts printing an underground bulletin calling for a general strike. The TUC is willing to call one, provided its French counterpart does the same. But all means of communication have been cut off. Here the other couple comes in, a reserve officer (one-time lover of the newspaper editor's wife ...) and his sister. The latter is able to carry a message from the French unions across the Channel. Tools are downed. The workers, led by the reserve officer,

Blow, Bugles, Blow, 1934; studio set

march into Downing Street to turn out the Cabinet. War has been prevented, a revolution accomplished.

Blow, Bugles, Blow reflects accurately the position of its makers in relation to the working-class movement. The leading middle-class characters of the film are pulling the strings *for* the workers and their organisations. Still the film also shows some important episodes depicting independent action by the workers. Railway workers fool the military authorities, thus enabling the strike bulletin to reach other parts of the country. Women workers at the telephone exchange refuse to connect the Whitehall authorities when they need telephone communication in order to remain in control of the situation. *Blow, Bugles, Blow* even glorifies an act of sabotage, showing the interruption of the Prime Minister's radio speech in order to spread the message of the general strike.

As a 'talkie', *Blow, Bugles, Blow* is an interesting film. Its use of sound and choice of music is often quite unnaturalistic, but one wonders whether financial constraints rather than aesthetic principles account for this. The films shows some examples of attempts at 'Soviet editing', with George Hicks literally speaking in images of cannons.

The SFC must have trodden on many a wrong toe in the Labour Party with *Blow, Bugles, Blow*. The Labour press virtually ignored the film.[25] Why was this? Because the film suggested a general strike as an effective means against war danger, while the scars of 1926 were still not healed? Because the film propagated pacifism, particularly among the armed forces? Or because *Blow, Bugles, Blow* was simply a bad film discrediting the labour movement? One wonders what part George Lansbury, a convinced pacifist, played in all this. In the meantime the SFC sought recognition from the Labour Party. Talks between representatives from the Labour Party and the SFC in December 1934 seem not to have led to any tangible results.[26] Was the SFC still regarded by Labour Party officials as the Socialist League Film Committee, and therefore a political maverick? The Labour Party's adverse attitude must have been a great disappointment to Messel and his colleagues. There was no chance of recouping the money put into *Blow, Bugles, Blow* without Labour Party support. Even though the print was on non-inflammable stock, an ordinary cinema had to be booked for its exhibition, as it was a 35mm sound film.[27]

The SFC must have been disbanded after this political and financial setback. Rudolph Messel tried to get *Blow, Bugles, Blow* distributed through other channels. In 1936 the Progressive Film Institute organised a trade-show of the film, but never released it.[28] In 1938 the ILP acquired it, according to its weekly *New Leader* because the film's producer 'has joined the Party and has placed the film at the disposal of the ILP'.[29]

Notes

1. Paul Rotha, *Documentary Diary, An Informal History of the British Documentary Film, 1928-1939*, London 1973, pp.109-10 (letter to Eric Knight dated 1 August 1933)

2. Charles Loch Mowat, *Britain Between The Wars 1918-1940*, Boston 1971, p.547.

3. G.R. Mitchison, *The First Workers' Government or New Times for Henry Dubb*, London 1934, p.34.

4. Letter written by Raymond Postgate and published in: *Sight & Sound*, Vol.II, No.5, Spring 1933, p.8.

5. *New Clarion*, 11 March 1933, p.267.

6. Raymond Postgate, author of *The Builders' History* (1923) and *A Short History of the British Workers* (1926), had been very active in the Plebs League (National Council of Labour Colleges). See Stuart Macintyre, *A Proletarian Science. Marxism in Britain 1917-1933*, Cambridge 1980.

7. *New Clarion*, 1 April 1933, p.327.

8. Ibid., 27 May 1933, p.486.

9. Ibid.

10. Ibid., 10 June 1933, p.7.

11. Ibid., 27 May 1933, p.486.

12. *Socialist Review*, Vol.V, No.6, September 1933, p.357. The surviving print of *What the News Reel Does Not Show* only contains footage shot by Messel on a tour through the Soviet Union. See Bert Hogenkamp, 'Workers' Newsreels in the 1920's and 1930's', in *Our History*, No.68 [1977], p.17.

13. *Daily Herald*, 29 July 1933, p.9.

14. *New Clarion*, 12 August 1933, p.158.

15. *Cinema Quarterly*, Autumn 1933, p.67.

16. Ibid.

17. *New Clarion*, 12 August 1933, p.158.

18. Ibid.

19. *Labour*, September 1933, p.21.

20. Cf. advertisement in *New Clarion*, 21 October 1933, p.328; see also *Plebs*, Vol.XXV, No.9, September 1933, pp.209-210.

21. *Labour,* September 1933, p.21.

22. *Daily Herald*, 29 July 1933, p.9; *Cinema Quarterly*, Vol.II, No.1, Autumn 1933, p.66.

23. *Labour Organiser*, October 1934, p.191.
24. *Kinematograph Weekly*, 4 October 1934, p.21.
25. *Daily Herald*, an influential Labour daily, for example did not publish a review of *Blow, Bugles, Blow*.
26. See Minutes, The Finance and General Purposes Sub-Committee, Labour Party, 7 December 1934.
27. *Labour Organiser*, October 1934, p.191.
28. See *Kinematograph Weekly*, 16 April 1936, p.27.
29. *New Leader*, 8 July 1938, p.8.

Chapter 5

Making Our Own Films: Kino and the Workers' Film and Photo League

The new 'sub-standard' film had more advantages than the exemption from censorship. The equipment was relatively easy to handle, light and comparatively cheap. This made it pre-eminently suitable for use by non-professionals. For Korea Senda and Heinz Lüdecke 'sub-standard' film was a prerequisite for the 'agitpropisation' of the cinema. In their view the German workers' theatre movement had proved how right they were in demanding such a move. But what exactly did this mean?

> We have to found *film agitprop troops*, i.e. small collectives, which are in very close touch with the factories and the agricultural workers. Their members must be 'worker film correspondents', who not only record demonstrations and other big campaigns of the workers, but also make regular film reports from the factories and the countryside. But their task will not be limited to the making of film reports. They will use the collected material for longer compilation films, which will criticise in a revolutionary way the existing conditions by means of the dialectical method. Self-evident are the favourable prospects of a collaboration with workers' theatre groups, worker cartoonists and proletarian writers, respectively worker correspondents.[1]

This 'agitpropisation of the cinema' fitted perfectly in the 'Class against Class' view of art and propaganda. The former must be at the service of the latter. Therefore, the contradiction between the professional and the amateur artist/writer had to be dissolved. Collective work was the best way to do this, unless

the artist or writer in question had a name and reputation to
offer to the movement. The basic political concept, from which
the other categories were derived, was the 'worker correspondent'. The German Communist Party had started organising a
worker-correspondents movement in the mid-1920s, after the
example of the Bolsheviks under the tsarist regime.[2] The worker
correspondent was 'the hinge between the communist press and
the masses', because only through his/her reports could the
party keep itself informed about what was going on in the
factories and because of his/her reports on specific conditions in
one or the other factory could it attract readers who would be
willing to learn from the examples in order to develop a critique
of capitalist society in general.[3] The KPD daily *Die Rote Fahne*
therefore organised its network of worker correspondents and
the step from workers using a fountain pen or typewriter to
working with a camera was soon made.[4] In 1926 an Association
of Worker Photographers was founded, which became very
active in the late 1920s and early 1930s.[5] Some worker photographers' collectives even started making films.[6] For this they
did not need the directives of Senda and Lüdecke, which got lost
in a Weimar Republic tottering on its last legs.

If the mighty German Communist movement did not succeed
in the 'agitpropisation' of its cinema, how could one expect the
tiny British movement to do so? The odds were certainly not in
its favour. Although the CPGB had been trying to organise a
worker-correspondents movement since 1928, it had remained
a very small one, with many weaknesses. An important flaw was
the unrepresentativeness of the correspondents for British
labour in general. Moreover, worker photography as an organised activity lagged far behind the movements on the Continent.
Although worker photography could be traced back to the
1890s (as we saw in Chapter One), the British Communist
movement was very slow indeed in organizing a network of
worker photographers in the 1930s. The basic concepts were
disseminated in a series of articles in the WIR monthly *Searchlight*, but the result, the Workers' Camera Club, never really got
off the ground.[7] One could certainly not expect the 'agitpropisation of the cinema' from the British worker photographers. Senda and Lüdecke also mentioned collaboration
with worker cartoonists and proletarian writers. Their organisations in Great Britain, the Artists International[8] and the

Writers' International,[9] did not come into being until 1933-34, and only became important after the international Communist movement had abandoned the 'Class against Class' policy for the Popular Front, a broad alliance against the fascist threat. Both the Artists and the Writers' international used *Left Review* (1934-38) as a forum for their ideas on literature and the arts.

This left the Workers' Theatre Movement as the only organisation capable of steering a British workers' cinema after the demise of the FOWFS. Chapter Three described the exhibition practice of the British workers' cinema, especially the contribution of the WTM. Charlie Mann, for example, considered the street corner exhibitions with a van in the East End of London as an extension of the WTM practice of performing theatre at street corners.

In their article on the 'agitpropisation of the cinema', Senda and Lüdecke dwelled only briefly on the kind of films to be made. They wrote of the recording of 'demonstrations and other big campaigns of the workers', and 'regular film reports from the factories and the countryside'. It seems they were trying to translate the concept of worker correspondence into cinematographic terms. To provide film reports from the factories or countryside would have required exceptionally favourable basic conditions, both cinematographically (filming interiors required more than the usual skills) and organisationally (as it was almost everywhere prohibited to bring a camera inside a factory). The keeping of a 'visual record of demonstrations, etc.' seemed the best solution.[10] Filming in the open air was relatively easy, while the importance of certain demonstrations was undisputed among the left. This was shown in the FOWFS newsreel *Workers' Topical News*, with its 1930 Hunger March and May Day demonstrations.

In 1932 a group made a film of the May Day demonstration which was focused on Japanese aggression in Manchuria. The Metropolitan Police kept an extensive record of all the preparations for the demonstration and were aware of the plan to film the demonstration, especially the march from Hyde Park towards the Japanese Embassy, near the Portman Hotel. The making of the film was invested with a much greater significance than it probably had:

In order that propaganda can be made out of the affair (and

incidentally prove to Moscow that the Communist Party in this country is not a spent force) stern resistance is to be offered to the police and a film taken of whatever might develop in consequence. A cinema camera, probably camouflaged and carried on a lorry, is to be in the vicinity of the Embassy, to photograph 'scenes of police batoning workers (men, women and children), when protesting against Japanese atrocities in China and war on Soviet Russia'.[11]

The WTM magazine *New Red Stage* published a report on 'Filming the May Day Demonstration', as experienced by one of the film crew ('S': most likely Ivan Seruya). One of the highlights of this report was the description of how the crew made the police believe they were pressmen. In view of the police report, quoted above, one wonders if the two camera crews mentioned in the *New Red Stage* article had really been able to mislead the police. The vital part of the May Day demonstration was described in *New Red Stage* as follows:

> Then came the march to the Japanese Embassy. The demo left the Park in an orderly manner, and suddenly came the baton attack by the mounties, who hurled the demo and crowd back. We were there right in the thick of it. What an opportunity! Up went the cameraman on the shoulders of the tallest in our party, and got an excellent shot of this.[12]

The result of these activities was a 'sub-standard' film, *Against Imperialist War – May Day 1932*, which may have been exhibited under the title *Workers' Topical News* No.4.[13] The extant version of this film testifies to the use of two camera crews, as mentioned in the article in *New Red Stage*. It shows marchers from the various parts of London, various speakers in Hyde Park (among them Harry Pollitt) and the march towards the Japanese Embassy.

Next year, in 1933, the May Day demonstration was covered in a similar way by a 16mm film crew: shots of marching participants, alternated by captions. The struggle against fascism had overtaken the struggle against the imperialist war as the most important slogan. But the film still proved the validity of the 'united front from below' thesis. It is not clear if this 1933 May Day film was shown publicly and if so, by which organisation. Like its predecessor, *Against Imperialist War – May Day 1932*, the 1933 May Day film seemed in the first place a

ETV

EDUCATIONAL & TELEVISION FILMS LTD

247a Upper Street, London N11RU   071-226 2298   Fax 071-226 8016

from *Stanley Forman*

WITH COMPLIMENTS

substitute of events the commercial newsreels did not show. Its strength was the conviction that the event filmed was important enough to be exhibited; its weakness lay in the traditional way in which the event had been filmed: columns of marchers, speakers in Hyde Park (unheard for want of sound film equipment). Conspicuously present in both May Day films were the police.

It is not quite clear what the exact purpose of the two May Day films was, given the fact that Kino had yet to be founded and that distribution outlets were therefore lacking. The significance of May Day itself was undisputed among the left, to the extent that both the Labour Party and the TUC and the Communist movement and its allies each organised their own May Day procession. Indeed, it may have been the purpose of both films to boost morale in the Communist movement by recording (and showing) its own May Day procession. The presence of hundreds of policemen could in that case be taken as an indication of the importance of the event. 'In our times, truth is revolutionary' – this adage, attributed to the French Communist writer Henri Barbusse, seems to have been the main concern of those involved in making the two films.[14] But how the process had to be carried on from there – from simply *showing* an event to *revealing* a conditon, from which the spectator could *learn*, as a result of which he/she would *act* – remained a mystery to them, unless they really had in mind to build up a library of film reports, from which 'longer compilation films, which will criticise in a revolutionary way the existing conditions by means of the dialectical method' (Senda and Lüdecke) were to be made. For, as the German playwright Bertolt Brecht wrote: '... less than ever a simple "reproduction of reality" tells something about reality. A photograph of the Krupp or AEG factories yields almost nothing of these institutions.'[15] Here Soviet theories of 'montage', or film editing, offered a number of possibilities and English translations (by Ivor Montagu) of the writings of the Soviet film director Vsevolod Pudovkin were of obvious importance.[16]

An exception to the simple May Day newsreels, made in the pre-Kino days, was *Liverpool – Gateway of Empire*, produced in 1933 by the Merseyside Workers Film Society. This 16mm film was a typical 'cross-section film', showing different aspects of life in the city and port of Liverpool. Undoubtedly its makers (among whom was the photographer John Maltby) had been influenced by the example of Walter Ruttmann and his *Berlin, The Symphony of a Great City* (1927). The German film theoretician Siegfried Kracauer defined 'the cross-section film' as 'the purest expression of New Objectivity on the screen. Their such-is-life mood overwhelmed whatever socialist sentiments played about in them.'[17] Kracauer's argument was simple: in order to provide a real cross-section, these films had to drop their political preferences, had to be neutral. Like some other films of this type, *Liverpool – Gateway of Empire* used the cross-section device as a means of taking sides rather than remaining neutral.[18] It shows the labour of the dockers, the shop windows with their riches from all the corners of the Empire, an unemployed demonstration, Labour leaders speaking at an open air meeting, the overcrowded tenement houses. The film lacked the direct political message that some might have hoped for, but it always kept a check on its artistic pretentions which might have led it astray politically.

The conference of the Cinema Bureau of the IURT in Moscow, May 1933 (see Chapter Three) did not have immediate results for the production of workers' films, as was the case with film distribution. At the conference, Hans Rodenberg stressed the possibilities for producing workers' newsreels and films, made in co-operation with the national workers' theatre movements. He did not mention the compilation films considered so important by Senda and Lüdecke. Once Charlie Mann got back from Moscow he started organising the distribution and exhibition side of the Film Section of the WTM. After it had been set up properly (and renamed Kino), a start could be made with the development of a production section. A special meeting was held for this purpose, on 9 December 1933.[19] The early history of the Kino production group is obscure. It is, for example, not known who exactly belonged to the group. The *Daily Worker* does not bring relief in this respect, as it concentrated, justifiably, on Kino's struggles with the authorities over the exhibition of *Potemkin*.

The first mention of a film produced by the Kino production section, the *Hunger March* film, comes in March 1934.[20] It did not differ much from the two May Day productions mentioned

above, or, for that matter, from *Workers' Topical News* No. 2, with
its film report of the 1930 Hunger March described in Chapter
Two. The footage for *Hunger March* was shot in three places:
Glasgow, Cambridge and London. The film starts with a brief
exposition of the reasons why the march took place. Through
pamphlets, mainly written by Wal Hannington, the leader of the
National Unemployed Workers' Movement (NUWM), the
viewer is introduced to the purpose of the march: the defeat of
the Unemployment Bill. Then it shows how the marchers
prepared in Glasgow, with Harry McShane addressing them.
The shots made in Cambridge focus on the solidarity between
students and clergy on the one hand and Marchers on the other.
Then the arrival in London is shown, with the usual processions
and speakers (including the indefatigable Tom Mann). The film
ends with a call for a United Front. In one of the shots made in
Glasgow, the ILP MP 'John McGovern tells Gaumont Graphic
why they march' (caption in the film). In 1932 the newsreel
companies had received a letter from the Commissioner of the
London Metropolitan Police, in which they were asked to
refrain from filming that year's Hunger March. With the
exception of Paramount, the newsreel companies complied to
this 'request', knowing that if they did not, certain privileges
could be withheld. Indeed, there was some talk of 'punishing'
Paramount in such a way. On 1 February 1934 a similar
'request' was sent to the newsreel companies. Whether
Gaumont Graphic made its interview with John McGovern as a
possible substitute for pictures of the Marchers, or as part of a
more rounded-off item on the March, is unknown. To the
certain satisfaction of the Commissioner the newsreel
companies Gaumont British, British Picture, British Paramount, Pathé and British Movietone News all abstained from
showing the 1934 Hunger March.[21] This makes the Kino
production *Hunger March* all the more important, as proof of the
adage that 'in our times, truth is revolutionary'. The film was an
act against the National Government's campaign to hush up the
plight of the unemployed.

Unemployment was also the theme of Kino's next release,
entitled *Bread*. It was quite different from *Hunger March* and the
newsreel films, in that it had a storyline and was acted. *Bread*
could be called a 'featurette', an alternative to the
hour-and-a-half feature-film, conforming to the practice of

Filming *Bread*, 1934

the workers' theatre of abandoning the traditional five-act play for the short but powerful sketch. The evidence shows that *Bread* was produced by a different group than *Hunger March*, an East London WTM group which had switched from agitprop theatre to the cinema. One of its members was Sam Serter, who recalled that a lecture by Eisenstein on 'montage' inspired him to make *Bread*.[22] Although Eisenstein visited London in 1929, it must be doubted if this was really the case (perhaps it was a lecture *about* Eisenstein). The important thing for Serter and his friends was the discovery of the 'montage' conception and its application in the cinema, the construction of meaning by putting certain images in juxtaposition. The film starts with a loaf of bread (in close-up) in a shop-window. It then brings the spectator to a back-to-back house, where the father is 'on the Means Test'. An interrogation scene at the Public Assistance Committee follows. Staccato close-ups of the faces of the commissioners are cut with a medium shot of the despondent father, sitting in a chair. The film shows the desperate father walking through an East End alley. He throws a stone through the window of the baker's shop and steals a loaf. He is caught by the police, leaving the bread on the street. In court two cases are heard. Students who have been spilling fruit off a cart are let off with a simple caution, while the father's argument (captions: 'Starving? Nonsense'; 'No need to starve') is not taken seriously. As a clear victim of class justice the father is sentenced to jail. The film ends with documentary footage of the 1934 Hunger March (though not of the solidarity shown by Cambridge students, which would have spoiled the film's argument). The message is clear: Only through organised action can the unemployed fight the injustice done to them. One cannot help but compare *Bread* with the Socialist Film Council's *The Road to Hell*. The latter film's pessimistic, individualist approach forms a marked contrast to the class-based story depicted in *Bread*, with its direct reference to the struggles of the NUWM.[23] It seems characteristic of the void that *Bread* tried to fill that the *Daily Worker* film critic never reviewed the film properly, whereas the paper devoted considerable space to the next Kino productions, *Workers' Newsreel* Nos. 1 and 2.

The first issue of *Workers' Newsreel* was released by Kino in August 1934, covering events during the first seven months of that year. The newsreel opens with the statement 'This is an attempt to present NEWS from the working class point of view.' In its presentation, *Workers' Newsreel* No.1 differed indeed from previous newsreels and documentary shorts. Its makers clearly considered news as a construction, which had to be presented in a certain way to the spectators. This clearly was a step forward from the previous notion that the revolutionary truth was there, waiting (even begging) to be filmed, which had to be done by workers' film groups, as the commercial newsreel companies were afraid of showing this truth on the cinema screens. The items of *Workers' Newsreel* No.1 are: the *Daily Worker* Gala in Plumstead, the building of a new store for the London Co-operative Society, the Hendon Air Display, the Youth Anti-War Congress in Sheffield and the anti-war demonstration in Hyde Park in August. According to *Daily Worker* film critic Dave Bennett, 'Blackshirt Olympia is shown and the workers' counter-demonstration', material that is missing in the extant print of the newsreel.[24] In a 'deadly parallel' the film shows how 'The Workers Create' (caption) – the construction of the new Co-op store – while 'Capitalism Destroys' (caption) – an air plane crash, the arrival of ambulances. The Hendon Air Display is used in a rapid 'montage' to introduce the Youth Anti-War Congress in Sheffield, arguing that 'Workers make these planes' ... 'to Destroy Workers' ... 'But the masses are Organising' (captions). Dave Bennett concluded:

> As their first effort the film deserves full praise and should be used immediately by working-class organisations as good, popular propaganda against Fascism and war. The weakness of the film is that the many strike actions of the workers this year are not brought in and the National Government is not depicted as the organiser of war and Fascism.[25]

Lack of money and the availability of only one camera was pleaded in excuse. This handicap might indeed have prevented the group from covering strike actions with its single camera. But Bennett did not indicate how the newsreel format, with its inherent limitations, could be used to expose the National Government 'as the organiser of war and fascism'. His critique can have been of little use to the Kino production group.[26]

The next issue of *Workers' Newsreel* appeared barely one and a half months later. Although the group managed to cover some very important events with the camera, *Workers' Newsreel* No.2 was a setback from the previous issue. With the exception of the item on the anti-fascist demonstration in Hyde Park on 9 September 1934, the 'deadly parallel' is not used and the film material is edited in the ordinary newsreel fashion. It simply shows some episodes of the struggle against fascism, like the 'Release Thaelmann' banner in Strand, which was removed by the police, (Thälmann, the leader of the German CP, had been jailed by the Nazis without trial) and the anti-fascist sports rally in Paris, where the Soviet athletes 'outclassed all nations' (caption).

On Sunday 24 September 1934 a serious mine disaster occurred at Gresford Colliery in North Wales, in which more than 250 miners died. With another Kino member, John Turner, Charlie Mann travelled overnight to Wrexham.

> We got there, when the dawn was just breaking. Terribly dramatic. There was a pithead gear silhouetted against this red, the trams, the women half weeping, half stolid. I'll never forget it. The atmosphere was tremendous. With Turner, we took shots of it.[27]

The Gresford episode offers a good example of the potential and the limitations of the Kino production group. The personal engagement and courage were beyond doubt. As Mann put it, 'we made ourselves available. If anything happened, we'd get a bunch of us to the spot.'[28] The result of the overnight trip was footage of what could be seen at the pithead, while it would have been more useful to have evidence of what caused the disaster. This, however, would have required a different approach, with long-term planning and the use of another visual language. Where the Kino crew had been able to prepare itself, as in the case of the anti-fascist demonstration in Hyde Park on 9 September, the results were definitely more successful. The item manages to show very clearly how the Blackshirts (who had announced their intention to march to Hyde Park) were swamped by masses of anti-fascist demonstrators and could only proceed thanks to police protection. It then switches to anti-fascist speakers, as if showing a May Day celebration.

In November 1934 a new organisation came into being, the Workers' Film and Photo League (WFPL),

> an offspring of Kino and the Workers' Camera Club, who have formed this organisation for the purpose of co-ordinating the activities of all workers, artists and technicians in films and photography and all those who appreciate the possibilities of the camera as a weapon in the class struggle.[29]

The distribution branch of Kino was not included in the merger. Close co-operation between the Workers' Film and Photo League and Kino was intended: Kino was to distribute the film productions of the WFPL. Moreover, Kino was to become a limited liability company, so that it would be less vulnerable in the jungle of the capitalist film trade. In the United States a (Workers') Film and Photo League had been active since December 1930.[30] Its success in combining film production and distribution, still photography, film criticism and educational activities had made it an example to be imitated. The film critic of the French Communist daily *L'Humanité* concluded his review of the film *Sheriffed* (produced by the New York Film and Photo League and directed by Nancy Naumberg and James Guy) with the wish: 'And when will there be a "French League for Workers' Films"?'[31] So the name Film and Photo League was held to be synonymous with success. Worker photography in Great Britain had been lagging behind developments in other countries, and it was hoped that the WFPL could provide British worker photographers with the impetus and enthusiasm they so badly needed.

By the end of October 1934 the distribution section of Kino still had the same two Russian feature films at its disposal as in February 1934: *Battleship Potemkin* and *The General Line*. Although it had been campaigning for funds to extend its small library with other Soviet films, the necessary capital had been lacking. There was mention of 'a minimum of £450' being required.[32] In the meantime, the production section had made steady progress, producing *Hunger March, Bread* and *Workers' Newsreel* Nos. 1 and 2. It seems that some members of the distribution section forced the split which resulted in the WFPL and Kino Ltd. They might have felt that Kino's first purpose, the distribution of Soviet films, was threatened by the successful development of the production group, which had about twenty members in November 1934. Professionalisation was the answer, but that would mean the end of the production section if done rigorously. The best solution seemed therefore to split the organisation, professionalising the distribution section and extending the base of the production group by merging it with the Workers' Camera Club. In their zeal they made some serious mistakes. Kino Ltd. was to keep its office in Gray's Inn Road, London, including equipment, funds, etc., while the WFPL had to start from scratch. It was even saddled with an old debt of £13, which had been incurred by the Kino production group.[33] This caused a lot of bad blood. Nevertheless, both organisations started leading their own lives, with the WFPL provisionally using Kino's premises. Inevitably, the difference between the two organisations remained somewhat indistinct. When Kino sent out a circular in February 1935 to those 'who had joined Kino in 1934' but whom 'we have not seen at our various group meetings for some time', [34] the reorganisation was indeed explained, but not directly linked to the activities listed in the circular which simply stated 'Still-Camera photography is now part of our work,' without specifying whose work – Kino's or the League's.

On 4 March 1935 Kino was incorporated as Kino Films (1935) Limited, with the aim of 'the promotion of sociological education by means of the cinematograph'.[35] It had no share capital, it being hoped to raise its working capital from subscriptions (minimum £2). The subscribers were to become members of the Kino Committee, the council of the new company but prospective subscribers were none too keen and the company had to raise its capital through loans from sympathisers.[36] It had been quite successful in extending its library of Soviet features. *Son of a Soldier* and *New Babylon* (see Chapter Three) were followed by the release of two Pudovkin films in March 1935, *Mother* and *Storm over Asia*. Both films had been banned by the BBFC, but after the favourable result of the Jarrow case Kino could afford to take the risk. In May 1935 it added *Heroes of the Arctic* to its list. The National Committee of the Friends of the Soviet Union made this new acquisition financially possible. These Soviet features were often exhibited in programmes that included WFPL shorts.

Notwithstanding the initial handicaps the WFPL started

The Film and Photo League camera car

energetically. Its secretary was Jean Ross, the *Daily Worker*'s film critic 'Peter Porcupine'. It soon had three active sections: newsreel, feature film and still photography groups. The first real test for the new organisation was not long in coming. In December 1934 the National Government published new scales for unemployment benefit under the Unemployment Act Part II. The Act provided for a uniform scale of relief for long-term unemployed through a national Unemployment Assistance Board (UAB). For many unemployed, especially those living in areas with Labour-controlled PACs, this meant a cut in their benefit. The NUWM organised a national campaign, which was supported by large sections of the labour movement notwithstanding TUC hostility. In South Wales in particular, united action against the Act was successful in bringing tens of thousands on to the streets.[37] The WFPL considered it as its duty to mobilise all its forces for 24 February, the NUWM's day of protest against the Unemployment Act. Through the *Daily Worker* Peter Porcupine appealed to

> any reader in the provinces [who] has got a movie camera, or can borrow one, will he make sure to get some shots of his local demo. The League will pay for all film used. Averge length needed is 25 feet (on 16mm stock). Same applies to all workers with ordinary cameras. If they will post their film right away to the Secretary, Workers' Film and Photo League, 84, Gray's Inn Road, WC1, the photographs can be printed and developed by the League in half a day. There will be a big demand for such photos in the Press.[38]

The WFPL sent four cameramen to Hyde Park to film the demonstration. It organised a competition for the best title of the film that was to be made; the prize was 'a copy of Marx-Engels-Leninism'.[39] The winner was George Philips, of North London, whose 'title is *Mass United Action Beat The UAB.* [A Slogan actually used for February 24.] It's a bit long for a title, some of the other entries were snappier and more original, but they didn't convey the actual subject of the film,' Peter Porcupine reported.[40] In WFPL circles it was known as 'the UAB film', while Kino released it as *Workers' Newsreel* No.3[41] From the extant prints one must conclude that the appeal to cameramen outside London to send footage of local demonstrations fell flat. The Hyde Park demonstration is covered with precision. The film uses newspaper headlines, especially those of the *Daily Worker*, as a running commentary. The film was considered by the Newsreel group of the WFPL 'technically and in every other way a hundred per cent improvement on all past news-reel work'.

With Pete Davis, who had been one of the cameramen of the UAB film, Frank Jackson made the next WFPL film to be released, *Transport*. Peter Porcupine devoted some space to this film in the columns of the *Daily Worker*, and considered it to be

> the most important and technically the best workers' film yet made in this country. It is a documentary film of Camden Town. Camden Town is shown as a centre of transport of all kinds. We see the wealth that passes through Camden Town and how little remains to the workers who handle this wealth.[42]

However, Porcupine was less satisfied with the film after its final cutting. She felt that

> the film would be improved by shots of a few maps showing the position of Camden Town in relation to the rest of London, showing bus routes, canals, roads, rail-roads and goods stations, to establish it as a centre of transport.

She was also annoyed by

> a rather serious political error. A sub-title refers to the workers' small share of the profits. To call any worker's wages his 'share of the profits', is, to say the least, a highly incorrect formulation. Its effect is reactionary, for in it the director implies that the workers do not get a big enough share in the profits of the capitalist system. It implies as a solution a continuation of the capitalist system with improved conditions for the workers under capitalism, instead of the overthrow of capitalism, the abolition of the profit system.[43]

This Marxist logic proved irresistible for the makers of *Transport*: Porcupine was later able to report 'that certain changes have been made in the film since it was first shown, including the title about "the workers' small share of the profits" to which we took exception'.[44] The League's productions were the subject of many debates among members, but this public rebuke over a particularly sensitive point, their political intentions, was to remain an exception. Still it may be asked whether it would not have been better for the WFPL to have devised some way of making its debates public, through the columns of the *Daily Worker* for example instead of just fighting them out internally which bred an atmosphere of suspicion.[45]

During the summer months British working-class organisations ran a wide variety of schools, lasting a day, weekend or week, where workers could not only educate themselves, but also enjoy each other's company, the countryside and various forms of entertainment. The League decided that a one-day school would be the ideal occasion to bring its members together, to make the outside world acquainted with its activities and to earn some badly needed hard cash. Lectures were to be given by Ivor Montagu ('Films and Modern Society'), Paul Rotha ('Making Films Without Money') and Stephen Harrison the editor of *The Private Life of Henry VIII*, the commercial success of film producer Alexander Korda; Harrison had just returned for a visit to Moscow. There was also to be an exhibition of British and foreign worker photography. In the evening a Flannel Dance was to be held, which would be adorned by a number of 'stars' (among whom 'Madame Tampuri, Finland's Sybil Thorndike').[46] Some 400 people attended the event on Sunday 7 July at the Studio Theatre in Hampstead. Rotha was not able to come, but 'Harold Lowenstein, a young director with new ideas about filmmaking' was found to replace him and talk on the same subject.[47] It seems the school was a great success, boosting the morale of the WFPL activitsts and providing the League with a financial profit which could be used to clear some debts.

During the summer of 1935 WFPL members were active on a number of projects. A fourth issue of the *Workers' Newsreel* was compiled from film reports of various events made by WFPL members. Responding to changes in the political climate, *Workers' Newsreel* No.4 included items on the ILP Summer School in Letchworth, the in 1935 May Day March, Soviet folk-dancers in London and Tom Mann's visit to a Pioneer's Camp.[48] Some of these items had also been edited into short films, for example of the performance of the Soviet folk-dancers in London.[49] WFPL members also filmed that summer, at the request of the camp committee, the holiday camp in Oxford for unemployed South Wales miners. The result, *A Holiday from Unemployment*, was taken by Kino on tour through South Wales in October 1935, with Pudovkin's *Storm over Asia*.[50]

Yet another film that the League was involved in was *Jubilee*. The Silver Jubilee of King George V was held on 6 May 1935. Newsreel cameras played an important part in turning the Jubilee into a celebration of national unity and a glorification of the Empire. Two North London teachers, the brothers H.A. and R. Green, made a film exposing the Jubilee event. Herbert Green was the secretary of the North London Film Society, a very active body which 'was formed early in 1934 to exhibit films privately on standard-size stock'.[51] Once they had made their film, with money from the North London Film Society, Herbert Green brought it to Kino as his own society could not distribute it adequately. Kino referred him to the WFPL. With the help of League members the film was recut and additional footage added.[52] The result was remarkable. As Peter Porcupine put it, *Jubilee* 'demonstrates clearly how the National Government used the Jubilee celebrations as a publicity stunt masking sinister preparations for war'.[53] The Green brothers used the 'deadly parallel' principle. *Jubilee* started with some fine shots of the East End Jubilee tour of the King and Queen, singling out the batteries of newsreel cameras covering this event. Then the captions read: '25 Years of Progress' ... 'Progress towards What?' The film switched to the day-to-day East End that the newsreel cameras never showed, with its slums, employment office, dole queues and depressing signs of 'No hands wanted'. A shot of disabled war veterans offered the film makers the opportunity to explain: 'Progress ... towards ... war', showing war preparations (recruitment posters, military parade, battleships at sea, etc.). *Jubilee* was more than a simple newsreel of the celebrations in May. Compellingly edited, it offered a political analysis by means of the cinema. It was the sort of compilation film that Senda and Lüdecke must have had in mind, when they suggested 'films, which will criticise in a revolutionary way the existing conditions by means of the dialectical method'.[54]

The only section of the WFPL without any finished films to its credit by the autumn of 1935 was the Feature Film group. A minute book of the group's meetings has survived, which gives some clues to its failure to live up to expectations. Like other sections of the League, the Feature Film group had to start from scratch. At its first meeting on 17 November 1934, several themes for films were discussed, a treasurer and secretary elected and an appeal for loans made. According to the minute-book '10/- was given on behalf of the Action Theatre', indicating the group's intention to establish closer relations with the theatre world. At a second meeting the position of the group within the League was debated. As the members present could not decide between two scenarios, 'it was decided to start work on one, using suggestions from both'. A sub-committee was elected for this purpose. By the end of 1934 the meetings of the group were marked by the concrete demands of film production: selection of actors, search for location, props, etc. Then follows a gap in the minutes. In March 1935 it was 'agreed that Feature Film Group continue to function when this film is done'. The problem was that the group could not finish its first production. Indicative of its failure to develop feature film production with assistance from left-wing theatre people was their absence from the programme of the WFPL one-day school in July. Barbara Nixon and Miles Malleson from the Left Theatre group were to preside over sessions. Malleson had to cancel his engagement, while Nixon only chaired Ivor Montagu's lecture.[55] In September the group met once more. It was reported by the directors that the film had been completed and accepted by Kino to be distributed in its present state. A lot of criticism of the production and the people involved in it cropped up. Ironically the film's title was *Fight!* It cost £12, of which only £8 17s. had been secured. It was hoped that the film's earnings could be used to cover the loss. However, the release of *Fight* ('showing the development of a young worker to class-consciousness'[56]) was postponed, because the League committee was not satisfied with the result. Incomplete minutes of a meeting on 3 April 1936 reveal that further changes in *Fight* were being contemplated.[57]

The production of *Fight* proved a good test of the flexibility of the League's organisational structure. A 'Manifesto of the Workers Film And Photo League' had been published to inform the outside world of the aims and activities of the League. Internally a (draft) constitution of the rules for the

WFPL was circulating. The key sentences in the manifesto were:

> Workers' Film and Photo League thinks the time has come for workers to produce films and photos of their own. Films and photos showing their own lives, their own problems, their own organised efforts to solve these problems. For this purpose there must be joint co-ordinated activity by all working-class film and camera club organisations, all individual workers, students, artists, writers and technicians interested in films and photography. Workers' Film and Photo League exists to provide this co-ordination.[58]

In the League's draft constitution its objects were described as follows:

> 1. To produce and popularise films and photos of working class interest, giving a true picture of the industrial and social conditions of the workers to-day and of their organised struggle to improve these conditions; 2. To carry on discussion and criticism of current commercial films and to expose films of a fascist, militarist or anti-working class nature.

In rules 3 and 5 the status of working groups of not less than ten members was described; such groups were to be autonomous and retain a proportion of the membership fees. The membership fee was fixed at 2s. 6d., and the working groups could keep 6d. per member. In rule 6 the powers of the Executive Committee (which turned down *Fight*) were defined; 'The function of the EC is to co-ordinate the work of the gorups; to assist them in every way possible: to arrange exhibitions of photographs; and to develop the WFPL as set down in the manifesto of the League.' Only in rule 7 the real power of the Executive Committee was laid down: 'Only films which have been approved by the EC and which bear the official leaderstrip may be shown as productions of the WFPL.'[59] As the Executive Committee was composed of the secretaries of the various WFPL working groups, one cannot but conclude that the Feature Film section was relatively isolated from the other groups. The kind of film making that had produced *Bread* came to a dead end with *Fight*.

In the autumn of 1935 the League organised a number of public events, hoping to continue the success of its one-day school in July. On 12 October 1935 *Jubilee* was shown, together with G.H. Sewell's *Gaiety of Nations*. Sewell, vice-president of the Institute of Amateur Cinematographers, introduced his own film.[60] On 27 November 1935 Francis Klingender and Ernest Lindgren debated the topic 'The Film: Propaganda or Art'.[61] In December 1935 the prefix 'Workers' was dropped, after the example of its American counterpart.[62] This marked a clear adaptation to the Popular Front policy of the international Communist movement, which could be traced back to the change from International Workers' Drama Union to International Union of Revolutionary Theatre in 1932.[63] Ironically, the first film shown by the League under its new name of Film and Photo League happened to be one made by some building workers on the job.[64] *Construction* was its title and it deserved the epithet 'workers' in every respect.

In October 1934 a nine-day strike had taken place at the Exeter House building site in Putney, London, over the sacking of a labourers' steward. But there had had been 'an accumulation of small grievances over a long period that caused the men to take drastic action'.[65] The strike was won and the steward reinstated, a victory due to rank-and-file trade union activity. Frank Jackson (no relation to Kino's Frank Jackson), a trade unionist of long standing who worked as a carpenter-foreman at Exeter House, had been closely involved in the strike.[66] He and his comrades extended their activities after the success of the strike. At lunch-hours Jackson and others led discussions on evolution and on current political topics, very much like Owen in Robert Tressell's *The Ragged Trousered Philanthropists* (of the abridged version of the novel then available, more than 200 were sold on the site after the strike). At one of these lunch meetings Alf Garrard, carpenter and amateur film maker, 'suggested the making of a film showing actual work on the job in progress'.[67] It was decided to do the job secretly, as it was unlikely that the manager would give permission. Jackson got Garrard a general maintenance job, so that he could move freely on the site. He put on 'a large sackcloth apron, instead of the usual linen one, cut a hole in it and took a number of photos. This resulted in some pictures coming out OK, but also many of them just showing the fibres of the sack.'[68] Garrard filmed the various activities on the building site in this rather haphazard way, and the workers also

Construction, 1935

re-enacted the strike of October 1934 in front of the camera. The film was edited with the help of some League members into a strong plea for trade unionism.[69] Both the FPL and Kino, which distributed the film, hoped that *Construction* would spark off the production of other trade union films.

Before the FPL held its first annual meeting on 21 February 1936, even more productions were on their way. A group specially set up for the purpose made a film on the defence policy of the National Government, entitled *Defence of Britain*. There are no prints extant of this film, which the Kino advertised by arguing that 'The National Government arms other nations, then demands arms for defence against the same nations.'[70] *Winter* was 'the first of a bi-monthly production schedule, agreed on by the League Committee', involving the participation of eight FPL members (among whom were Irene Nicholson, editor of the film magazine *Film Art*, veteran Ralph Bond and the editor R.Q. McNaughton, a member of the GPO film unit).[71]

The League also released a film on the unemployment in the South Wales mining valleys, the production of which it had encouraged by the loan of a film camera. It was entitled *Rhondda* and contrasted the destitution in the area with the mining population's spirited fight for a better future. The film makers – young, progressive, well-off – had been guided by men like Communist Councillor Jim Morton.[72] This may explain why *Rhondda* was more than a visitor's impression of the poverty in the valleys, more than a 'slumming' excursion with the camera. The film makers, however, went back to London to edit their film, taking with them cameras and film making skills, leaving local people without the necessary means to continue the film work. All the FPL productions so far had been based in London, a problem of which the League was acutely aware. A network of local FPLs would have been the best solution, but this required an organisational effort of which the League was simply not capable. Early in 1936 a Manchester FPL came into existence, and prepared as its first film, *Esperanto – The Workers' Weapon*.[73] The Hull Workers' Film Society, which had been founded in July 1935 with ILP support, also affiliated to the FPL.[74]

The first annual meeting of the FPL offered an occasion to assess its activities. Since November 1934, when it first started without any money, equipment or premises, some 80 members had joined the League and worked on a dozen films, photo exhibitions, etc. It published its own monthly bulletin *Camera Forward*. The League had also made great efforts to establish contacts with those working outside the small world of left-wing cultural activity. It had got in touch with organisations of amateur film-makers, which it had circularised in December 1935 with an appeal to submit scenarios.[75] But it considered the links with the professional film world even more important. Several members of the GPO film unit were drawn into its activities. The speakers at the first annual meeting formed a good indication of the League's interest: Irene Nicholson, editor of *Film Art*, was to speak on 'What's wrong with the cinema?' and Arthur Elton of the GPO film unit on 'Documentary Films'.[76] A report of the activities of the League's sections was sent to the members. It ended with the call: 'Let our first general meeting be a really fruitful one. Come armed with helpful criticism and fresh suggestions.'[77] How could the ordinary FPL member guess that the League's very existence was at stake?

What exactly happened at the first general meeting of the FPL on Sunday 23 February 1936 is difficult to reconstruct. It is clear that only a very small number of the 80 or so members attended the meeting. An urgent call in the *Daily Worker* two days earlier to members ('Matters vitally important') did not produce any results. On behalf of some members Albert Pizer proposed 'to dissolve the Film and Photo League and arrange for our members to be associated with the Kino Production Committee, and with adequate representation thereon'.[78] This resolution must have come like a bolt from the blue. After all, Kino had abolished its production section in November 1934 in order to concentrate on film distribution. Why was it so anxious to start its own production group now, taking over the FPL? At first sight Kino had little to gain from winding up the League. It would have to engage in financial risks, not to mention the time-consuming preparations for film production. As Pizer was not only a founding member of the League, but also treasurer of Kino, there had to be a catch somewhere. It was decided that a committee of three would consult the members who were not present, informing them of the differences of opinion. The FPL activists must have felt bewildered. They must have felt let down by the ordinary members whose absence at the AGM could not be ignored, while they could only guess at the reasons behind Albert Pizer's proposal to dissolve the League.

Sime Seruya (mother of Ivan Seruya, of Jarrow fame) was the first to take action. On 28 February she sent out a circular to those FPL members who had not attended the AGM. She made a case for continuing the work of the League.

> We have some 80 paid members and the help (as the F. & Ph. L. is absolutely nonparty) of an increasing number of professional technicians. Our main difficulty has been lack of premises and cash, and being saddled at the start with an old Kino debt of £13. Now that debt has been paid off, and we have a *fund specially earmarked for premises for the League*.[79]

A group of nine FPL members decided they would continue the League's work, whatever the result of the consultation of members. It is not clear whether Sime Seruya was among them. Their spokesman was Charles Gralnick. He argued that there was room for an organisation of voluntary enthusiasts beside the commercially run Kino Ltd. He believed that because it was a non-party organisation the League could attract wide sections of the population, while Kino, identified with the distribution of Soviet films, would find it difficult to achieve such a broad appeal. Gralnick also felt that Kino was after the money the League had put aside for new premises. He pointed out that there would be no room for a number of activities undertaken by the FPL, such as film education and criticism, in the Kino production group. Pizer argued that the FPL had failed to enlist support outside London, but Gralnick pointed out that Kino had not done any better in this respect. Gralnick concluded with the observation that, whatever his disagreement with Pizer, he still considered Kino 'an essential organisation'.[80]

In April 1936 the commission of three sent out a circular, summarising the differences of opinion regarding the future of the FPL.

> Kino Films (1935) Ltd. wish us to emphasise that the existence of a special production group will in no way affect their readiness to distribute such films as may be produced by the

> League. Their main reason for forming their own production group is that the League has in the past not been able to provide Kino with a sufficient number of good films to meet the demand from working-class and other organisations.[81]

It seemed the most practical solution: a party-based, (semi-) professionalised production group, beside a non-party, broad organisation of volunteer members.

Was the game worth the candle? It all depended on what one had expected from the League. The (W)FPL (and its predecessor, the Kino production group) never realised the formation of 'film agitprop troops', as outlined by Senda and Lüdecke. One gets the impression that the working-class element in the League was minimal, with the cameraman of *Construction*, building worker Alf Garrard, being the exception rather than the rule. Another weakness of the (W)FPL was its lack of planning. Most of its productions seem to have been made because a few individual members took a fancy to a subject. In fact, the two sections with a specific assignment fared pretty badly. The feature film section ran into trouble with *Fight* and the newsreel group found it impossible 'to produce up-to-the-minute newsreels' with cameramen only available during the weekends and without money to pay for transport. This led to the next question: the political usefulness of the (W)FPL productions. Kino had its doubts as to this. Still, the political relevance of the themes treated by (W)FPL productions could not be disputed. It is doubtful whether the transfer of the best part of the League to the Kino production section, as advocated by Pizer, could on its own have raised the level of left-wing political film making. Through his work with Kino Pizer must have been aware of the need to adapt the kind of film making that the League stood for ('making our own films') to the political requirements of the time.[82] While it may have been obvious to him that these requirements could only be met by Kino, he failed to convince others. The result was that suspicion reigned on all sides.

To end the confusion and get back to 'business as usual' the League's provisional committee decided to call the adjourned AGM on 22 April. Sime Seruya sent out a circular to that effect from the League's new address, 4 Parton Street, WC1. 'The League goes on!'.[83] There is no record of the attendance at the adjourned AGM, where a new committee was elected. This committee must have felt the need to let all concerned know that the FPL was continuing its activities. An insertion in the May Day issue of the *Daily Worker* was the occasion for this. It would prove that the League had not turned anti-Communist after the February events (some claimed that Pizer's move had been part of a Communist coup against the FPL). In the insertion the League greeted the *Daily Worker* staff, thanking it 'for the encouragement it has given to the League's efforts'. It greeted

the ever-widening masses of men and women of all classes and of all faiths in our country and throughout the world, who, WITH OR WITHOUT CAMERAS – often at the risk of their livelihood and their lives – are endeavouring to build up a clear picture of what is hidden beneath the now slowly decaying fortress of reaction, whether in the hands of financed dictators or profiteer democracies.

This message was accompanied by the assurance that

the League (now actively at work) is now technically, numerically and financially on a sounder basis than ever before, and asks for collaboration in all branches of its work from Trade Unions, Labour, Peace and other organisations in making pictures to expose present-day conditions as they affect the lives and aspirations of our own people.[84]

Notes

1. Korea Senda, Heinz Lüdecke, 'Agitpropisierung des proletarischen Films', in *Arbeiterbühne und Film*, Vol.18, No.5, May 1931, pp.8-11, here p.10.
2. The publication in the Communist monthly *Arbeiter-Literatur* (No.7/8, July/August 1924, pp.294-9) of two texts on the communist press by Lenin played a crucial part in the dissemination of the concept of 'worker correspondent' in Germany.
3. Paul Böttcher, *Der Arbeiter-Korrespondent. Winke und Aufgaben für Berichterstätter der proletarischen Presse*, Berlin 1927, p.20.
4. See Peter Kühne, 'Die Arbeiterkorrespondenten-Bewegung der Roten Fahne (1924-1933)', in Claudio Pozzoli (ed.), *Jahrbuch Arbeiterbewegung*, Vol.3, Frankfurt am Main 1975, pp.247-75.
5. See David Mellor (ed.), *Germany. The New Photographer 1927-33*, London

1978; W. Körner, J. Stüber, 'Germany: Arbeiterfotografie', in *Photography/Politics: One*, pp.73-81; *Creative Camera*, No.197/198, May/June 1981, pp.70-89.

6. This was mentioned by Senda and Lüdecke in their article (see note 1); the then secretary of the Association of Worker Photographers, Erich Rinka, confirmed this in a conversation with the author, East Berlin, 3 June 1981.

7. A series of articles, signed by 'Lens', in *The Searchlight*, May 1932, p.4; June 1932, p.2; July 1932, p.3; August 1932, p.8; September 1932, p.11.

8. See Robert Radford, 'When politics and art seemed to coalesce' in *Art Monthly*, No.20, 1978, pp.5-9; No.21, 1978, pp.7-10; Lynda Morris, Robert Radford, *The Story of the Artists International Association 1933-1953*, Oxford 1983.

9. See H. Gustav Klaus (ed.), *Marxistische Literaturkritik in England. Das 'Thirties Movement'*, Darmstadt/Neuwied 1973.

10. Korea Senda, Heinz Lüdecke, art.cit., p.10.

11. Public Record Office, London, Metropolitan Police, MEPO 2/3033 1a.

12. 'S.', 'Filming the May Day Demonstration', in *New Red Stage*, No.6, June/July 1932, p.4 and p.9.

13. On 4 March 1933 the Bethnal Green branch of Friends of the *Daily Worker*, organised a film show. In the ad the exhibition of an issue of *Workers' Topical News*, described as 'Shots of 1932 Demonstrations' was announced. See *Daily Worker*, 24 February 1933, p.3.

14. I have not been able to trace the original locus of the adage. In his dissertation Russell Campbell discusses the concept of revolutionary truth, as it was seen by the film makers of the American Film and Photo League. See Russell Campbell, *Radical Cinema in the United States, 1930-1942: The Work of the Film and Photo League, Nykino, and Frontier Films*, Ph.D., Evanston 1978, p.154. Although the members of the British left film production groups (Kino, Workers' Film and Photo League) must have had similar ideas, they never expressed themselves publicly on this matter.

15. Bertolt Brecht, *Gesammelte Werke 18. Schriften zur Literatur und Kunst I*, Frankfurt am Main 1967, p.161.

16. Vsevolod Pudovkin, *Film Technique*, London 1929 (revised 1933) and *Film Acting*, London 1935.

17. Siegfried Kracauer, *From Caligari to Hitler. A Psychological History of the German Film*, Princeton 1947, p.181.

18. One of the earliest examples was *Moscow* (1927), made by Ilya Kopalin and Michail Kaufmann. The latter's brother, Dziga Vertov, made the classic film *The Man with the Movie Camera* (1929), shown by many workers' film societies in Great Britain. The cross-section principle did not prevent Vertov from taking sides. A good example of an avant-garde film using the cross-section devise to express its sympathies with the working class is *Zijeme v Praze* ('We Live in Prague') (1934), made by Otakar Vávra.

19. *Daily Worker*, 9 December 1933, p.4.

20. Ibid., 20 March 1934, p.4.

21. Public Record Office, London, Metropolitan Police, MEPO 2/5507.

22. Sam Serter, interviewed by Gerd Roscher, for the West German television production *Wir machen unsere eigenen Filme* (We make our own films) (1978).

23. See Paul Marris, 'Politics and "Independent" Film in the Decade of

Defeat' in Don Macpherson (ed.), *Traditions of Independence. British Cinema in the Thirties*, London 1980, pp.70-95, here p.80.

24. *Daily Worker*, 24 August 1934, p.4.

25. Ibid.

26. There is no further information about the position of Dave Bennett as a possible adviser to the Kino production group – a position one would have expected the film critic of the party daily to hold. The fact that Bennett appeared in *Workers at their Summer School*, 'a film of the Socialist Summer School at New Milton (...) thinking out his film notes' (*Daily Worker*, 25 September 1934, p.4) might be interpreted that he was considered to be an important person by the group.

27. Charlie Mann, interview with the author, Somerset, 22 January 1979.

28. Ibid.

29. Daily Worker, 27 November 1934, p.4.

30. See Russell Campbell, op.cit.; William Alexander, *Film on the Left. American Documentary Film from 1931 to 1942*, Princeton 1981.

31. *L'Humanité*, 11 January 1935, p.4.

32. *Daily Worker*, 24 August 1934, p.4.

33. See circular from Sime Seruya to members of the Film and Photo League, 28 February 1936; memorandum, AGM Film and Photo League, 23 February 1936, by Charles Gralnick (?); statement of accounts of Production Group, 29 October 1934. The debt came to £12 17s. 3d., according to the last document. All documents are in Film and Photo League Archive (FPLA).

34. Circular, February 1935, sent by Kino to members (FPLa)

35. Kino Films (1935) Limited, First Annual Report, April 1936, p.2 (FPLa)

36. Ibid.

37. See Hywel Francis and David Smith, *The Fed, A History of the South Wales Miners in the Twentieth Century*, London 1980, pp.244-307; Peter Kingsford, *The Hunger Marchers in Britain 1920-1939*, London 1982, pp.202-5.

38. *Daily Worker*, 20 February 1935, p.4.

39. Ibid., 26 February 1935, p.4.

40. Ibid., 19 March 1935, p.4.

41. *Kino News*, Winter 1935, p.4.

42. *Daily Worker*, 14 May 1935, p.4.

43. Ibid., 28 May 1935, p.4.

44. Ibid., 18 June 1935, p.4.

45. The League published a monthly bulletin to keep its members informed about the activities of the various groups. Only one issue of this bulletin, *Camera Forward*, has been traced. League activists considered the lack of own premises as the biggest obstacle to a healthy internal climate.

46. *Daily Worker*, 9 July 1935, p.4.

47. Ibid.; for WFPL one-day school see also *Daily Worker*, 25 June 1935, p.4.; *New Leader*, 5 July 1935, pp.4 and 6; circular to WFPL members, concerning one-day school, instead of Monthly Bulletin, no date (FPLa).

48. *Kino News*, Winter 1935, p.4.

49. *Daily Worker*, 17 September 1935, p.4.

50. Ibid., 27 September 1935. p.4.

51. *Sight and Sound*, Vol.3, No.12, Winter 1934-5, p.188.

52. Notes on 'Production during 1935-6' (FPLa).

53. *Daily Worker*, 24 September 1935, p.4.

54. See note 1.
55. *Daily Worker*, 9 July 1935, p.4.
56. Survey of activities, sent to FPL-members for AGM, 23 February 1936 (FPLa).
57. Exercise-book with minutes of Feature Film group (FPLa).
58. 'Manifesto of the Workers Film and Photo League' (FPLa).
59. 'Draft Constitution for the Workers' Film and Photo League' (FPLa).
60. *Daily Worker*, 8 October 1935, p.4.
61. Ibid., 22 November 1935, p.7.
62. The first mention of Film and Photo League is in *Daily Worker*, 6 December 1935, p.7. The American League dropped the epithet 'Workers' ' in 1933-34, possibly simultaneously with the change of name of *Workers' Theatre*, which acted as the League's organ and became *New Theatre* with the September-October 1933 issue.
63. The new wording with its emphasis on 'revolutionary' rather than 'workers' made membership possible for a category previously excluded, such as professional playwrights and actors. Many such people might still have been repelled by the new wording, because it required a choice they did not want to make, but at least provision for their participation had been made.
64. *Daily Worker*, 20 December 1935, p.7.
65. Peter Latham, *Theories of the Labour Movement. A Critique in the Context of an Empirical Study of Building Trade Unionism*, Ph.D., London 1978, p.195; see also R.A. Leeson, *Strike. A Live History 1887-1971*, London 1973, p.132.
66. See Latham, op.cit., passim; Leeson, op.cit, pp.27-9, 52-6 and 92-3; Peter Latham, 'Rank and File Movements In Building 1910-1920', *Our History* No.69.
67. Frank Jackson, letter to the author, 21 November 1977.
68. Ibid; Frank Jackson, interview with the author, 7 March 1978.
69. Notes on 'Production during 1935-6' (FPLa); *Kino News* No.2 [Spring 1936], p.1; *New Builders Leader*, No.3, December 1935, p.7; No.7, April 1936, p.2; No.10, July 1936, p.2; see also Bert Hogenkamp, ' "Making Films with a Purpose": Film-making and the Working Class', in Jon Clark, Margot Heinemann, David Margolies and Carole Snee (eds), *Culture and Crisis in Britain in the 30s*, London 1979, pp.262-5.
70. *Kino News* No.2 [Spring 1936], p.3.
71. Notes on 'Production during 1935-6' (FPLa).
72. Donald Alexander, interview with the author, Dundee, 14 February 1986. From the League's Notes on 'Production during 1935-6' (FPLa) one might get the impression that *Rhondda* was made by a group based in South Wales, but Alexander's evidence refutes this.
73. *Camera Forward*, January 1936, p.5 (FPLa).
74. Ibid., *New Leader*, 27 September 1935, p.4.
75. *Daily Worker*, 6 December 1935, p.7; Circular from FPL to amateur film societies, 12 December 1935 (FPLa).
76. *Camera Forward*, January 1936, p.6 (FPLa); in the *Daily Worker*, 21 February 1936, p.8, Elton had been replaced by Thomas Baird (GPO Films).
77. Survey of activities, sent to FPL-members for AGM, 23 February 1936 (FPLa).
78. Motion proposed by Albert Pizer (FPLa).

79. Circular from Sime Seruya to members of the Film and Photo League, 28 February 1936 (FPLa).

80. Memorandum, AGM Film and Photo League, 23 February 1936, by Charles Gralnick (?) (FPLa).

81. Circular to members of the Workers' Film and Photo League, April 1936 (FPLa).

82. It seems that Pizer was not able to translate his views on the political reorganisation of left film-making in Great Britain in film aesthetic terms. In this respect a comparison with the American FPL is revealing. Essentially the same debate took place in the American FPL in 1934, but it was at least fought out openly on all levels (political, organisational and aesthetic). See Campbell, op.cit., pp.173-215; Alexander, op.cit., pp.65-112.

83. Circular to Friends and Members of the Film & Photo League, 9 April 1936 (FPLa).

84. *Daily Worker*, 1 May 1936, p.8.

Chapter 6

'The New Road to Progress'

'Those of us who stand for progress have no time to lose: to-day the road is steeper than before.' These words opened the editorial of *Kino News*, a four-page sheet published during the winter of 1935/36 by Kino Films (1935) Ltd. It pointed out that 'there are powerful forces working, not for progress but for reaction and decay.' Referring to the result of the recent general election, it continued:

> We cannot doubt that if the electorate had been convinced that the National Government stands for reaction and against progress, this government would have suffered an overwhelming defeat at the polls. Therefore, our first task is – Enlightenment. We have no illusions that this will be easy, but twentieth-century science has given us the most powerful instrument for our purposes which we have ever known – THE FILM. The film has been intensively exploited by the entertainment monopolies for super-profits. Now is the time to challenge the conception of the film which they have created. Now is the time for every individual and every group who realise the need for progress to use the film for its real purpose – for culture, for education and for enlightenment.[1]

Compared with Kino's previous declarations of intent, remarkable changes had occurred. There is, for example, no trace of the words 'workers' or 'working-class', whereas Kino's slogan in November 1934 went 'Workers! Hire Working-Class Films!!'[2] Another important change is the emphasis on 'progress' and 'enlightenment', in direct relationship between these notions and the results film could achieve. The editorial was an expression of the new political line adopted by the Communist International, the policy of the 'Popular Front'.

At its Seventh Congress in 1935 the Comintern decided on a major shift in its policy. Events in Germany after the seizure of power by the Nazis in 1933, who had outlawed the parties of the left, arrested and tortured thousands of Communists and Social Democrats and locked up working-class leaders without trial, convinced the Comintern leadership that the 'Class against Class' policy, with its inherent hostility towards the social democratic parties, was no longer appropriate. Fascism was identified as the principal enemy. At the Seventh Congress Georgi Dimitrov – the hero of the Leipzig trial – appealed for the formation of a 'popular front' against fascist aggression. Such a coalition, uniting working-class parties with progressive sections of the bourgeoisie, had already come into existence in France after an abortive attempt by royalist and fascist groupings to take power in February 1934. In its foreign policy the Soviet Union sought to isolate fascism by securing pacts with the leading democratic states. The signing of such a pact between the Soviet Union and France in 1935 was seen as an important step in this process. In 1934 the Soviet Union had joined the League of Nations, where it hoped to gain support for its foreign policy.

Already before the Seventh Congress, the Communist movement had started to correct some of the excesses of the 'Class against Class' policy. Some have suggested that it was writers and artists who actually paved the way for the Popular Front policy. Around 1932-33 many left-wing cultural organisations abandoned their exclusive working-class character and openly invited people with a different social background to join. Usually this change was expressed by dropping the epithet 'workers' in favour of 'left'. Not only the composition and name of the cultural organisations changed, but their practice too. One of the most conspicuous examples was the return to the curtain stage theatre by the workers' theatre movement. The Popular Front policy made superfluous an oppositional, exclusively working-class, cultural movement. Instead, the struggle against fascism became the rallying point for a broad cultural movement that attracted artists, writers and scientists of name and fame. It seems characteristic for the Popular Front era that France took over from Germany the role of providing ready-made organisational models through the prestige of its Association des

Ecrivains et Artistes Révolutionnaires (AEAR – Association of Revolutionary Writers and Artists).[3]

Unlike France, a Popular Front never came into existence in Great Britain. The basic condition for such an alliance – a united front of the working-class parties – could not be met. The CPGB had been making overtures to the Labour Party for a United Front (against fascism, against the National Government (since 1933, and with renewed vigour after the Seventh Congress. It even withdrew all but two of its candidates (one of whom, William Gallacher, was elected for West Fife) in the 1935 General Election. The Labour Party leadership, which may be characterised as 'right-wing', was not particularly impressed with the French example, loathed the idea of co-operating with Communists and met any approach by the CPGB with a blanket refusal. An application by the CPGB for affiliation to the Labour Party was turned down. A short-lived United Front between the CPGB, the ILP and the Socialist League came into being in 1935, as a first step, it was hoped, towards a real United Front. A rapid growth of Communist Party and Young Communist League (YCL) membership and rising sales of the *Daily Worker* were evidence of the success of the new line.

The organisation which had exemplified the cultural policy of the 'Class against Class' period in the United Kingdom, the Workers' Theatre Movement, disintegrated in 1934-35. It was internally divided over such issues as the return to the curtain stage and the enrolment of professional theatre people. Organisations like the Writers' International (British section of the International Union of Revolutionary Writers) and the Artists International (later AIA – Artists International Association), not so deeply rooted in the 'Class against Class' ideology, had fewer problems adapting to the 'Popular Front' policy and stepped into the breach left by the WTM. Particularly through the columns of the monthly *Left Review*, these organisations managed to mobilise a great number of British artists, writers and intellectuals. *Left Review* started in October 1934, promoting the idea of a British proletarian literature, but abandoned this approach after a number of issues for a more general concern for Marxist aesthetics. It stimulated much original thinking in this area, resulting in a series of important publications, some collective (5 *on Revolutionary Art*,

The Mind in Chains, Writing in Revolt), others written by talented individuals like Christopher Caudwell, Ralph Fox, Alick West and Francis Klingender.[4] Unfortunately this influence did not extend to the domain of film theory. Left Review only occasionally paid attention to the cinema. Perhaps this void can be explained by the almost general rejection by the left of fiction films in favour of the documentary. It seems no coincidence that the only profound film study published at the time – Money Behind the Screen (1937) by F.D. Klingender and Stuart Legg – is a factual account of how capital has taken control over the film industry.

After the result of the Jarrow case (see Chapter Three), Kino could start thinking of its future. To survive and extend its activities, it had to professionalise its operations. As a first step, it was incorporated as a non-profit-making company, Kino Films (1935) Ltd., in March 1935. This, however, did not resolve its financial worries. To a subscription scheme which made provision for a maximum of 200 members each subscribing £2 or more, only a pitiful sixteen responded.[5] Short-term loans from sympathisers brought temporary relief. The high initial costs involved in the acquisition of new films (copyright, negative and positive prints), had to be amortised as quickly as possible. For this purpose Kino organised so-called premiere or pre-release shows in London and important provincial centres. It booked a large hall (not licensed under the 1909 Cinematograph Act, of course!) for a number of nights, placed ads in the left press and pasted up its posters (often designed by AIA-members) all over town. Projection was carried out by Kino's own projectionists. By cutting down costs in this way, Kino was able to make substantial profits (£25, £50 or even £100) on these shows, allowing the loans to be repaid within a reasonable time.[6]

Contrary to common belief, the Soviet Union did not supply organisations which sympathised with the Communist cause with prints of Soviet films free of charge.[7] In fact, Kino experienced great difficulties in obtaining such prints. In the 1920s Berlin had been the centre for trade in Soviet films through Prometheus Film and Weltfilm. With Prometheus's bankruptcy in 1931, some Soviet studios began to deal directly with West European customers. After the Nazi take-over in 1933, Paris took over the role previously held by Berlin, but it never managed to monopolise the Soviet film trade. Soviet trade delegations in other countries also handled films. Another channel of supply was via the Soviet friendship societies. In a number of cases Kino was able to negotiate the rights for a Soviet film which was available on 35mm in the United Kingdom and could be reduced to 16mm by a simple order to the laboratory. In other cases prints had to be ordered from abroad, particularly from France. In the case of *The End of St Petersburg*, a film Kino was anxious to have 'as there was a very great demand for a good film to serve as effective propaganda against war', it was impossible obtain a print of the film. Kino even sent

> the necessary stock for making a print to Moscow. We then negotiated with Messrs. Garrison Films of New York, and were able to effect an exchange of a print of the film for a print of *The Ghost that Never Returns* which had not been shown in America.[8]

In its quest for Soviet films Kino had much support from the newly founded Progressive Film Institute discussed below.

The next important step in Kino's growth was the development of a national distribution network. So far, the bulk of Kino's activities had taken place in London. By concentrating a number of bookings, tours could be arranged to reach areas relatively remote from London. In order to consolidate the contacts made during such tours, it was Kino's policy to start a local group (rather than a sole agent who would most likely be unable to pay his way) representing the company in the area. Such groups came into existence in Birmingham (People's Film Service), Doncaster and Glasgow (Glasgow Kino).[9] South Wales proved a more difficult nut to crack. In October 1935 Kino toured the mining valleys with an attractive programme, consisting of Pudovkin's *Storm over Asia* and *A Holiday from Unemployment*, the short about a holiday camp in Oxford for unemployed Welsh miners.[10] The miners' lodges, workmen's institutes and welfare halls had been mailed systematically.[11] The tour was a success and Kino decided to organise another one in February 1936, with the famous *Battleship Potemkin*.[12] A Cardiff Kino Workers' Film Committee was set up to organise a special premiere screening in Cardiff on Sunday 5 January 1936. The Committee thought it had found a suitable unlicensed hall, but was outwitted by the

Cardiff police at the last moment.[13] The Committee – the nucleus of a Kino local group – never recovered from this blow. In the end, Kino used the left bookshop circuit to establish an agency in South Wales.[14] The development of Kino's distribution outside London involved a lot of hard work, but unfortunately no figures are available to assess what was achieved in this area.

It is difficult to ascertain the composition of the audiences which came to see Kino's films. In its First Annual Report Kino published a breakdown of its customers, which may be taken as an indication of the 'persuasion' of its audiences. One can assume that, if a local branch of the Friends of the Soviet Union (FSU) booked a Kino film, most of those attending the screening would be FSU members. In fact, FSU branches made up 30 per cent of the bookings. This is not so surprising, given the fact that Kino's film library held so many Soviet films and that it was virtually the sole 16mm distributor of Soviet films in the United Kingdom. Moreover, Kino acted as a distributor for those Soviet films which reached the country through the FSU. Thus it re-edited and titled *In the Land of the Soviets*, a film about the visit of workers' delegations to the Soviet Union in 1935. Film societies and film groups came second on the list with 12 per cent of the bookings. Next came United Front bodies and CPGB/YCL branches, each with 10 per cent. The other partners of the United Front, the ILP and the Socialist League, accounted for respectively 5 and 0.5 per cent. Given Kino's complete identification with the 'Popular Front' line, these figures are not surprising. They simply reflect Kino's numerous advertisements in the Communist *Daily Worker* and ILP's *New Leader* (ILP).

The Labour Party was more difficult to approach. Kino could not afford the rates of the *Daily Herald*, Labour's national newspaper, for a sustained advertising campaign. It decided to request Labour's national headquarters 'for facilities to circulate a publication in connection with their films to Divisional Labour Parties, and that it should be included in matter sent out from Head Office'.[15] If Labour's National Executive Committee had agreed to do this it would have been quite a feat, but the NEC's decision – 'That no action be taken' – will not have surprised the Kino people. Understandably, Labour's plans for a film service of its own

were watched closely (see Chapter Seven). Still, constituency
Labour parties and Labour League of Youth branches
accounted for 4 per cent of Kino's bookings. How carefully the
figures in Kino's breakdown have to be treated is shown by the
case of the Royal Arsenal Co-operative Society (RACS) in
London. Its educational secretary, Alderman Joseph Reeves,
was convinced of the need for film propaganda. As we have
seen, the RACS used Eisenstein's film *The General Line*
extensively as an example of what co-operation could achieve.
Reeves' contacts with Kino were very cordial indeed, with
important consequences for both parties in the years to follow.
The figure of 6 per cent on Kino's list for bookings by
Co-operative Societies and Guilds certainly doesn't do justice
to the importance of this development.[16]

It would be impossible to consider Kino's growth after
March 1935 without taking into account the development of
the Progressive Film Institute (PFI). This organisation had
been set up by Ivor Montagu with the deliberate purpose of
picking up any crumbs left by Kino or the commercial film
distributors. The PFI distributed for example the Pudovkin
films *Mother* and *Storm over Asia* on 35mm. Both films had been
banned by the BBFC, but the PFI was able to get a LCC
certificate for them, which guaranteed a few bookings from
London art cinemas. Commercial film distributors would
never have taken the risk. The PFI considered taking care of
the two films its duty. It handed over the 16mm rights (more
profitable, because not affected by the BBFC ban) to Kino.
Montagu was able to negotiate a deal with the Soviet trade
delegation, letting the PFI have all Soviet films not wanted by
anybody else.[17] The PFI's office was run by Eileen Hellstern,
Montagu's wife.

With its limited supply of 35mm Soviet films, the PFI only
had a very small number of potential customers. These
included art cinemas in London, Glasgow and a few other
cities and the cinemas of workmen's institutes or welfare halls
in the mining areas.

Despite the depression the miners' cinemas had been able to
expand considerably in the 1930s thanks to the backing of the
Miners' Welfare Fund. Under the 1920 Mining Industry Act a
levy of one penny per ton of coal produced had to be paid by
the mineowners into a special fund. By means of this so-called

miners' magic penny a whole range of social and cultural amenities for the benefit of the miners and the mining communities could be financially supported. The Miners' Welfare Fund was responsible for the installation of pit-head baths (from 1926 onwards financed by a levy on coal royalties), the opening of convalescent homes, the provision of recreational facilities and the support of miners' institutes and halls. Four-fifths of the proceeds had to be spent regionally, which meant that the regional welfare committees had a big say in the kind of welfare schemes they supported in their own area.

Though the national Miners' Welfare Committee 'strongly recommended in all schemes of suitable type ... the provision of cinematograph facilities', only the South Wales committee seemed to have followed a policy of consistent support to miners' cinemas.[18] In fact, there were more miners' cinemas in South Wales than in all the other mining regions together. The relative isolation of the mining communities in the Welsh valleys from centres like Cardiff or Swansea explains the need for local entertainment and the miners' halls and institutes – the social centres of the mining communities – took on the provision of cinema entertainment. Spurred on by the South Wales Miners' Welfare, 27 halls and institutes organised themselves into the Miners' Welfare and Workmen's Halls Cinema Association in 1939 in order to combine their forces.[19] After all, they formed the biggest independent circuit in Great Britain.

Film exhibition guaranteed the survival of the halls and institutes, which otherwise would have difficulties making ends meet due to high unemployment among members. With support from the Miners' Welfare, usually in the form of a loan, expensive projection and sound equipment could be purchased and necessary building alterations carried out. The miners' cinemas were equipped with 35mm projectors, licensed under the 1909 Cinematograph Act and run like ordinary cinemas with a paid manager.

In general film selection was left to the care of the manager, but often committees took an active interest in programme matters. They were anxious somehow to integrate the cinema programme into the policy of independent working-class education which the institutes and halls featured. Thus the

Montage from *Free Thaelmann*, 1935

committee of the Tredegar Workmen's Hall applied for membership of the British Film Institute as early as 1934 in order to obtain expert advice on educational cinema. The same committee spared no trouble to find a suitable anti-war feature. However, when Kino prepared its first South Wales tour in October 1935, the Tredegar committee had to decline its offer: 16mm projection was completely wasted in the huge cinema of the Tredegar Workmen's Hall; moreover, the screening of a film banned by the BBFC, *Storm over Asia*, might jeopardise the Hall's licence. The committee therefore decided to pass the Kino correspondence on to the local unemployed branch! This is why it was so important for the PFI to offer a 35mm alternative to the films distributed by the commercial companies, as the 'sub-standard' alternative was completely wasted on the miners' cinemas. The Tredegar committee would book the PFI's films in due time. With other committees it relied on distributors like the PFI for films in support of aid for Republican Spain. Soviet films, distributed on 35mm by the PFI, proved to be another attraction.[20]

Ivor Montagu was an active member of the Relief Committee for the Victims of German Fascism, so it is hardly surprising that the PFI released a film to support the Committee's campaign for the release of Ernst Thälmann, the imprisoned leader of the German Communist Party. This was *Free Thaelmann!*, a trimmed version of an American silent film entitled *Ernst Thaelmann – Fighter against Fascism*. Some traces of the film's American origins have remained: Thälmann is introduced by means of a title as 'a longshoreman' rather than 'a docker'. The film traces Thälmann's career, illustrating it with footage from the Weimar period. The second part shows the Nazi terror, the underground press and the international campaign for the release of Thälmann who was held without trial. When Montagu submitted the film to the BBFC, it took exception to one particular image, a photomontage showing Thälmann behind bars. The BBFC felt it would be wrong to give publicity to criminals; as Thälmann was shown behind bars, he evidently had to be a criminal! As the LCC also decided to ban the film, it was up to Kino to make the best of the situation by distributing the film on 16mm.[21]

Given the close relations between Kino and the PFI, it was only natural that Ivor Montagu was one of the main speakers at Kino's first Annual General Meeting on 26 April 1936 in London. Montagu took issue with George Elvin, the secretary of the Association of Cinematograph Technicians. Elvin had been making a case for the production of propaganda films which could be shown in the ordinary cinemas, in order to reach the unconverted. These films had to be 'films first and propaganda second'. Montagu pointed out that the expenses would be prohibitive, with £10,000 as the very minimum. Instead he recommended the production of documentary films: 'Kino was in a position to make true documentaries, whereas a good many so-called documentary films were forged documents.'[22] Montagu's authority in these matters was unquestioned: after all, he was not only the leader of the PFI, but he had been active in the Gaumont-British film studios, as associate producer for two Hitchcock films.[23] Why did Montagu emphasise the production of documentary films? Of course, there were eminently pragmatic grounds not to make feature films. Feature films called for very heavy investment and completely new standards of production (directing, acting, etc.) had to be met. Moreover, there was no guarantee that the commercial cinemas would take the film, even if the BBFC was willing to grant it a certificate.[24] But there was more to it. It was generally felt on the left that one had to oppose the commercial cinema, because it reduced film to mere 'entertainment', with a cinema that would educate and enlighten the spectator. True documentaries offered spectators the best chance of education and enlightenment. They could learn the facts from the screen and draw their own conclusions. In this way 'progress' could be realised.

Prior to Kino's first AGM another veteran, Ralph Bond, had put his arguments for the production of documentary films by Kino on paper. It was published under the title 'Making Films With A Purpose' in the first issue of *Kino News*. Bond summed up the requirements such films had to meet: they had to 'dramatise the lives and struggles of the workers' with subjects like 'unemployment, victimization, housing, children, strikes, hunger marches, war', without 'melodrama or false heroics and the message or lead must grow naturally out of the material'; they had to be 'positive in the sense that they must indicate the subjective factor of revolt and struggle against existing conditions'; they had to 'have unity and lead up to its motivating point in such a way that the audience will be carried with it naturally and logically'. Bond's conclusion:

> the documentary type is ... the one most suited to our aims ...
> We can take our cameras out into the streets, and at the expense
> of little more than film stock, patience and infinite capacity for
> taking trouble, photograph our material as it actually exists ...
> And if we do this, we are at the same time exposing the
> stupidity and false values of the commercial film.[25]

Bond's arguments were virtually the same as Montagu's: the need to make films in keeping with one's purse, i.e. documentaries, and by making documentaries combat the values of the commercial cinema.

Did the documentary need all this defence? After all, with a few (rather unsuccessful) exceptions, all the films produced by organisations like Kino and the (W)FPL had been documentaries. Did Montagu and Bond want to sound a warning against a misguided optimism reigning among certain young film makers? An optimism that arose from the general political climate of the time, or from the news that the Labour Party and the TUC were to start a film service of their own (see Chaper Seven). Rather than making a guess at the deeper intentions behind the Montagu and Bond statements, I would like to examine the films produced by Kino, the FPL and others in the light of their convictions.

Early in 1936 Kino decided to return to film production. The aims of the Kino Production Committee were described as follows:

> 1. To discuss and determine themes and treatments for films of
> social significance. 2. To form units throughout the country for
> their production, on sub-standard stock, and to act as a
> co-ordinating body to all such units and give assistance in every
> possible way. 3. To offer existing units a source of distribution
> for suitable productions in the sub-standard market, to assist
> and advise them on scenarios. 4. To undertake production for
> any organisations who feel that a film illustrating their work
> from a particular angle will aid them in their own sphere.[26]

How far was Kino able to achieve these aims?

In the summer of 1936 a Kino production unit worked on a new film, *Touch Wood*. According to its director Frank Jackson,

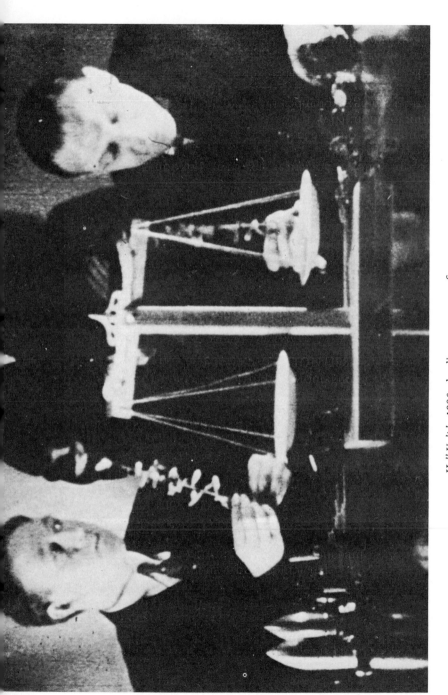

Hell Unltd., 1936; the disarmament conference

Hell Unltd., 1936

it was a 'working-class comedy'. The *Daily Worker* published a
publicity story describing how the film was shot in a timber
yard near King's Cross, with the leading part played by a
non-actor, the carpenter Tom Davies.[27] Obviously the unit ran
into difficulties completing the film. There is no trace of its
release in the contemporary press, nor can it be found in the
extant Kino catalogues. The failure of *Touch Wood* may have
been due to the high production standards needed for a
comedy film. It was the kind of failure of which Ivor Montagu
and Ralph Bond had warned. Frank Jackson evidently had
ambitions to become a 'real' film director, as was apparent, for
example, from his scenario 'A Portrait of John Keats', written
for the film periodical *Film Art*.[28]

It is difficult to say how far the Kino Production Committee
was actually involved in the formation of production units
throughout the country. It is, however, a fact that both the
Birmingham People's Film Service and Glasgow Kino
produced films of their own. Whether this was due to the Kino
Production Committee or a logical result of Kino's policy of
setting up local groups rather than appointing local agents, is
unclear. The Birmingham People's Film Service produced
films on important local events, such as the *Birmingham May
Day Procession*. Thanks to the presence of an attentive Detective
Sergeant, a witty description of this film has survived. The
policeman recognised his own person, 'taking notes of the
remarks made by Bert Williams, the District organiser of the
Communist Party'. Moreover,

> a touch of humour followed the caption, 'The Corporate State',
> when a photograph was shown of Councillor Victor Yates'
> stomach. Yates, is, of course, a rather portly gentleman.[29]

It seems that *Birmingham May Day Procession* and other films
produced by the People's Film Service were a strictly local
affair, and there is no indication that the Kino Production
Committee had any hand in their production.

Since 1935 Glasgow Kino had been responsible for the
distribution of Kino's films in Scotland, using Collet's
bookshop as its office. Its activities attracted two ambitious
young artists, Helen Biggar and Norman McLaren, who soon
developed plans for the making of films. A project on health
and environment ended in a failure, because the Glasgow

Corporation refused permission for filming inside a hospital. The night after Biggar and McLaren had received this bad news, McLaren wrote an enthusiastic letter to his collaborator outlining a new project. This would be the film *Hell Unltd.* It was made with the help of students and tutors at the Glasgow School of Art in about a month. *Hell Unltd.* was an anti-war film, using a great variety of techniques (documentary footage, fiction scenes and animated sequences). It tells the story of the arms dealer Mr Hell against the background of twentieth century history (First World War, Geneva disarmament conference, rise of fascism, etc.). The message of the film is simple: it appeals to its spectators to stop the arms race before it is too late, firstly by writing to their MP; then by demonstrating, if the first method has failed and finally by mass strike, if other means have proven unsuccessful. The film demonstrates how Mr Hell falls to the ground like a modern Dracula, as the result of such a strike. Glasgow Kino had little to do with the actual making of the film, but it provided a political focus for Biggar and McLaren. In August 1936 Helen Biggar took the film down to London to show it at Kino headquarters. The Kino committee suggested some changes, one of which, the omission of the caption 'Strike Now', McLaren refused to carry out, arguing: 'Other means have been failing for years. We need one-day strikes to protest against the present policy of governments and to show what resistance will have to be met with, in the case of the outbreak of war.'[30] Both Kino and Glasgow Kino distributed prints of the film, which seems to have been in steady demand, possibly because its length (about 20 minutes) made it a good match for Soviet features.

In May 1936 the Kino Production Committee had stated that it would produce 'a film for the Kensington Labour Party, dealing with infant mortality' and another one 'on Housing and Slums in co-operation with the builders' unions'.[31] This looked promising; the subjects were important, as was the fact that the Labour Party and a trade union were involved, but no more was heard of either of the projects. The only Kino production to have survived is a film commissioned by the London District Committee of the CPGB, *We are the English*. It is a film record of the History Pageant on Sunday 20 September 1936, showing the procession and its banners covering events from the Magna Carta to the Spanish Civil War; this film was released in October 1936.[32]

The record of the Kino Production Committee is far from impressive. It failed to fulfil any of the aims it had set itself. Perhaps even more important was its failure to react adequately and promptly to important political events of the day, like the Battle of Cable Street[33] or the 1936 Hunger March, not to mention the Popular Front in France or the Civil War in Spain. The Kino Production Committee ceased to function by the end of 1936, while the Film and Photo League, which the Kino Production Committee had been supposed to succeed, was still struggling on.

The year 1936 was not the most productive in the League's history. It had survived the crisis concerning its future (see Chapter Five), but was in a state of virtual stagnation. Its new committee was hardly energetic: it never met officially between the AGM of 22 April 1936 and 20 January 1937. No films were released, as far as can be ascertained, but the basic structure of the League remained intact and its various groups still met regularly to discuss their projects. The League also played an important part in the foundation of a new distribution company, International Sound Films (ISF). In June or July the League's treasurer discovered that the FPL had a deposit of £170 in the London branch of the Moscow Narodny Bank. He transferred the bulk of this money, £130, as a loan to Ivan Seruya to help him launch ISF, perhaps thinking that as the League's committee did not know of the deposit's existence, nobody would miss it. Once the committee found out about this dubious deal, however, it tried to get the money back from Seruya, who was in no hurry to redeem the loan, denying that the League had any greater right to the money, which he described as a 'windfall', than he had. It would seem that this money was a generous payment from the Soviet Union for some film footage sent there by the FPL.[34]

In the FPL archive footage of the Battle of Cable Street has been discovered. It proved that the League was still able to get its cameramen to the right spot at the right time. The handling of such material was the crucial issue. It would have been ideally suited for a workers' newsreel, but the FPL no longer produced workers' newsreels, so the Cable Street footage went to the League's vaults, waiting for a member to rescue it from oblivion.[35]

Collective work had always been the League's endeavour. In the autumn of 1936 it did the best collective job in its history, the filming of the 1936 Hunger March. This was the last national march organised by the NUWM. Unity was the order of the day and the March enjoyed a far broader support than its predecessors. The Labour Party and TUC did not ban support for the March, but advised their members against supporting it, advice that was ignored, or 'interpreted correctly' by virtually all the local Trade Councils and constituency Labour parties along the route of the March. The NUWM made £10 available for the production of a film record by the League. For the film the FPL got assistance from outside its own ranks: Helen Biggar (Glasgow Kino), Rudolph Messel (Socialist Film Council), H. Kay (Manchester FPL) and W. Richardson (Doncaster Workers' Film Society).[36] With this geographical spread the March could be covered in the various parts of the country.

With some delay, a two-reel film, *March against Starvation*, was edited from the material. This 'story of the National Protest 1936' (sub-title) commences with close-ups of books and pamphlets on malnutrition in Britain. By means of graphics the film depicts how much food people on the dole can actually buy. The NUWM is introduced as the organisation defending the unemployed against further cuts. NUWM leader Wal Hannington is shown, making prepartions for the March. The film then switches to Ellen Wilkinson and the Jarrow March, which preceded the National Hunger March and was not organised by the NUWM. An element of suspense is introduced: will Baldwin give way and receive a deputation of Marchers? The course of the March follows next, with many interesting details, ending with the huge turn-out in Hyde Park to receive the Marchers. The film ends on a high note: 'Mass Pressure Wins' (caption), referring to Baldwin's offer to arrange the reception of a deputation of Marchers by the Ministry of Labour. Of course, *March against Starvation* had its limitations, and its storyline (will Baldwin give way?) was rather weak, but it was an excellent piece of collective film-making, which must have improved the League's morale considerably. Released in March 1937, *March against Starvation* marked the League's resurrection.

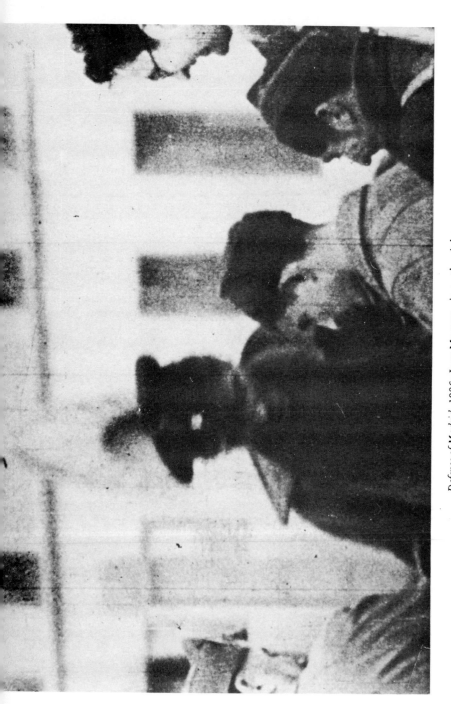

Defence of Madrid, 1936; Ivor Montagu is on the right

The year 1936 saw yet another production group make its appearance: The Vanguard Film Association. Its aim: 'To make films which by their art and entertainment will bring to those who see them an understanding of the lives and problems of the peoples.'[37] There was talk of making 'workers' films ... with the punch and power of Eisenstein'.[38] The presence of an American, C. Stoneham, 'one-time organiser of the Provincetown Theatre with Eugene O'Neill', was taken as a guarantee for success. Though the new association started shootings its first film, *Tomorrow, tomorrow*, dealing with unemployment, in May 1936, it obviously had no backing at all and disappeared without further trace.[39]

Not long after his intervention at the Kino AGM, Ivor Montagu could make an assessment of the production situation. There was no reason for optimism: the Kino Production Committee had not lived up to its promises, the FPL was struggling and the Vanguard Film Association was the misadventure Montagu had warned of. Montagu felt that the PFI had to step in the breach. There was an urgent need for a film on Spain. The British left sympathised with the Republican cause: numerous Spanish Aid Committees had sprung up all over the country and Britons were making their way to Spain in order to fight in what would become the International Brigades. Kino had hoped to get a film produced by the CNT in Barcelona, *Spain Fights for Liberty*, but it did not arrive when it was most needed.[40] On 8 November Franco started his carefully planned attack on Madrid. The fall of Spain's capital would only be a matter of days or even hours, it was predicted. But Madrid stood firm. As Montagu was free to go to Madrid, he decided not to wait another moment.[41] Norman McLaren, who had come down from Glasgow to work for Grierson's GPO Film Unit, was taken on as cameraman. They took two Kodak cassette cameras with colour and black and white 16mm film stock with them. By the end of November they had arrived in Madrid.

By the end of December 1936, *Defence of Madrid*, the film Montagu and McLaren had shot in Madrid, was ready for distribution. Because it was a 16mm film, its distribution was handled by Kino instead of the PFI. It was launched in four public screenings organised by the Relief Committee for the Victims of Fascism at Memorial Hall, Farringdon Street (seating 1,000) on 28 and 29 December.[42] Among the speakers was Isabel Brown who had worked with Montagu on the Relief Committee (which had dropped the epithet 'German' so as to include Spain as well). Brown would soon gain the reputation of being the best money raiser for Spanish Aid.[43] *Defence of Madrid* is divided into three parts. In Part I, 'The Assault on a People', the history of the war is explained, with its consequences: Italian airplanes bombing Madrid, the destruction of human lives and historic buildings, the rescue work. Part II, 'The Defence of Liberty', features the formation of the Republican army, the front line near the University City, the food queues and the evacuation of women and children to safer areas. Part III, 'The World Assists', shows the arrival in Spain of a Soviet food ship and the activities of the International Brigade, with footage of Ludwig Renn and Hans Beimler.[44] The film included two interviews (with captions quoting the statements instead of the spoken word, as *Defence of Madrid* is a silent film) with Eleanor Rathbone MP on Non-Intervention and Dr Christopher Addison on Medical Aid for Spain.

Defence of Madrid was anything but a masterpiece, but it was the film everyone on the left in Great Britain had been waiting for. It was estimated that the film raised £6,000 for Spanish Aid.[45] A sample culled from the pages of the *Daily Worker*:

Alexandria, a collection of £15 7s., the highest ever taken at a meeting in the Vale of Leven, was taken at a showing of the Film *Defence of Madrid* in the Co-operative Hall, Alexandria. (16 February 1937)

East Ham. A record crowd attended the showing of *Defence of Madrid* at East Ham (Minor) Town Hall. The sum of £12 4s. 5d. was collected to be sent to the Spanish Medical Aid Committee, together with the profits from the sale of tickets, which altogether amounted to over £13. This meeting and film show was organised by two members of the East Ham Ward Labour Party. As a result the official Labour Party are thinking of holding a similar film show in the future.

Rochdale. By showing the film *Defence of Madrid* the Rochdale Clarion Cycling Club raised £38 14s. for the Spanish Fund. The club have now formed a Spanish Aid Committee, and intend to carry on the good work for Spain. (18 February 1937).

Shettleston. Showing the film *Defence of Madrid* the Shettleston branch of the Communist Party collected £7 and a gold badge from an audience of 250 people. The branch will hold another show early in March and anticipates a big attendance.

Bermondsey. A deep impression was created on an audience of 300 trade unionists at Bermondsey Library Hall by speakers and by *Defence of Madrid*. A collection of £20 was taken at the meeting, which was organised by the Bermondsey Trades Council (19 February 1937).

But *Defence of Madrid* did more than raise money for the Spanish cause. It introduced Kino to the kind of 'Popular Front' audiences it had been anxious to reach: constituency Labour parties, Trades Councils, Clarion Clubs, etc. Moreover, it made people aware of the importance of film news, as provided by the commercial newsreel companies, and of the need to counteract its influence. It was no coincidence that reports on Spain by the commercial newsreel companies were watched more closely after *Defence of Madrid*.[46] The next film on Spain was awaited anxiously, and a number were released in the spring of 1937. On 14 April 1937 a 35mm sound film *News from Spain*, with a commentary spoken by Isabel Brown, was premiered.[47] It was another PFI production, compiled from Spanish government footage, and a 16mm version was released through Kino. A 16mm silent film, made by Vera Elkan for the PFI, entitled *International Column* or *International Brigade*, came next.[48] It was a 'home movie' which became a political document due to circumstances, and showed the day-to-day life of the Brigaders. *Call to Arms* (previously known as *Spain Fights for Liberty*), the CNT film Kino had been waiting for, also arrived.[49] As it had dated considerably, Kino decided to re-edit it with more recent material. This version was released in July under the title *Crime against Madrid*.[50] Ivan Seruya's ISF had brought into distribution *They Shall Not Pass*, a compilation film made by the Spanish Ministry of Public Instruction.[51] None of these had the success of *Defence of Madrid*, of which twenty prints were in distribution,[52] but as a body they contributed considerably to people's understanding of the war in Spain.[53]

Another boost for Kino was the interest the Left Book Club (LBC) had taken in film shows. The LBC had been founded in the spring of 1936 by the publisher Victor Gollancz. A committee composed of Gollancz, John Strachey and Harold Laski selected a monthly choice which members could buy for 2s. 6d. The LBC was an instant success and had 39,400 members by March 1937. The LBC was in certain respects the most tangible result of the 'Popular Front' policy in Britain. As a book club it produced some remarkable political alliances indeed, although the Labour Party soon withdrew its initial support (Clem Attlee's *The Labour Party in Perspective* was the 'Book of the Month' for August 1937) and refused any further co-operation. A network of LBC groups was built up, with the monthly *Left Book News* (from December 1936 *Left News*) as a liaison bulletin. From the LBC headquarters in London an effort was made to stimulate the cultural life of the groups. A very successful Left Book Club Theatre Guild was set up, organising around 250 amateur theatre groups all over the country.[54] In January 1937 John Lewis, the convenor of the LBC groups, drew the groups' attention to Kino's existence. He foresaw the possibility

> that enterprising groups will soon be able to arrange for periodic film shows as part of their programme. Not only will this further the kind of education we are concerned with, but it will add interest and variety to group meetings and greatly aid recruiting.

Lewis outlined the following scheme: district organisers would book a number of film shows in their area, which would then be called at by a travelling projection unit.[55] In *Left News* of March 1937, Lewis specified that these regional organisers 'would be in charge of the apparatus, the projector, a car for transport, and the operator'.[56] Truly a demanding job, but one that was considerably eased by the expansion of Kino's national network. By June 1937 Kino had agents in Belfast, Birmingham, Blackpool, Bradford, Cardiff, Doncaster, County Durham, Glasgow and Nottingham.[57] John Lewis decided to set the example himself. In connection with the Book of the Month for February 1937, Frank Jellinek's *The Paris Commune of 1871*, he held several lectures, illustrated by *New Babylon* (a silent Soviet film on the Commune, distributed by Kino since January 1935). The London lecture was sponsored by Collet's.[58] Lewis was particularly happy with the combination of Jellinek's book and the film. The book was 'strictly academic, factually accurate and, for the ordinary reader at that time, a rather difficult book'.[59] The film could present it in an attractive way. Kino probably felt just as happy about the combination. A film it had had in its collection for more than two years was given a new lease of life.

'The film is the machine-gun of ideological warfare, and can be fed from the scenes from everyday life recorded on celluloid by an intelligent amateur.'[60] These words were written by a LBC member, and heartily welcomed by the Film and Photo League. Even more than with Kino, the LBC established a close relation with the FPL, facilitated by a remarkable renaissance of the latter. The new secretary of the FPL, the Reverend Hugh Cuthbertson, must get much of the credit. Cuthbertson took over the League's secretariat in January 1937. One of his first acts was to settle the League's administrative affairs prior to the AGM on 13 February 1937. Since the FPL committee had decided to vacate the premises at 5 Great Ormond Street, Cuthbertson had taken the paper muddle to his own place at Somerset Terrace. This was to remain the League's correspondence address until its winding-up. The AGM offered the opportunity to sift the chaff from the wheat. Cuthbertson invited all the people on the League's mailing list, giving them a chance to pay up their subscription. unfortunately, no attendance figures of the AGM are known, but it seems clear that many of the hundred or so on the League's mailing list did not turn up nor renew their subscription. The League needed reinforcements and the LBC had to provide them. The FPL had to couch its activities in a language that would appeal to the LBC groups and therefore often compared itself with the LBC Theatre Guild: amateur, but amateur without being ashamed of it.[61]

For publicity purposes the FPL badly needed some new films. It only had some films like *Bread, Jubilee, Winter* or *Construction* available, which had been in its library for some time, plus *Revolt of the Fishermen*, a documentary on the 1935 fishermen's strike in Hull, made by Adrianne Hanné and Michael Burke, which had received little attention.[62] The priority was to get the film on the 1936 Hunger March ready. *March against Starvation* was available by March 1937 and had its London premiere on 26 April.[63] Wal Hannington delivered a speech that night; the League had paid its debt to the NUWM. But the only other way to extend the League's film library was by starting new projects. May 1937 offered two excellent subjects; the May Day procession and the Coronation of King George VI.

For many years there had been two May Day demonstrations in London. The 'official' demonstration, organised by the Labour Party, was traditionally held on the first Sunday of the month (in 1937 it fell on 2 May). Labour had rejected an offer by the 'left' May First Committee for a joint demonstration, as this might be interpreted as a step towards the 'united front'. Therefore the 'left', including the CPGB and some militant trade unions together with the LBC, Unity Theatre and the FPL, held its May Day demonstration on 1 May.[64] The League displayed a cinema screen with the words 'Show Workers' Films' and a giant FPL camera on tripod. Along the route – from the Embankment, to Hyde Park – FPL cameramen were lined up. They had been given detailed instructions about what to film. Youth, joy and happy expressions were considered to be the true spirit of May Day. With only three to four minutes of film available to each cameraman, shots had to be short, with 'plenty of close-ups'. The Kodachrome colour stock was used for filming 'massed red flags ... wherever they appear, and in various positions and angles'. New was also the use of 9.5mm cameras, a home-movie format not previously used by the FPL.[65] The Coronation of George VI took place while the London busmen's rank-and-file movement was on strike for a seven-and-a-half-hour day. The FPL decided to make a satire, combining May Day and the Coronation. Of course, it referred to the busmen's strike. Both films were released in the autumn of 1937, the former as *The Spirit of May Day*, the latter as *Coronation May Day* or *The Merry Month of May*.

In the meantime the LBC and the FPL continued their consultations for further co-operation between the groups and the League. A special conference was convened for this purpose. To show John Lewis that the League meant business, it organised an impromptu film show in Lewis's office, which was reported by the convenor of the LBC groups in *Left News*:

> The League invaded my office a few days ago with their apparatus, and in less than five minutes were projecting on to the wall an excellent film on 9[.5]mm. of the Coronation and of

the street festivities in East London, in colour. Needless to say, the whole point of this Coronation film is to contrast the glitter and show of a celebration which diverts us from our real tasks, with the determination, purpose and virility of the great May Day demonstration.[66]

The aforementioned conference took place in London on 7 June 1937. FPL committee member Michael Burke opened the day's proceedings with a brief history of the left film movement, calling

> attention to the need for further effort in the production and distribution of films 'with a purpose'. Dr John Lewis then gave a most stimulating talk on the value of the film in supplementing the printed word. Because of the easier assimilation of facts presented through the eye, social education by this means can, he said, prepare the way for the appeal of literature. He would like the League's film *March against Starvation* to be shown to every one of the six hundred LBC branches throughout the country ... In the documentary sphere, the land or factory worker, seeing things from his own angle, can contribute more for our purpose than the most expert professional artist approaching the same subject lyrically and from the outside. Such effort must be enthused, trained and assisted in a way that only such a society as the FPL can do.

Could these two approaches to film – the cognitive and the creative – be accommodated in a working scheme? And where would it leave the FPL and the LBC?

The conference agreed to set up amateur film making groups to work on and show shorts in conjunction with other political and cultural groups. The activity of these groups was to be co-ordinated by the League, which would help by bulk-buying film-stock, providing editing and studio space in London, and in other ways. The local groups were to collaborate on projects with a national dimension, like Hunger Marches, and while the subjects to be filmed were the standard ones for left-wing film making groups of the time, the prospect of making films for children was also raised, uniquely for the period, though nothing came of this.[67]

It was an ideal rather than a workable scheme that was presented. The drafters had presupposed the political unity of the left as a working condition. But by mid-1937 the chances for a 'United Front', let alone a 'Popular Front', were slimmer than before. The scheme left the FPL with the burden of the work without any assessment of the financial consequences. The League would have to be professionalised if it were to cope with the job. But this would have been in contradiction with the ideology of amateurism the FPL had recently embraced.

This notion of amateurism prevailed in the first (and, as far as can be ascertained, last) issue of the League's bulletin *Left Film Front* of July 1937. Hugh Cuthbertson pointed out that the FPL had 'come to a mutual understanding with Kino that we [the FPL] shall chiefly be catering in the normal way for shows in rooms and small halls of silent films to illustrate talks'. He dealt with the question of the 9.5mm format, correcting a mistake in *Left News*, which had given the impression that the FPL worked largely with 9.5mm films. Evidently, Cuthbertson had received a lot of requests for 9.5mm films, which the League did not have. The choice between the two formats had little to do with technical particulars, it was an ideological choice: 9.5mm was the pre-eminently amateur format. But the League stuck to 16mm as its main format. It had, however, a 9.5mm version of the 1937 May Day film, *Spirit of May Day*, for hire. *Left Film Front* also announced the making of a series of films, entitled *Building the People's Front in England*. They consisted of 'seven separate films intended to run progressively in the style of *The March of Time*, including much historic material and aspects of political and ideological struggle from month to month'.[68] *The March of Time* was an American monthly screen magazine, which caused quite a stir by its unorthodox documentary approach (mixing newsreel footage with enacted material) and its treatment of controversial topics (for example American fascist groups, distressed areas in Britain, conditions inside Nazi Germany). There is sufficient footage of events in 1937 in the FPL archive to suggest that the production of *Building the People's Front in England* was actually started, but neither People's Front nor film series materialised.

The League's ideological positions of amateurism and political unity of the left were under considerable pressure, but the LBC summer school in Digswell seemed the ideal place to forget such problems. For some time, the FPL had considered making a film about the LBC and the summer school was an ideal location, with many LBC authors present. As the school lasted a fortnight, Cuthbertson and others felt there was enough time to initiate some of the students into the practice of film making, hoping that this 'practical experience [would] enable them to set up autonomous groups of the FPL in their own localities'.[69] The result was a comedy film entitled *Red, Right and Bloo*. A 'Bloo' Lady, on her way to a Blue Book Club Conference in Prigswell, is misdirected and arrives in Digswell during a lecture on the USSR by John Lewis. The Lady in question finds out about the mistake, but cannot leave the meeting. Two naughty boys fix her car, so that she is forced to stay the night. She gets carried away by a LBC book on *The Position of Women in the USSR* and takes a fancy to a young student. In the end, the Lady is converted to the LBC cause. *Red, Right and Bloo* is a disappointing film. It simply does not succeed as a comedy, and can have been amusing only for those who made it. Politically, it was just too naïve. Did the LBC really stand for the conversion of nobility to its cause? Still, *Red, Right and Bloo* seems to have been well received by the LBC people involved.[70] How far the practical experience acquired during the making of *Red, Right and Bloo* enabled the students to set up local FPL branches is an open question.

In the autumn of 1937 the FPL released some more films. One of them was *Strife*, a film the FPL had been sitting on for much too long. It had been started as *Fight* by the Feature Film Group of the then WFPL (see Chapter Five). Its theme was trade union organisation as experienced by different members of one family. Trade union organisation was the subject of another FPL production, *Dockworkers*, made by H.A. Green. This film appears to have been shot a couple of years before its release and is very much in the same vein as the early (W)FPL productions. *Dockworkers* presents a documentary enquiry into the casual labour system as practised in the port of London and ends with an appeal to support the dockers' demand for abolition of the system. From Castle Film in the USA the FPL bought some issues of *The News Parade*, and made its own commentary for these films, to be read during the screening. Another film, *The Spanish Dance* or *Spanish Travail*, was distributed with a disc of the mass declamation of Jack Lindsay's poem 'On Guard for Spain', to be played during the screening. *Challenge of Youth* was yet another FPL production, made in conjunction with the Socialist Youth Camp, including scenes of the Herne Hill Youth Festival. Two more films on 9.5mm were also made available: *Workers' Excerpts from Metropolis* and *Russian Journey*.[71] The League's connection with the LBC remained close. The LBC Group in Pontypridd contacted the FPL about a film on the distressed areas, to be made as an illustration to Wal Hannington's forthcoming *The Problem of the Distressed Areas* (LBC choice for November 1937). The League appealed for financial support: if someone would provide the raw film, it would send a cameraman. Unfortunately not enough money was collected and the project had to be called off. Instead, the League proposed the UAB film, *Bread* and *March against Starvation* as suitable productions for showing in conjunction with Hannington's book.[72]

From 21 to 25 January 1938 the FPL held a five-day film school, with lectures by a wide range of speakers, film shows, practical sessions, the AGM and a dance. Michael Burke stressed the need for 'films dealing seriously with British problems' and thought that the League 'should devote all [its] energies and considerably more money to the production of essentially "home" films'.[73] Hugh Cuthbertson wanted more active groups working under the guidance of the League. It had to become a truly national organisation. The newly-elected Central Committee, which included Cuthbertson as secretary and Burke as assistant secretary, should work towards this end, but this plan proved far too ambitious for an organisation run on a voluntary basis. If too much labour was put into organisational work, production suffered and vice versa. Moreover, Kino had once more revived its Production Committee to stir some unrest in the FPL. This time the FPL committee opted for co-operation instead of confrontation. Undoubtedly they were aware of the League's weaknesses. Perhaps they hoped to save the national organisation by sacrificing the production department. 'After a series of discussions, the FPL Central London Branch and Kino producers have decided to co-operate in a first step towards the unification of all Left Cinema work.'[74] Political unity, so cherished by the League, was saved. The loss of its most experienced camera crew still did not incapacitate the League's work among local FPL and LBC groups all over the country. A final irony: at the end of its 1937 May Day film, the FPL had added a trailer advertising next year's May Day film. 'Ask your

Secretary to book this film Now.' The first film of the new production unit was ... *May Day, 1938.*

Kino's attitude towards the FPL was certainly marked by an air of conspiracy. It can be explained (but not excused) by the difference in purpose and practice of the two organisations. Kino was a national distribution company, which was trying to operate as professionally as possible on a limited budget. The amateurism promoted and embodied by the FPL was completely alien to its outlook. Politically, Kino closely followed the line of the CPGB. It could not see any of the aims the CPGB had been campaigning for adapted to the screen by the FPL. Kino felt, for example, that there was an urgent need for a film propagating the slogan 'Chamberlain must go, no Cabinet reshuffle, a People's Government' and decided to start working on such a film, without waiting for the outcome of the talks with the FPL.[75]

After the signal success of *Defence of Madrid* and other Spain films, Kino had been working towards its conversion to sound. 'Talkies' had been announced as far back as the winter of 1935-36. The considerable investment needed had held up the operation, which was finally made possible by the success of *Defence of Madrid.* Ivan Seruya's International Sound Films had been one step ahead, but in view of ISF's limited collection (including Ekk's *The Road to Life,* for which Kino could also obtain the rights) it was only a matter for Kino of getting some 'hits' to catch up with ISF. One of these 'hits' was the Soviet children's film *Torn Shoes,* which was situated in pre-Nazi Hamburg. The film had been made in 1933 by the woman director Margarita Barskaya. *Torn Shoes* was premiered on 1 March in the Besant Hall, London, together with the Spanish film *Call to Arms.*[76] In its selection of 'talkies' Kino took care to find a balance between 'entertainment' and 'campaign' films. G.W. Pabst's *Kameradschaft* (1931), an epic celebrating workers' solidarity crossing national borders after a pit disaster, fitted very well in this strategy. Kino also publicised the Irish feature *The Dawn* (1936) widely. This remarkable sound film had been produced and directed by Tom Cooper, a garage owner in Killarney. *The Dawn* tells a story of the Irish War of Independence, centred around a feud between two local families. The film was inspired by nationalist sentiments and had nothing to do with Irish Communism or the kind of left-wing republicanism symbolised by International Brigader Frank Ryan. Still, Kino felt that *The Dawn* could contribute to the left's views on the 'Irish question' and therefore qualified *The Dawn* as 'revolutionary'.[77] In the autumn of 1937, a number of Soviet 'talkies', such as Pudovkin's *Deserter* (1933), were released.[78]

Kino acquired some important 'campaign' films through Garrison Films in new York. *Millions of Us*, a sound film secretly and anonymously shot in Hollywood, was released in the autumn of 1937. It tells the story of an unemployed worker who is stopped from scabbing and joins the strikers on the picket line. Another trade union film in Kino's library had come from France, *Stay-In Strikes*, a Ciné-Liberté production on the famous strike in June-July 1936. Again from Garrison Kino obtained the sound documentary *China Strikes Back*, with cameraman Harry Dunham's famous footage of the Chinese Red Army. The film was released after the publication of Edgar Snow's *Red Star over China*, LBC's Book of the Month in October 1937. The popularity of Snow's book and the interest in the Chinese struggle for freedom (often equated with the Spanish Civil War) created a considerable demand for *China Strikes Back*.[79]

The war in Spain was still in the limelight. Every day meetings on Spain were held all over the country, organised by relief organisations such as the Spanish Medical Aid Committee, the Basque Children's Committee, the Milk for Spain Committee, etc. (co-ordinated by the National Joint Committee for Spanish Relief) or by the left parties, the LBC, etc. Many of these meetings were enlivened by a film show. Kino was in most cases the supplier of the films and often of the projection equipment too. By 1938 about a quarter of Kino's library consisted of films on Spain, ranging from ten-minute silent shorts to 'talkies' of almost one hour. Two of these were films commissioned directly by the National Joint Committee for Spanish Relief: *Modern Orphans of the Storm* (1937) and *Help Spain* (1938). The former was made to support the relief campaign for 4,000 Basque refugee children who had arrived in Great Britain after the fall of the Basque Country in May 1937. *Modern Orphans of the Storm* was the only film on Spain made by one of the established documentary units (i.e. Realist, a film unit led by Basil Wright); a failure which clearly calls in question the documentary movement's progressive character.[80] *Help Spain* was a Kino production on the work of the National Joint Committee for Spanish Relief in England and in Spain. Cameraman James Calvert had been sent to Spain in late 1937 or early 1938 to film the Committee's work there. He was reported to have shot a large part of the film in colour, but with no prints of *Help Spain* extant it is not clear if this colour footage was integrated into the final version.[81] A highly acclaimed film on Spain was Joris Ivens' *Spanish Earth* (1937), with a commentary written and spoken by Ernest Hemingway. The BBFC had some objections to the film, which had been sponsored by leading American intellectuals and artists, but it got its certificate in the end.[82] Kino did not have exclusive rights on *Spanish Earth*, but it was nevertheless a very successful film for the company.[83]

The lion's share of Kino's Spain films was provided by the PFI. Relations between the two organisations were very cordial. They recognised each other's activities of production and 35mm distribution (PFI) and 16mm distribution (Kino). Politically they were very much on the same line, putting into practice the 'Popular Front' policy.[84] Starting with *News from Spain*, the PFI had been working on English-language version of films produced by the Republican government. These included *Madrid To-day*, on the bombardment of Madrid, *Non-Intervention*, on the proof of Italian intervention found after the battle of Guadalajara, and *Sunlight in Shadow*, on care for children made homeless by the war. At one point the Republican government felt it might be more effective from a propaganda point of view for the PFI to shoot some films in Spain, instead of making English-language versions of Republican productions. Otto Katz, with whom Montagu had worked closely in the days of the Relief Committee for the Victims of German Fascism and who now worked in Spain handed Montagu £3,000 in cash on behalf of the government. Montagu picked his crew from members of the Association of Cinematograph Technicians (ACT), who were willing to go to Spain with only their expenses paid for. They were Thorold Dickinson and Sidney Cole (directors), Alan Lawson and Arthur Graham (cameraman), and Phil Leacock and Ray Pitt (assistants). Montagu himself acted as producer. After an intervention by Attlee they were granted the necessary papers

Spanish ABC, 1938; a wall-newspaper for Spanish soldiers

to go to Spain, as the Foreign Office had been extremely suspicious of the crew's intentions.[85]

The crew arrived in Barcelona on 14 January 1938, and were treated the next day to a series of air raids.[86] They stayed until the end of March, intending to make three films: one on the educational system, another on the formation of the army and a third on the parliamentary system in the Republic. In fact, only the first film could be finished (it would become *Spanish ABC*), while the material for the two others only allowed one film to be edited from it (*Behind the Spanish Lines*). The military situation simply did not allow Montagu and the others to film as they would have liked to. As Dickinson put it:

> We could not make a scenario but worked from statistics and local information arranged as best we could. You see, we only had a couple of hours in any given spot – just time to look around, concoct a plan of action in a couple of minutes and then shoot.[87]

In Barcelona Montagu was able to film with a hidden microphone (in those days observers did not automatically associate filming with the recording of sound) interviews with German and Italian prisoners of war. After their strenuous trip, the crew found themselves in Barcelona when the Italians started their bombing raids on 16 March, lasting until 18 March, leaving 1,300 killed and 2,000 injured.[88]

Back in London, Ivor Montagu edited some of the footage of the interviews of Italian and German prisoners of war into a newsreel film, *Prisoners Prove Intervention in Spain*. It was quite successful, Montagu remembers, with about fifty cinemas all over the country taking it.[89] The film was also shown at the Emergency Conference for Spain on 28 April 1938, one of the last efforts to support the Republican government by denouncing the German and Italian violations of the 'Non-Intervention' agreement.[90] A longer version was later released under the title *Testimony of Non-Intervention*. *Spanish ABC* and *Behind the Spanish Lines* were premiered on 26 June 1938.[91] The former presents the Republican government's literary campaign being pursued vigorously under most difficult circumstances. The latter shows how democracy worked in Spain and how Italy and Germany were making a farce of 'Non-Intervention'.

In close collaboration with the PFI, Kino could offer a great number of 'campaign' films on Spain. It should be mentioned that none of these films presented the war in Spain as a revolutionary struggle. It was seen as a struggle for the democratically elected 'Popular Front', against fascism, particularly German and Italian fascism. With these films on Spain, with the package of 'entertainment' films, the gap in Kino's film library became only too obvious: 'campaign' films on British issues. *Hell Unltd*, and *We are the English* had been the most recent acquisitions, with the latter soon struck off the list. Kino had not taken over any of the FPL's more recent productions for reasons one can only guess at. Hence the urge to revive its defunct Production Committee and the talks with the FPL, resulting in the joint May Day project. But *May Day, 1938* was made with only limited means. What Kino needed were well-made sound films on topics concerning the British labour movement, which could only be made if the movement was willing to sponsor them.

Notes

1. *Kino News* No.1, Winter 1935, p.1.
2. *Daily Worker*, 7 November 1934, p.4.
3. For the AEAR See Nicole Racine, 'L'Association des écrivains et artistes révolutionnaires (AEAR)' in *Le Mouvement Social*, No.54, January-March 1966, pp.29-47; J.-P. Bernard, *Le Parti communiste Français et la question littéraire (1921-1939)*, Grenoble 1972; Arno Münster, *Antifaschismus, Volks front und Literatur. Zur Geschichte der 'Vereinigung revolutionärer Schriftsteller und Künstler' (AEAR) in Frankreich*, Hamburg and West Berlin 1977. The AEAR as 'export model' has been documented in the case of the Belgian Association Révolutionnaire Culturelle (Revolutionary Cultural Association) in Bert Hogenkamp et Henri Storck, *Le Borinage. La grève des mineurs de 1932 et le film de Joris Ivens et Henri Storck*, Brussels 1984, issue No.6-7 of *La Revue Belge du Cinéma*, pp.27-32.
4. An extremely useful selection of texts is available in German in H. Gustav Klaus (ed.), *Marxistische Literaturkritik in England. Das 'Thirties Movement'*, Darmstadt and Neuwied 1973. Some of the original works have, of course, been reprinted. Good essays on this period have been published in Jon Clark *et al.* (eds), op.cit. and Frank Gloversmith (ed.), *Class, Culture and Social Change. A New View of the 1930s*, Brighton 1980. For the relationship with the Artists International see Lynda Morris and Robert Radford, *The Story of the AIA Artists International Association 1933-1953*, Oxford 1983.
5. Kino Films (1935) Limited, *First Annual Report*, April, 1936, pp.2-4 (FPLa)

The profit and loss account of Kino for the year ending on 4 March 1936 gives the following figures:

Receipts from shows	£693 10 8
Less: Expenses in	
connection therewith	£336 12 11
	£356 17 9

6. In the balance sheet as at 4 March 1936, the following loans are listed:

Stich	£103 17 6
C.F. Chance	40 0 0
A. Marshall	111 9 3
Mrs Seruya	41 10 2
C. Williams Ellis	25 0 0 +
	£321 16 11 (FPLa)

7. Ivor Montagu who dealt for many years with Soviet films in Great Britain, summed up the position in an interview: 'I should emphasise that we always had the utmost difficulty getting Soviet films, because they are handled in this country – and have always been – by commercial organisations. Sometimes 16mm films are sent to friendship organisations for teaching, documentaries of one kind or another, and a few 16mm films were sent in the early days by trade union organisations or political organisations to Kino. But in general, they would sell their art films through their trade delegations and when you approached them for a film – for nothing, even for the Film Society – they would say: 'We are here only to buy and to sell.' They hadn't the authority to do anything else, they hadn't the machinery: it was a trade delegation. We had to argue – we argued for twenty years or more: 'Well, all right. Sell. Please sell. But if you can't, we'll put them on and that will help to create an interest in Soviet films and make it easier for you to sell other films. We don't want it, if you can find anybody else, only if nobody else wants it.' This, of course, was entirely strange to them and what happened was that after the fellow had been here for four or five years and hadn't sold a single film, he began to understand and let us have the pictures. But then his tour of duty would end and a new one would come out, determined to do better, and we would have to wait for years again. I want to make this perfectly clear that it wasn't political, let us call it human nature, but the idea that Soviet films are just for propaganda and that anybody can have them, is absolutely false. We never could get the damn things. It was a very thankless task.' Ivor Montagu, interview with the author, Watford, 6 September 1974.
8. Kino Films (1935) Limited, *First Annual Report*, April, 1936, pp.3-4 (FPLa).
9. Ibid., p.5.
10. *Daily Worker*, 27 September 1935, p.4.
11. The Tredegar Workmen's Institute for example received correspondence from Kino. Cf. minutes Cinema Committee, Tredegar Workmen's Institute, 3 October 1935 (in University College Swansea, referred to hereafter as UCS).
12. *Daily Worker*, 10 January 1936, p.8.
13. The Cardiff Kino Workers' Film Committee had booked the unlicensed Lesser Hall of the Stacey Road Hall for Sunday 5 January. The larger hall on the same premises was licensed for dancing. The police interpreted this

licence in such a way that it covered the Lesser Hall too. A Cardiff by-law banned the exhibition of films on licensed premises on Sunday. *Daily Worker* 4 January 1936, p.2.

14. Kino's agents for South Wales were Gilbert Taylor and John Harris (*The Left News*, June 1937, p.392; October 1937, p.543) Both operated from Collet's Bookshop, 26 Castle Arcade. Taylor left for Spain, where he died as a member of the International Brigades. The combination of Kino and Collet's was quite logical from a distribution point of view (in Glasgow, Glasgow Kino had operated from the local Collet's late 1935, early 1936). In South Wales Taylor and Harris seemed to have combined not only the supply of books and films from London, but their distribution into the mining valleys as well. Thus the Mardy Workmen's Hall decided on 30 June 1937 to 'invite Collets man to the Committee to explain the supply of Films + also the running of a Book Club'. Within days the 'Collets man appeared re Book Club + Films, + gave particulars of how to procure books + also Films.' Cf. minutes Committee, Mardy Workmen's Hall and Institute, 30 June 1937 and 7 July 1937 (in UCS)

15. Minutes, National Executive Committee, Labour Party, 22 January 1936, p.28.

16. See Joseph Reeves, 'A Co-op Success. *General Line* shown to 40,000 People', in *Kino News*, Winter 1935, p.1.

17. See note 7.

18. Viscount Chelmsford, *The Miners' Welfare Fund*, London 1927, p.29.

19. The minutes of the Miners' Welfare and Workmen's Halls Cinema Association are kept at the South Wales CISWO office in Cardiff.

20. This paragraph is based on Bert Hogenkamp, 'Miners' Cinemas in South Wales in the 1920s and 1930s' in *Llafur*, Vol.4, No.2 (1985), pp.64-76.

21. Contemporary reviews in *Daily Worker*, 30 July 1935, p.4; 1 August 1935, p.4; for the origins of *Free Thaelmann!* see Bert Hogenkamp, 'Thaelmann's Trail', in *Jump Cut* No.21, November 1979, p.27; Ivor Montagu, 'The Origin of *Free Thaelmann!*', in *Sight and Sound* Vol.49 No.2, Spring 1980, pp.130-1.

22. *Kino News* No.2, [1936], p.1; cf. *Daily Worker*, 27 April 1936, p.8.

23. Montagu was associate producer for *The Man Who Knew Too Much* (1934) and *The Thirty-Nine Steps* (1935).

24. These arguments were given by Montagu in an interview with the author, London, 8 March 1978.

25. Ralph Bond, 'Making Films With A Purpose', in: *Kino News* No.1, Winter 1935, p.1.

26. 'Film Production', in *Left Review* Vol.2 No.8, May 1936, p.415; leaflet on 'Film Production' (in FPLa).

27. *Daily Worker*, 6 August 1936, p.3.

28. Cf. *Film Art*, Vol.3 No.8, 1936, p.40; in 1938 Jackson wrote some short stories, based on what he had experienced as a Kino projectionist, 'Only 6 Miles out of London', in *Daily Worker*, 4 May 1938, p.2, and 'The Veteran Shows His Treasures', ibid., 7 July 1938, p.7.

29. Public Record Office, London, Home Office 45/17068.

30. Letter cited in Anna Shepherd, 'Helen Biggar and Norman McLaren. Based on a MS "Helen Unlimited" ', in *New Edinburgh Review* No.40, February 1978, p.26; see also Bert Hogenkamp, 'Making Films with a Purpose: Film-making and the Working Class' in Jon Clark *et al.* (eds),

op.cit., pp.265-7. A video of Helen Biggar's work, *Traces Left*, was released by the Birmingham Film and Video Workshop in 1985.

31. 'Film Production', in *Left Review* Vol.2. No.8, May 1936, p.415.

32. *Daily Worker*, 31 October 1936, p.6.

33. On 4 October 1936 tens of thousands of anti-fascists prevented Mosley and his Blackshirts from parading through the East End of London. In Cable Street barricades were put up and a street battle was fought with the police. See Phil Piratin, *Our Flag Stays Red*, London 1978, pp.19-24.

34. Minutes of Committee Meeting, Film and Photo League, 20 January 1937 in (FPLa).

35. It can now be seen in the film *Workers Films of the Thirties* (1981), directed by Victoria Wegg-Prosser.

36. A title card (not used in the film?) in the FPL archive lists the following people: Helen Biggar (Glasgow School of Art), Michael Burke, S. Feld (FPL), H. Kay (Manchester Workers' Film League), H. Ludlow (Independent Films), Rudolph Messel (SFC), W. Richardson (Doncaster Workers' Film Society), Ivan Seruya, Sime Seruya, E.D. Stich (FPL).

37. *Daily Worker*, 20 April 1936, p.7.

38. Ibid., 13 April 1936, p.7.

39. Ibid., 1 June 1936, p.7.

40. Ibid., 31 October 1936, p.6.

41. Montagu: 'In 1936, I was working temporarily at Gainsborough as an associate producer and it was agreed that I should direct a film with Paul Robeson called *King Solomon's Mines*. I went, with Hell, to Moscow, to discuss the battle sequences with Eisenstein. I felt very uncomfortable about them. While I was there, there was a terrible drought. I got ill. I came back with this illness, so I got taken off the subject and another director was put on it. That freed me. While we had been on our way to Moscow, the actual news of the revolt of the generals in Spain had come through. And so I was free to go to Spain at once.' Interview 6 September 1974.

42. *Daily Worker*, 18 December 1936, p.7. 'Three thousand people saw the film', according to a Kino advertisement (*Tribune*, 8 January 1937, p.15). It is not clear if this was the actual premiere of *Defence of Madrid*. A Kino leaflet, announcing the first performance of the film on Tuesday 22 November (a misprint for 22 December, which fell on a Tuesday) in Besant Hall, London, is in the South Wales Miners' Library, Swansea. If this screening took place, it left no traces in the contemporary press.

43. For Isabel Brown see May Hill, *Red Roses for Isabel*, London 1982.

44. Hans Beimler was a Communist Reichstag deputy from Bavaria, who had managed to escape from a Nazi concentration camp. He was killed near Madrid on 13 December 1936. The footage of him in *Defence of Madrid* is the only known of his stay in Spain.

45. *Daily Worker*, 9 June 1937, p.4.

46. See for example Jane Morgan, 'Spain on News Reel', ibid., 15 February 1937, p.7. See also Anthony Aldgate, *Cinema and History, British Newsreels and the Spanish Civil War*, London 1979.

47. *Daily Worker*, 16 April 1937, p.5.

48. Ibid., 3 May 1937, p.7.

49. Ibid., 22 February 1937, p.7; *Tribune*, 26 February 1937, p.15.

50. *Daily Worker*, 19 July 1937, p.7. The more recent material added to *Call*

to Arms was also available as a separate film, *Madrid To-day*, with a commentary spoken by Herbert Marshall.

51. *Daily Worker*, 2 June 1937, p.5.
52. Ibid., 9 June 1937, p.4. *Defence of Madrid* was also shown abroad. International Brigader Frank Ryan presented the film in Dublin, where it resulted in a collection of £10 for Spanish Aid (see Seán Cronin, *Frank Ryan. The Search for the Republic*, Dublin 1980, p.105). The film was 'cut by the Australian censors, who removed scenes of children being killed by the fascist bombing of Madrid' (Charles Merewether, 'Towards a Radical Film Practice, Part 1 – Australian Left Film History' in *Filmnews*, August 1981, pp.8-10, here p.10).
53. In his biography of Jack Roberts (*No Other Way. Jack Russia and the Spanish Civil War*, Port Talbot 1981) Richard Felstead tells the story of Wilf Winnick: 'In April 1937, Wilf and Anne went to see a special workers' newsreel of the bombing of Guernica. A week later Wilf was in Arles' (on his way to join the International Brigades p.64.) Guernica was bombed on 26 April. Of the commercial newsreel companies, only Gaumont paid attention to it, in its issue of 6 May. There is no record of any workers' newsreel covering the bombing of Guernica.
54. Cf. John Lewis, *The Left Book Club: An Historical Record*, London 1970.
55. *Left News*, No.9, January 1937, p.196.
56. Ibid., No.11, March 1937, p.263.
57. Ibid., No.14, June 1937, p.392.
58. *Daily Worker*, 27 February 1937, p.6.
59. Lewis, op.cit., p.38.
60. *Left News*, No.12, April 1937, p.309.
61. Ibid., No.14, June 1937, p.392.
62. *Revolt of the Fishermen* showed the history of the Hull fishermen's strike of Easter 1935, ending with the recognition of the union and a victory for the strikers. Hanné and Burke paid a lot of attention to the composition of the film's images. These were edited so as to contrast by their aesthetic character with the straightforward story of the strike, narrated by means of captions. In many ways *Revolt of the Fishermen* was reminiscent of John Grierson's famous silent film *Drifters*, which showed the life of the high sea fishermen. Grierson, of course, never mentioned the existence of a union. *Revolt of the Fishermen* escaped, quite undeservedly, the attention of the contemporary press.
63. *Daily Worker*, 23 April 1936, p.6.
64. Cf. John Saville, 'May Day 1937' in Asa Briggs and John Saville (eds.), *Essays in Labour History 1918-1939*, London 1977, pp.232-84.
65. 'Film and Photo League, Notes for May-Day Camera Men' (in FPLa).
66. *Left News*, No.14, June 1937, pp.392-3.
67. Ibid., No.16, August 1937, pp.479-80; *Left Film Front* No.1, July 1937, p.2 (in FPLa).
68. *Left Film Front* No.1, July 1937, p.5.
69. 'Commentary for *Red, Right and Bloo* to read beforehand' (in FPLa).
70. *Left News*, No.19, November 1937, p.572.
71. *Left Film Front* No.1, July 1937, p.5; 'Film List. Film and Photo League', ca. October 1937 (in FPLa).
72. *Left News*, No.20, December 1937, p.624.
73. 'FPL 5-Day School in London' (in FPLa).

74. *Left News*, No.27, July 1938, p.906.
75. Minutes, Meeting 22.3.38 at 84 Gray's Inn Road to discuss formation of organisation for amateur 16mm production (in FPLa).
76. *Daily Worker*, 22 February 1937, p.7; *Tribune*, 26 February 1937, p.15.
77. *Daily Worker*, 2 October 1937, p.2. In the *Daily Worker* of 15 February 1937 (p.4) *The Dawn* had been praised as 'excellent anti-imperialist propaganda as well as an exciting film'.
78. Ibid., 9 October 1937, p.7.
79. *Left News*, No.22, February 1938, p.703; Frank Jackson, 'China Strikes Back', in *Left Review* Vol.3 No.13, February 1938, pp.808-9.
80. See Nicholas Pronay, 'La Non-Intervention de l'Ecole documentariste anglaise' in *Les Cahiers de la Cinémathéque* No.21, January 1977, pp.23-7.
81. *Daily Worker*, 12 January 1938, p.2.
82. Ibid., 12 November 1937, p.5.
83. Especially as Kino was able to release an uncensored 16mm version of the film in the summer of 1938.
84. Perhaps the most conclusive proof of both companies' adherence to 'Popular Front' politics was the composition of Kino's General Council and the PFI's Board of Directors. The Kino General Council of 1937 had the following members: J.D. Bernal; Aneurin Bevan, MP; The Bishop of Birmingham; Alberto Cavalcanti; Sir Stafford Cripps, KC, MP; Maurice Dobb; Havelock Ellis; Victor Gollancz; Viscount Hastings; Professor Lancelot Hogben; Professor Julian Huxley; Professor H. Levy; Ivor Montagu; D.N. Pritt, KC, MP; Alderman Joseph Reeves; Paul Rotha; Bertrand Russell; Lord Strabolgi; H.G. Wells. Whether this illustrious body ever met in full is not known. The PFI had as directors the superintendent of the London Zoo, Geoffrey Veevers, Lord Listowel, Alderman Joseph Reeves (a key figure!), Wilfrid Roberts MP, John Jagger MP and Dorothy Woodman, with D.N. Pritt giving legal service and Ellen Wilkinson MP helping Montagu on many occasions.
85. Ivor Montagu, interview 6 September 1974.
86. Thorold Dickinson, 'Spanish ABC' in *Sight and Sound* Vol.7 No.25, Spring 1938, p.30.
87. Ibid.
88. Sidney Cole, 'Shooting in Spain' in *The Cine-Technician* Vol.4 No.15, May-June 1938, pp.1-2. Cole gives the figures 1,400 killed and 3,000 wounded as a result of the bombardment. The figures of 1,300 killed and 2,000 wounded are given by Hugh Thomas, *The Spanish Civil War*, Harmondsworth 1971, p.658.
89. Ivor Montagu, interview 8 March 1978.
90. *Daily Worker*, 26 April 1938, p.3.
91. Ibid., 25 June 1938, p.4.

Chapter 7

Labour Cinema Propaganda: One Man's Affair

Since its abortive 1920 'Labour Cinema Propaganda' circular, the Labour Party had given little further thought to the idea of propaganda by means of the cinema. Its main adversary, the Conservative Party, had not shown such reserve in film matters. The Tories felt that cinema propaganda had enormous advantages over more traditional forms of publicity if they wanted to reach certain sections of the population, particularly the so-called unconverted working-class. Since 1925 the Conservative Party used cinema vans to enliven its election campaigns. With these vans programmes could be screened in broad daylight at any street corner. By means of short films, a clever mixture of entertainment and propaganda, the crowds would be stopped and the message to vote Tory hammered home. The Conservative Films Association produced some twenty films for this purpose, including some cartoon films ridiculing their opponents. By 1930, twelve cinema vans were in use, with another twelve for the transport of projection equipment to be used at indoor meetings.[1]

The existence of this fleet of Tory cinema vans and their success in attracting the attention of the crowds on the street could scarcely go unnoticed by the Labour Party. It had given priority to the expansion of its national newspaper, the *Daily Herald*, now published by Odhams Press. In 1933,

> when the *Daily Herald* was approaching a circulation of two million, the assistance of the Labour Party and the General Council [of the TUC, B.H.] was sought in order to speed up the

reaching of the two million mark. In return it was promised that when this figure was achieved, the *Daily Herald* would present for the joint use of the TUC and the Labour Party a talkie film propaganda van.[2]

It seemed an ideal present, with one form of propaganda (newspaper) generating another (film). In fact, the Labour Party was thoroughly embarrassed by the present. A second-hand van, offered to the *Herald* for £600, did not meet with the approval of Labour Party and TUC representatives. They were taken aback too by the extra costs involved in running the van, estimated at £625 per year. But it was the expense of the provision of suitable films, approximately £2,000, that came as the biggest shock. 'Consequently, we have refrained from pressing the *Daily Herald* for delivery of the van,' as TUC secretary Walter Citrine reported.[3] The cinema van was never delivered, never used.

The Labour Party seemed indifferent to this lost opportunity. The TUC, however, decided to study the question of film propaganda. It may possibly have been pushed into this by some unions like, for example, the Amalgamated Engineering Union which had put in a strong plea for a 'Workers' Cinema' in 1934 in its *Monthly Journal*.[4] In March 1935 a report on 'Cinema Film in Trade Union Propaganda' was presented to the General Council of the TUC. It related the unfortunate episode of the *Herald* cinema van. The costs involved in making and showing propaganda films were listed in some detail. Particularly interesting was section 12 of the report. It concerned the formation of a documentary unit along the lines of Grierson's Empire Marketing Board and GPO film units. Such a unit could, if supported by the Labour Party, produce 'either free of charge or at very low costs propaganda films for the movement'.[5] Still, the report cited the figures of £3,000 as capital costs for the first year and £2,000 for recurring annual charges. As there was no prospect of an increase in overall membership, the report recommended the General Council to look for 'other means as will ensure that the publicity and propaganda work of the Council can be adequately financed'. Rather than being the actual starting-point for a trade union film service, the report resulted in yet another committee, made up of representatives of the TUC General Council and the Labour Party National Executive Committee. Thus the 1935 General Election went by without a Labour cinema van, without Labour cinema propaganda.

In April 1936 the committee published a circular on 'Labour Cinema Propaganda' on behalf of the TUC and the Labour Party. Evidently the 1920 'Labour Cinema Propaganda' circular had been unearthed for this purpose. Not only is the 1936 circular's motto – from Heraclitus – the same, but the same opening sentence is used: 'During the war the cinematograph became a powerful instrument of propaganda in the hands of the government.' The next sentence brought the reader up-to-date: 'Since then, with the development of talking films and the immense improvement in cinema technique, film production has become nothing short of a fine art, the propaganda value of which has been multiplied a hundredfold.' This, the circular explained, made it imperative for Labour to organise its own film propaganda. But the circular only put forward one concrete suggestion: the formation of film societies by local Labour parties. A questionnaire was added to the circular, asking for data on the local situation. Given the work of a special committee ('composed of representatives of the Labour Party Executive, the General Council of the Trades Union Congress, and a number of friendly experts'), and given the 'many discussions, during which the subject has been exhaustively studied', the result was very meagre indeed. If local Labour parties decided on the formation of a film society, the circular promised that they could count on 'a central organisation for the supply of information, projectors and films'. To avoid preaching to the converted, the circular recommended the opening of Labour film societies 'to members of other non-party organisations with interests of an educational and cultural character, as well as to individual members of the general public.'[6]

Why did the circular propagate the film society idea? Was preaching to the converted not inherent to a society with its membership regulations? Given the self-evident alternative – the use of non-flam 16mm film – the circular seemed completely anachronistic. One can understand the Committee's political objections to quoting the example of the Socialist Film Council or Kino in these matters, but by 1936 the documentary film units – and even such a highly respectable body as the British Film Institute – were using

16mm stock on a large scale. Without Labour propaganda films there could be no Labour cinema propaganda. This was another major flaw of the circular: there was not a word about the films the proposed Labour film societies could exhibit. Not even the promise of a future Labour film production. Nobody expected a British equivalent to *Battleship Potemkin*, but some indication as to the films the committee had in mind (either available through existing distribution companies or yet to be produced), would certainly have made the circular a more inspiring document.

Kino welcomed the 'Labour Cinema Propaganda' circular, but could not help making some remarks. Inevitably Kino felt it had been ignored by the circular, which it considered 'the response to the growing demand of the rank and file of the labour movement for new forms of propaganda.' It added,

> We can cite many instances of local Labour parties and trades unions who were well ahead of Transport House and who have run shows in co-operation with us. We can safely claim that we have not been an unimportant factor in the production of the circular.

Kino was afraid that the circular's silence on the question of film format (inflammable 35mm vs. non-inflammable 16mm) could be interpreted as a tacit indication of the intention to produce expensive 35mm films for theatrical distribution. Kino made a plea for 16mm production and distribution: 'There is no reason why this should cut down the effectiveness of the propaganda or why large sections of the general public cannot be drawn in.'[7]

In *Left Review* Kino's Frank Jackson provided some further arguments in favour of the 'sub-standard' format. He pointed out that the making of feature films would cost the labour movement over £10,000, that it could not expect any help from film producers as Labour propaganda films would stand the 'chance of being banned by the Censor', and that therefore 'making films on this scale would mean squashing out every trace of propaganda or education; it would mean that the films would defeat their own purpose.' Interestingly, Jackson also opposed the production of one- or two-reelers

> dealing with such subjects as 'A Day in the Life of a Railway Worker' [which] would stand a chance of being shown fairly

extensively, on condition that there was no 'propaganda' in them. And if these films are going to be in the tradition of the 'English school' of documentary they would be shown only in the specialist cinemas, and again would not reach that wider public at which the circular aims.[8]

There were no grounds for Kino's anxiety that the 'Labour Cinema Propaganda' circular would inaugurate an era of expensive feature films. Labour never had the intention of putting a lot of money into its film service. It had no personal relations with important film producers, as the Tories had.[9] Perhaps even more importantly, it knew that any feature film propagating its cause would necessarily be rejected by the BBFC. But for some time, the Joint Film Committee had been in touch with Paul Rotha, next to John Grierson the most important documentary film maker in Great Britain. Rotha was a dedicated supporter of the Labour Party. With his friend, the *Herald* reporter Ritchie Calder, he tried to win Labour for the documentary. Rotha had proposed the formation of a documentary unit to produce free or low cost propaganda films for the movement.[10] For this purpose, he organised a film show at the Labour Party's annual conference in Brighton in 1935. In 1936 Rotha took the authorities and the film trade by surprise with his three-minute *Peace Film*.[11] By editing images of modern arms and the destruction caused by them, Rotha argued for the importance of halting the arms race by writing to one's MP. The success of this venture against all the odds – the *Peace Film* was shown as part of the ordinary programme in hundreds of cinemas all over the country – should have given Labour food for thought. Rotha was the main speaker at a Special Conference on Film Propaganda, held prior to the 1936 Labour Party Conference in Edinburgh. Another speaker was Labour Party secretary J.S. Middleton who outlined

the provisional plans of the Joint Committee, both for the production and the exhibition of special Documentary and Labour Propaganda Films, the establishment of Film Societies, the provision of suitable Portable Projectors, and the organisation of a Centralised Service of Film Programmes.[12]

Last but not least, a programme of films was shown, screened by the 16mm sound projector which the Committee recommended as suitable for purchase by local Labour organisations.

Rotha's speech at the conference was published as a pamphlet, *Films and the Labour Party*. In it Rotha dwelled on the propaganda aspect of the cinema, quoting numerous examples. His conclusion: 'no film dealing with any contemporary subject from a working-class point of view can be made under the existing conditions of commercial film production.'[13] The documentary offered an alternative, but documentary films could not 'be regarded in themselves as an antidote to the propaganda of the story-film in the public cinemas'.[14] Given the fact that radio was a closed monopoly, Rotha recommended the organisation of a Labour film movement, to complement the Labour newspapers and other forms of propaganda, 'Spreading working-class propaganda throughout the country by making and showing films'.[15] The kind of films Rotha had in mind were inexpensive documentaries, made by professional people,

> designed to appeal to three kinds of public: (i) To the community as a whole, in order to make the ordinary person socially and politically interested in the government of the country. (ii) To people already politically-minded from a working-class point of view, to instruct them further in Labour and working-class principles. (iii) To the unconverted, to make them culturally minded, and to make them realise the short-sightedness and injustice of Conservatism.[16]

Of course, Rotha hoped that he would be invited to produce these films. His friend Ritchie Calder supported him by selecting a still from Rotha's film *Shipyard* to illustrate his article on Labour film propaganda, published in the monthly *Labour*. Calder's arguments were exactly the same as Rotha's, apart from the journalistic bravura with which they were delivered.[17] To convince his readers Calder referred to the recent success of the Swedish social-democratic party, which had made extensive use of film propaganda during its election campaign.[18]

Calder and above all Rotha were to be cruelly disappointed in their expectations. Nothing happened at all after the 1936 Labour Party Conference and the party's leadership remained completely indifferent to the question of film propaganda which it considered an administrative matter to be dealt with by the Labour Party and TUC secretariats. The Joint Film Committee continued its existence, but it had no money and consequently no power to do anything. In retrospect Rotha complained that 'Labour did not even have an aesthetic approach (to film), let alone a social one.'[19] Rotha turned his back to the Film Committee, not just because he personally felt offended by the course of affairs, but also because he was completely bewildered by Labour's refusal to take the film medium seriously. By its inertia Labour lost the services of one of the outstanding documentary film makers of the time.

Rotha had tried to get the Labour Party to take a serious interest in film, but failed and resigned from its Joint Film Committee. By the end of 1936, entirely new perspectives for Labour film propaganda arose. The National Association of Co-operative Education Committees published as a pamphlet a speech by Joseph Reeves on *The Film and Education* and launched the idea of establishing a National Co-operative Film Society: film as a means of education instead of propaganda, supported by the Co-operative movement instead of the Labour Party and TUC. There were obvious advantages, ideological and financial, attached to this. The main difference, however, between this and the 'Labour Cinema Propaganda' scheme was a personal one: Joseph Reeves.

Since 1918 Joseph Reeves had been the Education Secretary of the Royal Arsenal Co-operative Society (RACS). From 1922 onwards Reeves integrated film into the educational activities of the RACS. The Tooting Co-op Hall, owned by the RACS, was equipped with a projection booth to act as a base for these activities. It will be remembered that the hall was a temporary home for the London Workers' Film Society in 1929, when the LCC refused permission for the use of a cinema covered by an LCC licence (see Chapter Two). The Tooting Co-op Hall was not adapted to 'talkies', instead the RACS obtained a portable 16mm projector. With this projector Eisenstein's *The General Line* was shown to thousands of co-operators. The RACS even bought a film camera to record its activities.[20] Reeves wanted the example of the RACS to be followed by other Co-operative societies. So far the Co-operative movement had only produced advertising films to increase the sales of its products. Reeves delivered his speech on 'The Film and Education' at a conference organised by the National Association of Co-operative Education Committees on 5 September 1936. He argued convincingly for the involvement of film in the educational activities of the Co-ops. On Reeves's recommendation a circular was sent by the National Association

> to all co-operative societies asking whether they would be prepared: (i) To donate the sum of £10 with the object of establishing a National Co-operative Film Society. (ii) To purchase (a) equipment outright, or (b) equipment on a hire-purchase basis, and (iii) To guarantee to rent weekly programmes of films from the National Co-operative Film Society at a cost of approximately £3 to £5 per week, or (iv) If unable to guarantee to hire films for a period of 26 weeks, to agree to arrange a certain number of film exhibitions, all equipment and films with operators being supplied by the National Co-operative Film Society for the sum of £6 to £8 per exhibition.[21]

Except for its detail, this circular was not very different from the 'Labour Cinema Propaganda' circular. But Joseph Reeves made sure that it was taken seriously. About fifty Education Committees subscribed to the society, donating the substantial sum of £500. The Joint Film Committee could not help but invite Reeves as the secretary of the National Co-operative Film Society to attend its meetings, hoping that the financial resources of the Co-ops and Reeves's persistance would succeed where its own inertia had failed.[22]

From now on the initiative passed to Reeves. He knew that it would be pointless to wait for a move from the Labour Party and/or the trade unions in film matters. If the National Co-operative Film Society could be strengthened, then it could become the future film service for the whole labour movement. Through his personal contacts with Kino and the PFI, Reeves had access to an extensive 16mm film library (and, if necessary, 35mm films too). In September 1937 the Film Department of the National Association of Co-operative Education Committees started its activities. By December the Department had arranged more than 400 film shows, consisting mainly of educational films rented from various film libraries. They included three films distributed by Kino: *Kameradschaft, News from Spain* and *War is Hell*.[23] The next step was the production

of films. For this purpose Reeves approached the four big
Co-ops in Metropolitan London with the request to finance
the production of five films, at the rate of one a year. Each film
would cost approximately £1,000 and Reeves managed to
convince the Co-ops of the need for this 'five-year plan'.[24]
Soon the first of these 'five short documentary films putting
co-operation's romantic story on the screen' was on its way.[25]

While Reeves was lobbying for the big money, young film
makers were producing pictures for the Co-operative
movement on shoestring budgets. Not surprisingly, their
background was the (Workers') Film and Photo League. In an
article in the *Millgate* of October 1936, Frank Cox argued in
favour of 16mm sound film production by the Co-operative
movement. He warned against the simple copying of 'the
methods of existing film companies in production [because]
these are wasteful in the extreme.' Cox: 'We have learned from
Russia how to make use of natural acting by picking types to
take those parts which they themselves fill in their daily life.'
He was further thinking of 'a very modest outlay' as a studio,
where these films could be shot.[26] Cox's article was followed by
a contribution from Sidney Moir who had 'made four films for
the "unofficial" Co-operative Film Council' (unfortunately no
titles are mentioned).[27] 'The satisfactory planning of this [type
of film production, B.H.] would necessitate the calling together
of those who understand both the aims of our Movement and
the particular technique of 16mm film.'[28] In other words, Moir
was pleading for a Co-operative equivalent of the FPL.

Frank Cox did not wait until this body got together. He
managed to get money from the Political Committee of the
London Co-operative Society to produce 16mm sound films.
The Peace Parade (1937) was 'a newsreel of the Great
Co-operative peace demonstration in Hyde Park on
September 19'.[29] *The People Who Count* (1937) was a more
ambitious production, trying to show the meaning of
co-operation. The commentary to the film was read by
Co-operative MP A.V. Alexander. The film gives a good
impression of the various aspects of Co-operation, ranging
from Women's Guilds to parliamentary representation. To
match this rather serious film with something more
entertaining, Cox made *?Utopia* (1938), which was described as
'an entertaining skit upon the Tory point of view about slums,

rehousing, malnutrition and rearmament, and gives the irrefutable Socialist answer'.[30] When *Reynolds News*, the popular Co-operative Sunday paper, organised a scenario competition, Cox was asked to adapt the prize-winning screen-play, 'The Dream of Christopher Cole', the story 'of what happened in his sleep to a man who firmly believed that everything should be privately owned'. *Reynolds News* assured readers that it was 'highly amusing, and has many apt social pointers'.[31]

It was no surprise that one of Frank Cox's films (*?Utopia*) was included in a two-hour film programme demonstrating the possibilities of 16mm sound projection, at Transport House on 22 March 1938.[32] It was another example of how important the input of the Co-operative movement was in these matters. In January 1938 the Joint Film Committee decided to establish 'a Central Office and Library'.[33] A sub-committee, which included Joseph Reeves, was formed to further work out this decision. Its report on 24 March 1938 clearly bore Reeves's mark. The Labour Film Service was modelled after the Film Department of the National Association of Co-operative Education Committees. The new organisation would be responsible 'for the circulation and production of films'; it would have a General Committee consisting of an equal number of representatives from TUC, Labour Party and National Association of Co-operative Education Committees; it would employ a secretary-organiser and an assistant who would have to work in 'suitable offices', consisting of one room for the secretary and another for the assistant and the storage of the films. The costs were estimated at £1,000 per year, but it was hoped that after two years the film service would become self-supporting. The report dwelled on the supply of suitable 'sub-standard' sound films, listing the various companies offering these. Necessarily more vague was the section on production. It recommended co-operation with trade unions in the provision of documentary material of special interest. The report ended with the recommendation to start the new organisation in the autumn,[34] and the Joint Film Committee adopted the report at its meeting on 28 March 1938.[35] Now it was up to the General Council of the TUC, the National Executive of the Labour Party and the Committee of the National Association of Co-operative Education Committees to approve the scheme without further delay, so that the new organisation could be launched in the autumn of 1938.

Local Labour parties and trade union branches were sometimes ahead of the decisions made by the Joint Film Committee. For example, during the 'Milk for Spain' campaign (winter 1937-38), a fair number of local Labour parties actually hired projectors from Co-ops to show films about Spain.[36] Kino was, of course, still doing business with Labour organisations. Unfortunately, there are no figures available to show the percentage of local Labour parties, trade union branches or Co-operative education committees among its customers, but one gets the impression that by 1938 the left in general had come to an *awareness* about the importance of the film medium, as a source of information, education and propaganda. A brief look at Glasgow Kino will make this clear.

In September 1937, at the start of the new season, the Glasgow Kino Film Group claimed: 'Bookings so far give ample evidence that the Labour and Co-operative Conferences' decisions on the necessity for socialism to be spread by film propaganda is bearing fruit.'[37] This was a rather bold claim but one the group nevertheless sought to live up to. The group not only acted as a distribution agency in Scotland for Kino and International Sound Films, it also organised premiere screenings in Glasgow and toured the regions with portable projector and film programmes. When Mrs Cicely Munro, Labour candidate for the St Stephen's Ward in the Edinburgh municipal elections, opened her campaign, Glasgow Kino was present with *Hell Unltd.*, which 'fetched many non-socialists' to the meeting.[38] When the Govanhill and Shawlands branches of the Scottish Socialist Party decided to organise a series of five Sunday film shows, Glasgow Kino was put 'in charge of the programmes.'[39] Many of the films shown every Sunday by the Glasgow Clarion Scouts were provided by Glasgow Kino. In December 1937 and January 1938 Glasgow Kino made an extensive tour with a programme specially aimed at co-operators, which included the Scottish Co-operative Wholesale Society's film *Tea.*[40] At the same time, it supported the 'Milk for Spain' campaign by organising shows with *News from Spain* and *Modern Orphans of the Storm.*[41] The group claimed that of the bookings for the last quarter of 1937, 'Co-operative guilds and education committees are second on the list with 14 per cent.'[42] Last but not least, Glasgow Kino organised its own premiere shows of *Millions of Us* and *Hey Rup!* (a Czech comedy distributed by ISF) on 8 October 1937 and *The Dawn* together with various shorts on 16 January 1938.[43]

With this broad support (and, obviously, a healthy group life) Glasgow Kino felt the time had come to produce a film of its own. May Day 1938, with a procession jointly organised by the Glasgow Trades Council and the Burgh Labour Party, was the natural subject. Glasgow Kino appealed for donations from the organisations taking part in the procession and from the public: 'The sum of £50 is required but if the Group receive more, the making of a sound film, costing about £100, will be considered.'[44] Evidently, this target could not be reached. The Group was afraid that participants and public would react unnaturally to the presence of its camera units at the May Day procession and therefore placed an ad in the press, asking them: 'Please resolutely ignore the camera!'.[45] In the end, the film was not marred by the unnaturalness of the people in front of the camera, but rather by its general conception. Directed by Helen Biggar and filmed by three motorised camera units, the film, entitled *Challenge to Fascism!* (a direct reference to the majority of the slogans carried in the May Day procession), is rather disappointing. It shows the preparations of the May Day committee, the morning of the day itself as experienced by a working-class family, and the procession itself. The three parts are separate entities; consequently the film remains not much more than a newsreel. Film making was beyond Glasgow Kino's abilities, but otherwise the group had professionally proven the value of a film service for the labour movement in Scotland.

While Helen Biggar and her friends were filming the May Day demonstration in Glasgow to make *Challenge to Fascism!*, a Realist film unit, directed by Ralph Bond, was doing the same in London for the film *Advance, Democracy!*, the first in the five-year plan of the London Co-ops. Apart from the different financial conditions under which both films were made, they have something in common. Both viewed the 1938 May Day in the context of the struggle against fascism, for democracy. *Advance, Democracy!* starts with a sequence showing the difference between rich and poor in London. The film then introduces the main protagonists: Bert, a craneman at the London docks, who earns £4 a week when working, and his wife May, a staunch member of the Co-operative Women's Guild. Bert (by contemporary standards a prime example of the 'sexist' husband) does not give a damn about the ideal of Co-operation, but is persuaded by May to listen to A.V. Alexander MP on the radio. There is a droll interlude with the radio forecasting 'a deep depression over mid-Europe, heading westwards'. Bert gets carried away by Alexander's speech, particularly his analysis of the current political situation, and therefore appeals to his comrades in the docks to join the May Day demonstration. The film ends with shots of Bert and May marching in the May Day procession, edited with songs rendered by the Co-operative Choir and orchestrated by Benjamin Britten.

With *Advance, Democracy!* Ralph Bond had once more proven his qualities as a film maker for the labour movement.[46] It was the best opener Joseph Reeves could wish for for the new Labour film service, the Workers' Film Association, of which he had been appointed Secretary-Organiser in August 1938. The first public appearance of the new organisation was in the form of a film show at the TUC annual conference in Blackpool early September 1938. The programme included *Advance, Democracy!* and *Spanish Earth*.[47] In November 1938 Joseph Reeves left the RACS after almost twenty years as its education secretary. His new offices were at 145 Wardour Street (also the premises of the Association of Cine-Technicians). Reeves and his Workers' Film Association (WFA) set to work at once. The WFA offered an 80-minute film programme for £2, charging another pound (or more, depending on the size of the hall) for projection equipment and the services of an operator. It offered a 15 per cent rebate on the price of sound projectors, cash or hire-purchase, for organisations associated with the TUC, Labour Party or Co-operative movement. Apart from *Advance, Democracy!*, its film library included political films from Kino, educational films from Gaumont British Instructional and travel films from the Workers' Travel Association.[48] Thanks to Joseph Reeves, Labour had finally opened its eyes.

Notes

1. See T.J. Hollins, 'The Conservative Party and Film Propaganda Between the Wars' in *English Historical Review*, 1981, pp.359-69; 'Politics and the Film', in *Sight and Sound* Vol.1 No.2, Summer 1932, pp.49-50.
2. Walter M. Citrine, 'Cinema Film in Trade Union Propaganda', report to TUC General Council, 25 March 1935, p.1 (in TUC Library).
3. Ibid.
4. J.W. Smith, 'Why Not a Workers' Cinema?' in *AEU Monthly Journal*, June 1934, pp.16-7.
5. Citrine, loc.cit., p.3.
6. 'Labour Cinema Propaganda', circular, Labour Party, April 1936.
7. 'Labour Opens Its Eyes' in *Kino News* No.2, 1936, p.1.
8. Frank Jackson, 'Films for Labour' in *Left Review* Vol.2 No.9, June 1936, p.477.
9. See T.J. Hollins, loc.cit., particularly p.364.
10. See note 5.
11. See 'Interview: Rotha on Rotha', in Paul Marris (ed.), *Paul Rotha*, BFI Dossier 16, London 1982, pp.10-1.
12. 'Special Conference on Film Propaganda', circular, Labour Party, September 1936.
13. Paul Rotha, *Films and the Labour Party*, 1936, p.11 (reprinted in Marris (ed.), op.cit., pp.47-54, here p.51).
14. Ibid., p.12 (reprint, p.52).
15. Ibid., p.15 (reprint, p.54).
16. Ibid., p.14 (reprint, p.54).
17. Calder formulated, for example, the three kinds of publics (note 16) thus: 'In the first, come films which are not directly political but designed to make people "outside" socially conscious and alive to the need for reform. In the second, come films which educate the converted in the ideals and objectives of Socialism. In the third, come films which are straight-from-the-shoulders propaganda using hard-hitting arguments which carry conviction among the unconverted, and win elections.' Ritchie Calder, 'We Must Learn to Shoot' in *Labour*, October 1936, pp.35-6, here p.36; 'Federation of Film Guilds for the Labour Party' in *World Film News* Vol.1 No.8, November 1936, p.29.
18. For the election films of the Swedish Labour Party, see Ingmari Eriksson, 'Kyss Till För Partiet! En Studie Kring Kärlek och Ideologi i Arbetarrörelsens Filmer' in *Film & TV* No.1-3, 1975, pp.26-32. Of the two films mentioned by Calder (in *Labour*, October 1936, p.35), *Our Country for the People* and *Here We Build a New Sweden*, Eriksson only refers to the former, originally entitled *Landet för Folket*. She makes clear that the SAP, the Swedish Labour Party, had been using films in its election campaigns as far back as 1928.
19. Paul Rotha, *Documentary Diary. An Informal History of the British Documentary Film, 1928-1939*, London 1973, p.281; see also Rotha's reminiscences in Marris (ed.), op.cit., pp.17-8. In this interview Rotha

confuses the 1934 halfpenny levy imposed by the TUC for the commemoration of the Tolpuddle Martyrs (with £10,000 spent on a theatre tour with Miles Malleson's play on the Dorsetshire labourers) with TUC proposals to impose a similar levy for film propaganda. Rotha's final break with the Joint Film Committee must have had other grounds than the money spent on Malleson's play.

20. See Joseph Reeves, *The Film and Education*, Stoke-on-Trent [1936]; John Attfield, *With Light of Knowledge. A Hundred Years of Education in the Royal Arsenal Co-operative Society, 1877-1977*, London 1981, passim.

21. *Scottish Co-operator*, 26 December 1936, p.1383.

22. Report, Trades Union Congress and Labour Party Joint Film Committee, 22 July 1937.

23. *Daily Worker*, 3 November 1937, p.3.

24. Ibid; *Scottish Co-operator*, 4 December 1937, p.1347; Reeves had announced the plan already long before to the Joint Film Committee, see Report, Trades Union Congress and Labour Party Joint Film Committee, 22 July 1937 (in TUC Library).

25. *Scottish Co-operator*, 4 December 1937, p.1347.

26. Frank H.W. Cox, 'A National Co-operative Film Society' in *The Millgate* Vol.32 No.373, pp.39-40, here p.40.

27. S.E.L. Moir, 'Co-operative Films – When?' in *Millgate*, Vol.32 No.376, pp.200-1, here p.200.

28. Moir, loc.cit., p.201.

29. *Reynolds News*, 31 October 1937, p.12.

30. *Daily Worker*, 28 March 1938, p.7.

31. *Reynolds News*, 3 July 1938, p.15.

32. Ibid., 20 March 1938, p.15.

33. Minutes, Joint Film Committee, 28 January 1938 (in TUC Library).

34. Report, National Joint Film Committee, 'National Film Service. Central Office and Film Library', 24 March 1938 (in TUC Library).

35. Minutes, Joint Film Committee, 28 March 1938 (in TUC Library).

36. See Report, National Joint Film Committee, 'National Film Service. Central Office and Film Library', 24 March 1938, p.1 (in TUC Library). According to the *Daily Worker* (8 December 1937, p.3) a special sound trailer had been made for the campaign, 'in which Mr. A.V. Alexander, MP, makes clear the reason for the "Milk for Spain" campaign and appeals for assistance'.

37. *Forward*, 25 September 1937, p.10.

38. Ibid., 2 October 1937, p.10.

39. Ibid., 13 November 1937, p.10.

40. *Scottish Co-operator*, 11 December 1937. p.1375; 1 January 1938, p.4.

41. Ibid., 1 January 1938, p.4.

42. Ibid., 15 January 1938, p.73.

43. *Forward*, 2 October 1937, p.12; *Scottish Co-operator*, 15 January 1938, p.73.

44. *Forward*, 26 March 1938, p.11; see also *Daily Worker*, 4 April 1938, p.8; *Forward*, 23 April 1938, p.11.

45. *Forward*, 30 April 1938, p.12.

46. In 1937 Ralph Bond had co-directed, with Ruby Grierson, the film *To-day We Live* on the work of the National Council of Social Service. Bond and his assistant Donald Alexander had handled the part of the film set in the

Rhondda Valley with great skill and understanding. He even managed to get a statement from a miner, demanding real work instead of the palliatives offered by the National Council of Social Service, into the film. *To-day We Live* differs in this basic criticism from many other films produced by the established documentary units. Ralph Bond wrote on the making of the film in *World Film News*, Vol.2 No.6, September 1937, p.39.

47. *Daily Herald*, 30 August 1938, p.11.

48. Joseph Reeves, 'You Can't Ignore the Taste for Pictures' in *Labour Organiser*, February 1939, pp.33-4.

Chapter 8

For Peace and Plenty

In September 1938 the British Prime Minister, Neville Chamberlain, was carrying on negotiations with the German Führer Adolf Hitler (then still referred to by British statesmen and the media as 'Herr' Hitler) over the fate of Czechoslovakia, which Britain and France were bound by treaty to assist against foreign aggression. Hitler's demands amounted to the extinction of Czechoslovakia's independence and the dismemberment of its territory. It seemed that Europe was on the brink of war. Chamberlain flew to Munich, sacrificed Czechoslovakia, and proclaimed 'Peace in our time'. He returned to a hero's welcome in the media.

From 16 to 19 September 1938, while the Munich crisis was at its height, the CPGB was holding its Fifteenth Congress at Birmingham Town Hall. The slogan of the Congress was 'For Peace and Plenty'. PFI cameramen were present to record some of the proceedings. Harry Pollitt, in his main report, analysed the Chamberlain government, its composition, its policies, its hidden aims. He called for the building of a great popular movement against Chamberlain, which could defeat the government, secure peace abroad through an alliance with the Soviet Union and the Western democracies, and create plenty at home by implementing new economic and social policies. The shadow of war hung over the Congress, but the Communist Party had actually been living with war since 1936, when British contingents joined the International Brigades in Spain. In the tense political situation of the time, the Congress was a convincing public demonstration of the party's morale and unity. Chamberlain's return from Munich in the following weeks confirmed the party's analysis and added urgency to its message.

The material shot by the PFI crew was edited into a

ten-minute sound film, the *XVth Congress Film*. This film does
not so much report the actual proceedings of the Congress as
give an impression of the general atmosphere, with shots of
well-known Communists, of wall decorations painted by
AIA-members and of community singing. The film was
'accompanied [by] music, drums, singing',[1] and was advertised
as 'a fully professional production'.[2] This perfectly sums up the
policy of the PFI: to support the anti-Chamberlain alliance by
producing professionally-made films. Until then the PFI had
only produced films which were actually shot indoors (*XVth
Congress Film*) or abroad (*Defence of Madrid, Spanish ABC* and
Behind the Spanish Lines). But, if it were to record news items in
Britain, its cameramen could get into trouble with the police
for filming without a pass. So Eileen Hellstern wrote a letter to
Scotland Yard, asking them to supply Christopher Brunel with
a Police Pass to pursue his employment as a newsreel
cameraman. On 12 October 1938 the Commissioner of Police
replied that the request was refused, because 'the issue of Press
cards to cinematograph cameramen is restricted to established
newsreel companies'.[3]

Not satisfied with the reason given for refusal, Montagu
enlisted Clem Attlee's support. The PFI had worked previously
with Attlee, producing a short film, *Attlee in Spain*, on the
Labour leader's visit to Spain with Ellen Wilkinson.[4]
Wilkinson, MP for Jarrow, was closely involved in the activities
of the PFI. Attlee had intervened with the Foreign Office when
Montagu had trouble obtaining the necessary papers for
himself and his camera crew to go to Spain in late 1937 (see
Chapter Six). Again Attlee intervened on behalf of the PFI, this
time with Sir Samuel Hoare, the Home Secretary, and Hoare
promised to have enquiries made. This led to a revealing
correspondence between the Commissioner of Police, the
Home Office and Scotland Yard, of which neither Attlee nor
PFI were aware.[5] Perhaps surprisingly, a flexible conclusion
was arrived at: '... concerns like the PFI will not be seriously
handicapped by the refusal of a pass and ... it may be wiser to
give them one.'[6] This was duly notified to Attlee by the Home
Office: '... if they will communicate with the Commissioner
again he will be prepared to reconsider the matter,'[7] but it is
not known if the PFI bothered to do this.

While the *XVth Congress Film* had been made with an
essentially Communist audience in mind,[8] the next PFI

production, *Britain Expects*, aimed at large cinema audiences. Made under the auspices of the shipowners' organisations and the National Union of Seamen, it set out to show how the lives of British seamen were endangered as a consequence of the Government's policy on Spain.[9] It showed 'authentic pictures of the bombing of British vessels'.[10] By means of graphic diagrams the film made clear 'that many British trade routes are now within the radius of German and Italian aerodromes on the coasts of Spain'.[11] *Britain Expects* revealed that Chamberlain's policy of 'leniency' towards Franco only led to a decline in British sea trade with that part of Spain, as the Germans were shipping the minerals needed for their rearmament directly to Germany. *Britain Expects* was 'made in such a way as to bring home the real meaning of Chamberlain's policy to the unconverted and non-political, to the person who is not quite sure what's it all about'.[12] The PFI therefore released it on 35mm, hoping that as many ordinary cinemas as possible would take it. This commercial version was, however, 'censored of vital facts about German and Italian bombing of ships'.[13] Perhaps most surprisingly, *Britain Expects* also served as an election film for the 'Red' Duchess of Atholl, who stood unsuccessfully as an independent candidate in the West Perth by-election in December 1938.[14] As usual Kino handled the 16mm distribution of the film.

On 7 December 1938 the bulk of the British Batallion of the International Brigades returned to the country. In January 1939 a big welcome rally was organised in the Empress Hall in London. A crew of ACT members, including Ivor Montagu, made a film of this moving event.[15] In the past, the PFI had always mobilised the ACT in order to get personnel for its Spain films, now the initiative had been taken by the union itself, a clear sign of the growing interest taken by the ACT in film politics.

Since George Elvin had taken over as secretary of the Association of Cinematograph Technicians in 1935, this union had made remarkable progress, reflected in its excellent journal *Cine-Technician*. The ACT had not only organised and defended the interests of studio personnel, laboratory workers and even documentary film makers (to Grierson's annoyance), it also took an active interest in the future of the British film industry. The discussions in 1938 around the renewal of the

1928 Quota Act – which prescribed the quota of British films to be produced, distributed and exhibited – prompted the union to look for support from the politicians.[16] The new Quota Act was followed by some successes like *Pygmalion, The Citadel* and *The Lady Vanishes*, but the general situation was far from brilliant, with much unemployment among ACT members. Thoughts turned towards the Left Book Club with its mass membership. So far the LBC had only mediated between Kino and the FPL on the one hand and the LBC groups on the other. To provide a forum for LBC members and sympathisers working in the film industry was a new step. On 15 December 1938 the first meeting of the LBC Film Group was held in London. The speaker was Professor J.B.S. Haldane with a lecture on Air Raid Precautions (ARP) and their application to film studios in time of war.[17] It was the ideal subject to open with: the LBC had been campaigning vigorously for ARP (Haldane's *ARP* had been the Book of the Month in September 1938), yet it had never been related to the specific interests of the film trade.

But the LBC Film Group stood for more, as became clear in January 1939 when Thorold Dickinson gave a talk. He made the

> suggestion that the Left Book Club should make its own films, for use and not for profit, thereby helping if only in a small way to stem the tide of ruin in the British film industry ... It would be possible, he said, for the Club to tackle subjects of a lively political and social kind that the commercial cinema will not touch, not only documentaries but cartoons, satire and acted subjects.[18]

Dickinson referred to the making of the Popular Front film *La Marseillaise* as a means of raising the necessary money, though he was thinking of a less ambitious project. *La Marseillaise*, a film on the French Revolution directed by Jean Renoir, had partly been financed by popular subscription: a two franc share entitled the holder to a deduction of the same amount on the price of a ticket after release of the film.[19] Dickinson's plan met with ready approval. The group decided to approach the LBC with the proposal for 'a fiction film of life in the Distressed Areas ... based on Miss Ellen Wilkinson's forthcoming book, *Jarrow: the Biography of a Town*'.[20] The choice of Wilkinson's book was unfortunate as it would only appear in September 1939 under the title *The Town that was Murdered*, but it is open to doubt whether the outbreak of war was the only reason for the failure of Dickinson's plan.

In the meantime, the LBC Film Group met every month. In April 1939 Wilfrid Roberts MP, director of the PFI, spoke on 'Film Propaganda in the Countryside'. In January 1938 Roberts had made 'an experimental tour of villages in [his] constituency in North Cumberland', showing a number of Kino films and some documentaries to various audiences.[21] Based on these experiences, Roberts proposed a national organisation for showing suitable films to audiences in the countryside. The Group took up Roberts's point and expressed its anxiety 'to arrange special programmes of films which can be available up and down the country and will have a very special appeal to the unconverted'.[22] In May, Cedric Belfrage proposed along similar lines the formation of an organisation of film audiences.[23] The French organisation of film spectators Ciné-Liberté had played a crucial part in getting the *Marseillaise* project off the ground, in close co-operation with the Syndicat Général des Travailleurs de l'Industrie du Film (the French equivalent of the ACT). The LBC Film Group kept on meeting, even after the start of the war, but the ideas it floated – however original and stimulating – were seldom put into practice. Typically, one of the most concrete plans – 'a new scheme for the provision of a selected programme of Left films for Left Book Club Groups' – entirely depended for its realisation on the co-operation of Kino, which became the sole supplier of films to the LBC Groups after the demise of the FPL.[24]

Kino adapted itself remarkably well to the special needs of the time. In the summer of 1938 it held a conference of its provincial representatives on the ways and means to make its, and therefore their, work more effective.[25] There is no report of this conference, so one can only guess at the meaning of the word 'effective'. Advertisements and reports in the left-wing press give some impression of how Kino saw its own work. In the first place, Kino stressed the quality of the product it was offering: 'a fully professional Film Service' and, above all, sound films.[26] Obviously, silent films were now considered to be inferior, a sign of amateurism. When, for example, Glasgow

Kino acquired a new sound projector, this was highlighted in the press.[27] In the spring of 1939, Kino even bought a daylight cinema van, which it sublet to the *Daily Worker* and the WFA.[28]

Politically, Kino was still closely following the line of the CPGB. Its new acquisitions included *If War Should Come*, a 50-minute Soviet film showing how the Red Army would beat back an attack from Nazi Germany; *Czechoslovakia*, an issue of the American screen magazine *The March of Time*; *Martyred Towns*, produced by the International Peace Campaign, compiled from newsreels, an indictment of the mass slaughter in Manchuria, Abyssinia, Spain and China; *Tenants on Strike*, the first issue of the American series *The World Today* (1936), an enacted film on the mortgage interest strike in Sunnyside, New York; *Fight to the Last*, a film on the Japanese aggression in China.[29] The British-produced films have already been mentioned: *XVth Congress Film*, *Britain Expects* (both PFI) and *Advance, Democracy!* (four London Co-ops). In 1939 two series of short films were added to the list: *Inside Nazi Germany*, *Nazi Conquest No.1 (Austria)*, *New Schools for Old*, *Juvenile Crime (USA)* (all from *The March of Time* series) and *New Moscow*, *Places and People*, *Soviet Parliament*, *Animal, Vegetable and Mineral*, *Soviet Sports*, *For the Young*, *Growing Up* and *Palace of Wonders* (showing a cross-section of life in the Soviet Union).[30] Conspicuous is the absence of 'entertainment' features among the new acquisitions. All were 'campaign' films, none longer than an hour. Because of their subject and length, they perfectly met the requirements of a typical left-wing meeting – allowing sufficient time for a speaker, singing, maybe a short theatre sketch and, inevitably, a collection for the good cause (Spain, China, refugees, etc.). With good reason Kino praised its films as crowd-pullers and money-raisers.

There is no doubt about the value of these film shows for the organised left. But a problem which kept haunting Kino was the impact of its films on the unconverted. When a *Daily Worker* reader complained, after having seen *If War Should Come*, about 'the same comrades attending, as usually attend these private shows,'[31] Kino's Frank Jackson immediately took up his pen, indignant at this accusation. He argued that 'the value of films is that they attract the outsider much more than an ordinary meeting, and make it very easy to get people outside the organised movement to come and hear what we have to say.'

Jackson pointed out that 'private' was a false denomination for 16mm film shows. Though they were not held in ordinary cinemas, they were nevertheless public events. He concluded:

> If at the moment the films do not reach as wide a public as those shown in the ordinary cinemas, this is not because of any defect inherent in 16mm films, but simply because the working-class movement in this country has not woken up to the enormous assistance films can be to them in their work.[32]

In the same vein, it was argued a few months later in *Left News* that 'films ... mobilise the hitherto disorganised but vaguely progressive feeling which is at present without a voice in the land'.[33] Notions on the relation between film aesthetics and politics and on the diversity of audiences (with films aiming at so-called target-groups), common property in 1970s and 80s film theory, are conspicuously absent. Therefore the embarrassment when Kino was faced with questions about the appeal of its films to the unconverted. To some extent, Kino anticipated this by designating some of its films (for example, *Britain Expects* and *The March of Time* series) as particularly suited to persuading the unconvinced. This, of course, did not solve the problem, which Kino still considered one of organisation.

Since the Jarrow case with its verdict on non-flam stock (see Chapter Three), Kino had experienced only relatively few problems with local authorities over contravention of the 1909 Cinematograph Act. In fact, there was a legal vacuum concerning non-flam stock. Some local councils felt that bluff could get them their way and a pretext was usually not difficult to find in order to ban a left film show. Surrey County Council went even further. It simply did not recognise the Jarrow verdict, declared all film stock inflammable and consequently required from organisers of 'sub-standard' film shows a licence as under the 1909 Cinematograph Act. By refusal of a licence, a number of Kino film shows in Surrey were effectively banned. Once more the National Council of Civil Liberties took up the case. In the end this resulted in the setting up of an Advisory Committee to the Home Office in October 1938. This committee, better known as Lord Stonehaven's Committee, asked various bodies concerned with the use of non-flam film for evidence. Kino and the PFI testified to the Commitee and submitted a nine-page joint memorandum.[34] The NCCL did likewise.[35] Both pleaded in favour of the status quo, that is freedom from the BBFC and the licensing authorities for 'sub-standard' film. In their memorandum Kino and PFI recommended the sending out of 'a simple memorandum to local authorities from the Home Office designed to secure consistency and end arbitrary pretensions such as those of the Surrey County Council'.[36] In August 1939 the Committee presented its conclusion to the Home Office. It argued that 'risk of panic amongst audiences at "non-flam" performances was extremely small', so there was no need for new legislation. Moreover, it held the view that

> those who are concerned with the production and exhibition of slow-burning films may in present circumstances be safely left with the responsibility for the contents of the films, and may be relied upon not to produce or exhibit films distasteful or offensive to the public.[37]

Whether the Home Office agreed with this conclusion is unknown. It hardly mattered, because war broke out within weeks of the appearance of the Stonehaven Committee's report.

A General Election was due to take place in 1940 at the latest, but some observers reckoned with an earlier date, given the mounting opposition to Chamberlain, even from within his own ranks. Late in 1938 Ivor Montagu was approached by the CPGB to make an election film for the party. It had to be a professionally-made sound film, but produced as cheaply as possible, as the CPGB's financial resources were limited. This meant that the film could only be made with a lot of outside assistance. The film's central theme – the struggle against the Chamberlain government – met with the approval of many, which eased Montagu's task of coaxing them into lending a helping hand. The mother of actress Elsa Lanchester made a puppet of Neville Chamberlain, which was to play an important part in the film. Bandleader Van Phillips composed a special score, which was used to great effect. Cameramen like Arthur Graham made themselves available for shooting. The Unity Theatre Mobile Group supplied actors for some short enacted sequences. Even Harry Pollitt went to the studio, to make a short speech which Montagu shot on 35mm colour stock. Pollitt's speech was the climax of the film; Montagu wanted the audience to be startled by the colours, so that they would not have the time to think 'another boring speech ...' To a great extent the film was composed of stock shots, taken from films in the libraries of Kino, PFI and the documentary film units, and of stills. This choice was not entirely determined by financial restraints. Stock shots and stills were a lot cheaper than freshly shot footage, but in addition the use of stills (Montagu went through hundreds of them) gave the film a special cachet.[38] The title of the film, *Peace and Plenty*, was derived from the slogan of the CPGB's XVth Congress. The film was a very powerful audiovisual adaption of Harry Pollitt's main Congress report.

Peace and Plenty starts with a shot of the cliffs of Dover. 'Our country,' says the commentator's voice, 'with its wealth,' (shots of the countryside) 'its industry,' (shots of industrial towns) 'it's traditions' (shots of a soccer match). This last illustration comes as a surprise. Of course, soccer was the popular game *par excellence*, but the spectator might have associated Britain's traditions with something more 'traditional' (the Changing of the Guard or the Boat Race). 'All this is ruled by Mr Chamberlain and the members of his National Cabinet', continues the commentator's voice. The Ministers are each introduced by means of a still, which does not show them at their most favourable. The film then sets out to examine the government's record, at home and abroad. The result is devastating. No wonder, demonstrates the film, because 'the National Government is a government for and of rich men'. This is shown by means of a series of 'deadly parallels'. For example, Lord Winterton. *Commentary*: 'Here is Lord Winterton. This property belongs to him.' *Image*: a portrait of the gentleman on the left side of the screen; on the right side a street with slum houses. *Commentary*: 'It was his wife who said the other day it was a pity the unemployed leaders had not been shot in Spain. The government has appointed Lord Winterton to deal with refugees.' *Image*: the same portrait of Lord Winterton on the left side, the shot with the slum dwellings on the right side fading. *Commentary*: 'He and his uncle own 28,000 acres.' *Image*: on the right side appears the figure 28,000 acres.

The film then examines Chamberlain's personal role, ending

Peace and Plenty, 1939; the Chamberlain puppet

with Munich and 'Peace in our time'. It demonstrates how
ridiculous the government's defence policy is, because: 'All
they really care about is this' (*commentary*), a blackboard with
profits and dividends of the big armament companies (*image*).
Then follows a speech choir: 'Stop! This government has done
enough. How can we get rid of them?' It is Harry Pollitt who
gives the answer, in a short outline of the party's programme:
the election of a democratic government with a works
programme, and an international anti-fascist alliance. When
Pollitt says 'End profiteering ...' the blackboard with the
profit and dividend figures is wiped clean; when he says
'Chamberlain must go', the puppet of Chamberlain is kicked
out of the frame.

Peace and Plenty is an exceptional film. It breaks completely
with the realist conventions which dominated left film making
in the 1930s. The only other film which had done so, was *Hell
Unltd.* by Helen Biggar and Norman McLaren (see Chapter
Six). The contemporary left press was very enthusiastic about
Peace and Plenty, and even *The Times* was favourably disposed.
Elizabeth Young of *Tribune* called it the 'Film That Flays
Chamberlain'.[39] Remarkably, none of the critics mentioned the
election film of the French Communist Party, *La Vie est à Nous*
(1936), which had been directed by Jean Renoir. In its theme,
its unorthodox use of filmic conventions and its agitprop
character, *Peace and Plenty* closely resembled the French film.
There is at least one direct 'quote' from *La Vie est à Nous* in
Peace and Plenty: a shot of Maurice Thorez, the General
Secretary of the PCF. Still, *Peace and Plenty* is far from a carbon
copy of the French film.[40] Kino released the film in March
1939, so that it could be used immediately in the struggle
against the Chamberlain government, even before the calling
of a General Election. There was a slight ambivalence about
this. If an organisation booked the film rightaway, would this
not spoil the film's use when it was really needed, during the
General Election campaign? In many cases, Communist Party
branches booked *Peace and Plenty* for internal use in order to
find out what it looked like. Thus they would be better
prepared for the public exhibition of the film during the
election campaign. MPs did not have to wait that long. On 14
June 1939 William Gallacher entertained them with a
screening of the film in the House of Commons. Quite a few

Tory MPs were highly impressed by the film, saying that the Conservative Party ought to have such an eloquent piece of propaganda.[41]

The Sussex County Communist Party showed *Peace and Plenty* on 27 August 1939, a special bonus for its members and sympathisers after the second Sussex People's History March, held that day in Eastbourne.[42] This would hardly have been worth mentioning if it had not been for the date (a few days after the signing of the Soviet-German non-aggression pact and a few days before the declaration of war) and for the fact that Sussex was the only Communist District to have its own newsreel crew. This People's Newsreel was composed of the Sussex District Organiser of the CPGB, Ernie Trory, of the artist Ralph Sydenham and amateur film maker Norman Trearson, who was not a party member. The group started in August 1938 and in the thirteen months of its existence shot material for two short films: *People' Scrapbooks 1938* and *1939*. The idea was very simple: to record with a 9.5mm camera events such as the 1938 Sussex People's History March, the celebration of the twenty-first anniversary of the Russian Revolution, the return of three International Brigaders, Brighton unemployed demonstrations, May Day 1939, Labour officials joining the CPGB and the second history march. The *People's Scrapbooks* were shown at party meetings and congresses, an attraction to new members and a means of putting heart into existing members. Unique was the concern, expressed by these newsreels, to record one's own history.[43]

The Film and Photo League would have had reason to cherish the People's Newsreel group, but after the departure of its London production group in the spring of 1938 (see Chapter Six) it had drifted helplessly towards its end. Political disillusion (the Soviet trials, the extermination of the POUM in Spain, the failure to build a Popular Front in Britain) was rampant.[44] Still photography could have been an ideal solution to the League's film production problems, especially in relationship to the LBC. But the League had always been more a Film than a Photo League. When it launched the idea in *The Left News* to promote still photography and photo montage, the response was negligible.[45] That the revival of the FPL had owed everything to its secretary became evident after Hugh Cuthbertson's departure from London. In 1939 even the membership fees were no longer collected. The League's financial situation was desperate. It had never set out to make a profit on its operations. With virtually no reserves and a restricted membership (in 1938 the FPL had 92 paid-up members), it became impossible to make ends meet. In March 1939 Cuthbertson made a last effort to get back the money loaned to ISF, so as to ease the situation. On behalf of ISF Ivan Seruya made clear that the company was in no position to repay its debt. Seruya showed no remorse: after all, the money had come from a particular windfall and how could the future of the FPL depend on windfalls?[46] In the end, the Committee decided to wind up the FPL. There was understandable reluctance to transfer the League's possessions to Kino. Instead, Cuthbertson approached Joseph Reeves of the WFA. A scheme for incorporation with the WFA was proposed, on condition that the basic aims of the League – to co-ordinate and direct amateur film making and to provide films for small groups at a low rate – would be maintained.[47] By that time the League's debts ran to £100, although Cuthbertson optimistically predicted they could be written down to £35. The sale of the League's Bolex film camera would make up for this sum.[48] It is not clear if the WFA accepted the offer, but the days of the Film and Photo League were definitely over.[49]

In his first year as Secretary-Organiser of the Workers' Film Association, Joseph Reeves had developed a great number of activities, and the WFA even made a small profit during its first year of operation. In the Annual Report it was stated that the Association did well in the sale of equipment and the production of films, but was still weak on road shows and film hire. This is confirmed by the figures on the balance sheet. Unfortunately, neither report nor balance sheet reveal the identity of the organisations (and individuals?), which had bought equipment from the WFA. On the production side, the WFA received commissions from the whole spectrum of the labour movement. Its first production was ordered by the RACS (a farewell present to Reeves?): a £1,200 film, showing past and present of the educational work undertaken by the Co-operative movement, entitled *People with a Purpose*. It was another example of the special interest in education held by the RACS, which had already produced a sound film on its own educational work, *Workers' Education*, in 1937.[50]

The Kino daylight van in 1939

People with a Purpose was made by the Realist Film Unit and directed by Ralph Bond. The Realist Film Unit also signed for the second production in the five-year plan of the London Co-ops (now five in number, instead of the previous four). It was *The Voice of the People* (directed by Frank Sainsbury and produced by Ralph Bond), a history of the struggle of the British people against oppression from the early nineteenth century onwards. *People with a Purpose* and *The Voice of the People* were released after the war had started, which seriously handicapped their distribution, despite a sympathetic review in *The Times*.[51] Reeves personally directed a 16mm film, commissioned by the Camberwell Borough Council, *Camberwell is Prepared*. The title referred to the Borough's Air Raid Precautions and it was also known as the 'ARP Film'. The WFA hired Kino's daylight cinema van in the summer of 1939 and toured the country for a month, exhibiting *Camberwell is Prepared* everywhere possible. Two trade unions commissioned films from the WFA, which could not be finished because of the outbreak of the war: *The Jubilee* for the National Society of Operative Printers and Assistants, and *The Builders* for the Amalgamated Union of Building Trade Workers. A special *WFA-Newsreel*, which included colour footage of the 1939 London May Day procession (with a WFA tableau!), was compiled. Furthermore, the WFA produced two silent films: *Sport* for the British Workers' Sports' Association and *The Children's Republic* for the Woodcraft Folk. The most unusual production – typical of Reeves's ingenuity – was a trailer, which could be used by Co-operative societies ordering regular weekly programmes from the WFA. This trailer, set to the music of Parry's 'Jerusalem', appealed to the audience to find out more about their local Co-op. Twenty copies of it were sold. The WFA too had been making preparations for the General Election: a film on the Labour Party leaders was ready and only needed a topical commentary to be added. A remarkable record for what was virtually a one-man operation.[52]

On the distribution side, the WFA did not meet with the same success. Although its own library was growing, it was still very much dependent on other companies for its films. Kino was one of these. In January 1939 Kino was also 'appointed projection agent for the London and Home Counties area' to the WFA.[53] In a similar way the PFI handled all the WFA's 35mm films. Reeves knew that such outside assistance would be needed until the labour movement started taking film seriously and using it on a large scale. When he circularised all the trade unions with the request to organise a film show in the period of their annual meetings, only two replied favourably. The WFA also organised two film conferences, in association with the Leeds and Newcastle Divisional Labour Parties respectively. As a result of the Newcastle Conference, 'trade unions in the County of Durham were circularised for contributions towards a "Film Fund" which would enable the workers' movements in that county to have their own film units'. This 'Film Fund' project never got off the ground as a result of the outbreak of the war.[54]

After Chamberlain's return from Berchtesgaden with his famous piece of paper, many people really believed that the Prime Minister had secured 'Peace in our time'. This illusion was soon eroded, when Hitler made his way into Czechoslovakia. On the left, warnings against Chamberlain's appeasement policy were sounded over and again. The right-wing Labour leadership, however, did not hesitate to expel members like Sir Stafford Cripps, Aneurin Bevan and G.R. Strauss for the heresy of advocating a Popular Front against the Chamberlain Government.[55] In the summer of 1939 the international situation again deteriorated. Hitler had set his eyes on Poland, which Great Britain and France were bound by treaty to assist in case of foreign aggression. While Britain and France were protracting negotiations with the Soviet Union over a collective security alliance against Germany, they were taken by surprise when the Soviet Union and Germany signed a non-aggression pact on 23 August. Their hope that Germany would exhaust itself in a war with the Soviet Union was shattered. On 1 September Germany invaded Poland and on 3 September Great Britain and France declared war on Germany.

The war had disastrous consequences for the left-wing film movement. From the beginning it became impossible to continue business as usual. In the first weeks of the war all cinemas and theatres were closed by the Home Office. After this ban was relaxed, it was followed by the black-out, evacuations and the call-up. Moreover, within weeks the

Ministry of Information took complete control over all film activities in the country. This meant that 'sub-standard' films which displeased the Ministry could now be banned or censored without any problems. The supply of films from abroad also came under its control. It goes without saying that the import of films from the Soviet Union came to a complete halt.

But the most far-reaching consequences stemmed from the differing interpretations of the war within the labour movement. Was it an anti-fascist or an imperialist war? The Labour Party and TUC condemned the signing of the Soviet-German pact in August, and loyally supported the war effort. This policy paved the way for the entry of the Labour Party into a coalition Cabinet with the Tories. This happened in May 1940, after Churchill had replaced Chamberlain as Prime Minister. On the other hand, the CPGB opposed the war as an imperialist one. It came to this interpretation after initial support for the war, and under strong pressure from the Comintern. It was based on the Soviet Union's neutrality with regard to what was considered a conflict between the European imperialist powers: a conflict from which the working class had nothing to gain; on the contrary, it had to defend its rights and standard of living against attacks from its own government. This volte-face by the CPGB created much confusion and it made the arguments presented in a film like *Peace and Plenty* completely obsolete.[56]

After Kino had overcome the initial surprise created by the war and the consequences of the new CPGB line, it managed to adapt its operations to the new exigencies. It released a new Soviet film, *The Rich Bride* (1938), a musical set in a Ukrainian collective farm. The film had previously been available on 35mm from the PFI. For the rest, Kino offered films dealing with rent struggles (including a film on the rent strikes in the East End of London, *Tenants in Revolt*), trade union recruitment and anti-fascist work. Kino kept a low profile with regard to the political conflicts between Labour and CPGB.[57] In spring 1939 the PFI had released the Soviet feature film *Professor Mamlock* (1938). It was initially banned by the BBFC, but later permitted in a censored version. *Professor Mamlock* (1938) was based on a play by Friedrich Wolf, a German doctor and playwright living in exile in the Soviet Union. The film treated the persecution of the Jews in Nazi Germany. The PFI did not withdraw it after the CPGB's new position on the war had become clear.[58] Interestingly, *Professor Mamlock* became a film which united audiences: those who believed in the anti-fascist character of the war wanted to see it because it denounced Nazi anti-Semitism; those who considered the war as an imperialist one were no less anxious to see it, because it was after all a Soviet film.[59] When Germany invaded the Soviet Union in 1941, a new propaganda effort began in favour of British-Soviet friendship and the establishment of a Second Front. This required a new alignment and concentration of resources, resulting in the winding-up of Kino and the PFI.

The only organisation to survive the war was the WFA. In September 1939, it had adapted its activities to the needs of the time by organising film shows for evacuees, using the seven portable projectors owned by the five London Co-ops and its own film library.[60] But the WFA soon lost Joseph Reeves to the Ministry of Information (where his talents were never really appreciated). Due to the war, the WFA had to stop film production, undoubtedly its most successful activity. The five-year plan of the London Co-ops could not be completed. The departure of Reeves and the interruption of the production activities fundamentally changed the organisation's character: it became respectable rather than dynamic. In 1942 the WFA was registered as a Co-operative Society. Grants from the Labour Party and TUC kept it afloat. Distribution of films and organisation of film conferences were its main activities until the end of the war.[61] Ironically, the election of a Labour government in 1945 made a return to pre-war conditions impossible for the WFA: Labour in power in fact ruled out the oppositional film practice the WFA had tried carry out before the war, especially in the realm of Labour film production.

There is no doubt that the war acted as the great divide for the left-wing film movement in Great Britain. It is only with great difficulty that one can find examples in the post-war period of film making of the kind practised by Kino, the Film and Photo League, the Progressive Film Institute or the Workers' Film Association. Ralph Bond (again!) tried to set the example in 1945 with *Unity is Strength* for the Amalgamated Engineering Union, but the trade-union movement failed to respond. Derek York and Walter Lassally made *Smith, Our Friend* (1946) in the vein of a Film and Photo League production. This silent 16mm film on a demobbed soldier who returns to a slum, gets nowhere with the housing authorities and therefore joins the squatters in Bloomsbury, contains enacted parts and documentary footage. But these films where the exception which confirmed the rule.

The workers' and left film groups of the 1930s had sprung from direct political needs. The Comintern's 'Class against Class' policy, for example, implied a struggle by the workers on the cultural front, which led to the foundation of workers' film societies and the making of workers' newsreels. The use of 16mm stock offered a way around the censorship problems with Soviet films. Moreover, the 16mm format was relatively cheap and easy to handle, so that the groups could produce their own films to complement the Soviet films. In the second half of the 1930s the 16mm format turned out to be eminently suited for use in anti-fascist campaigns. Compared to attendances in the commercial cinemas, the audiences these films attracted were limited, but there is no doubt that these film-shows served their purpose, as was shown by the £6,000 *Defence of Madrid* raised for aid to Spain.

During the war anti-fascism became the government's official policy. The 16mm format was used by the Ministry of Information in order to reach ordinary citizens in factory canteens, schools, clubs, etc. But do these changes explain the almost complete disappearance of left-wing film-making after the war? Of course, with Labour in power after the 1945 elections, the need for an oppositional cinema could easily be dismissed by a party (and trade union movement) which had always shown a great reluctance to use the film medium in the furtherance of its cause. Moreover, the Communist movement, while retaining a strong interest in the distribution and exhibition of Soviet films, no longer saw the absolute need of a film production of its own. In the 1930s it had encouraged (or at least tolerated) a type of amateur film-making trimmed to its financial limitations, but by setting professional standards for its films in the post-war period it virtually killed any prospects. Last, but not least, one gets the impression that the general cultural climate after the war did little to encourage political expression in the arts.

It was with the student revolts of the late 1960s and the resurgence of working-class militancy of the early 1970s (the work-in at the Upper Clyde shipyards, the 1972 and 1974 miners' strikes) that film production comparable to that of the 1930s emerged, with the activities of groups like Cinema Action, Berwick Street Collective, Amber Films, Newsreel Collective and others. Since video has offered favourable conditions for use in political campaigns – it might be considered the 16mm stock of the 1980s: cheap, easy to record and distribute – a whole range of video collectives and groups has sprung up. If one may speak of lessons learnt from the 1930s, it is in the video area that one can find the most outstanding example: the Miners' Video Campaign Tapes. Six tapes were produced from footage shot by a number of film and video collectives all over Great Britain, supported by the Association of Cine and Television Technicians and the National Union of Journalists and endorsed by many National Union of Mineworkers areas, in support of the 1984-85 miners' strike. The tapes, distributed in enormous quantities to local NUM branches, constituency Labour parties, trade unions and the like, remind one of the 1930's films in their agitprop style. But I think it is more than symbolic that one finds the names of the late Ivor Montagu and of Ralph Bond among those who contributed financially to the making of the videos, on the credits of the Miners' Video Campaign Tapes. After all, to paraphrase the words of Ralph Bond, they are 'videos with a purpose'.

Notes

1. *Daily Worker*, 29 October 1938, p.5; for a review see *Daily Worker*, 5 October 1938, p.5. Unfortunately the prints of the *XVth Congress Film* which have survived are silent.
2. *Daily Worker*, 29 October 1938, p.5.
3. Public Record Office, London, Home Office 45/17415.
4. 'Kino Presents ...', catalogue published by Kino [1938], p.1 (in MWCML).
5. Reports from Commissioner of Police (28 October 1938), from Home Office to Commissioner (29 November 1938) and from Scotland Yard (30 November 1938), in Public Record Office, London, Home Office 45/17415.
6. Public Record Office, London, Home Office 45/17415.
7. Ibid.
8. Cf. Kino advertisement: '[the *XVth Congress Film*] will greatly help you to

recruit to the Party and get a mass sale of the Congress Reports.' (*Daily Worker*, 29 October 1938, p.5).

9. *Daily Herald*, 9 December 1938, p.5.

10. Ibid.

11. Ibid.

12. *Left News* No.33, January 1939, p.1136.

13. *Tribune*, 27 January 1939, p.19.

14. *Daily Herald*, 14 December 1938, p.13. The Duchess of Atholl was a Conservative MP who went into opposition against her party's policy on Spain. In 1938 she published *Searchlight on Spain*, a Penguin Special. Because of her sympathies for Republican Spain she often shared the platform with left-wingers and was nicknamed the 'Red' Duchess.

15. Ivor Montagu interview, 8 March 1978. Only a silent workprint of this film has survived, which still conveys something of the atmosphere of the event.

16. See for example, G.R. Strauss, 'British Film Racketeers: Sordid Facts Behind Studio Glamour' in *Tribune*, 19 November 1937, p.16. ACT activist Ralph Bond wrote an excellent article, 'A Bit of Gristle for the Starving Dog: The British Film Industry Between Life and Death' in *Left Review*, March 1938, pp.845-9. For a history of the ACT in the 1930s see Michael Chanan, *Labour Power in the British Film Industry*, London 1976, pp.23-44.

17. *Left News*, December 1938, p.1094; *Tribune*, 2 December 1938, p.15. The *Daily Worker* published a report of the meeting in its issue of 22 December 1938, p.2.

18. *Tribune*, 27 January 1939, p.19.

19. See Goffredo Fofi, 'The Cinema of the Popular Front in France (1934-38)' in *Screen*, Vol.13 no.4, Winter 1972/73, pp.5-57; Pascal Ory, 'De "Ciné-Liberté" à *La Marseillaise*: Espoirs et limites d'un cinéma libèrè (1936-1938)' in *Le Mouvement Social* no.91, April-June 1975, pp.153-75; Elizabeth Grottle Strebel, *French Social Cinema of the Nineteen Thirties: A Cinematographic Expression of Popular Front Consciousness*, New York 1980.

20. *Cine-Technician*, March-April 1939, p.182.

21. For a report of this tour see Wilfrid Roberts, MP, 'Films for the Countryside' in *Left Review*, March 1938, pp.852-3.

22. *Tribune*, 12 May 1939, p.6.

23. *Left News*, June 1939, p.1302; *Tribune*, 26 May 1939, p.18.

24. *Left News*, July 1939, p.1331, p.1338.

25. *Forward*, 18 June 1938, p.11.

26. *Tribune*, 3 February 1939, p.16.

27. *Forward*, 8 October 1938, p.2; 29 October 1938, p.2; *Scottish Co-operator*, 22 October 1938, p.1180.

28. *Daily Worker*, 5 August 1939, p.3; Workers' Film Association, *Annual Report and Balance Sheet for the year ended with September 30th, 1939*, p.1 (in TUC Library).

29. Cf. Kino advertisements in the *Daily Worker*, 29 October 1938, p.5; *Tribune*, 3 February 1939, p.16.

30. *Left News* March 1939, p.1205.

31. *Daily Worker*, 28 December 1938, p.2.

32. Ibid., 4 January 1939, p.2.

33. *Left News*, March 1939, p.1205.

34. Public Record Office, London, Home Office 45/21109.

35. Public Record Office, London, Metropolitan Police 2/5073.

36. Public Record Office, London, Home Office 45/21109.

37. *Daily Herald*, 8 August 1939, p.10.

38. Ivor Montagu, interviews with the author, Watford, 6 September 1974 and London, 8 March 1978. An article, signed by 'A Helper', on the making of *Peace and Plenty* appeared in the *Daily Worker*, 21 April 1939, p.2.

39. *Tribune*, 31 March 1939, p.19. Other reviews appeared in the *Daily Worker*, 21 April 1939, p.2, *New Statesman and Nation*, 22 April 1939, p.607, *The Times*, 20 April 1939, p.12.

40. It would be interesting to make a comparative study of *La Vie est à Nous, Peace and Plenty* and the Dutch CP's election film *Land in Zicht* (1937), directed by Joris Ivens' assistant John Fernhout. Each film embodied the Popular Front idea in a typically national way. Each clearly shows the hand of its director, yet these films resemble each other closely.

41. Ivor Montagu, interview with the author, Watford, 6 September 1974; *The Times*, 15 June 1939, p.8.

42. Ernie Trory, *Between the Wars: Recollections of a Communist Organiser*, Brighton 1974, p.158.

43. Paragraph based on an exchange of letters between the author and Ernie Trory, and Trory, op.cit., passim.

44. Already in the summer of 1937 an FPL member, cameraman Pete Davis, expressed his doubts. He had been asked by Cuthbertson to be present at the LBC summer school, but replied: '(...) As for holding aloft the FPL torch, with things as they are at present, and with all respect and appreciation of the work you and a few others have put in, I feel I must say "why hold it aloft any longer? Don't your arms ache? Anyway, have we a torch? Can Kino or any left film organisation still claim to be a "Progressive Movement"? Apart from all this, my views on Spain are pretty sure to prove unpalatable to respectably conservative Communists of the LBC. (...)' (in FPLa).

45. *Left News*, July 1939, p.907.

46. Ivan Seruya to Hugh Cuthbertson, postcard, 8 March 1939 (in FPLa).

47. Hugh Cuthbertson to Joseph Reeves, typewritten letter, 5 July 1939 (in FPLa).

48. Hugh Cuthbertson to Joseph Reeves, handwritten letter, 5 July 1939 (in FPLa).

49. There is no mention of incorporation of the FPL in the WFA's *Annual Report* for 1939. It seems more likely that Cuthbertson himself somehow cleared the League's debts, in exchange for which he became the custodian of its heritage. Shortly before his death in 1976, Jonathan Lewis and Elizabeth Taylor-Mead of Metropolis Pictures rescued the FPL archive, consisting of some 90 reels of film and two boxes of paperwork.

50. Attfield, op.cit., p.55.

51. *The Times*, 26 September 1939, p.6.

52. Workers' Film Association, *Annual Report and Balance Sheet for the year ended with September 30th, 1939* (in TUC Library).

53. *Tribune*, 3 February 1939, p.16.

54. See note 52.

55. Interestingly, Cripps, Bevan and Strauss were all involved in the left film movement. Cripps was a member of Kino's General Council, as was Bevan

whose name also figured on the letterhead of ISF. Strauss was an amateur film maker, whose films on his trips to the Soviet Union and Spain, Russia, 1936 and Spain To-day, were distributed by Kino.

56. See John Attfield and Stephen Williams (eds), *1939: The Communist Party and the War*, London 1984.

57. C.f. an undated circular (1940?) from Kino Film Services, W.G. Alexander, London, quoting examples of film shows held by the North Hackney Labour Party, Brighton CP, Russia Today Society and Civil Servants LBC.

58. *Professor Mamlock* may have been withdrawn at a later stage at the request of the Soviet authorities. Hetty Bower who worked for Kino at the time, the 16mm distributors of the film, has recalled how she got the news of the withdrawal in Attfield and Williams (eds), op.cit, pp.60-1. In his classic history of the Soviet cinema, *Kino*, Jay Leyda confirms this: [After August 1939] 'all films attacking the German government and Hitler's brand of fascism were withdrawn from Soviet distribution. Abroad, the same films were removed from circulation whenever the distributor operated on terminable lease. In those circumstances where *Mamlock* had been sold outright, it continued to be shown for a while, giving courage to the badly shaken anti-fascist forces ...' Jay Leyda, *Kino: A History of the Russian and Soviet Film*, London 1973, p.356.

59. See Ernie Trory, *Imperialist War: Further Recollections of a Communist Organiser*, Brighton 1977, pp.57-8, for reactions to the exhibition of *Professor Mamlock* in Brighton. The Tredegar Workmen's Institute booked the film in November 1939; see Minutes of the Cinema Committee, Tredegar Workmen's Institute, 12 October and 16 November 1939 (in UCS).

60. *Daily Herald*, 27 September 1939, p.3.

61. See *Annual Conference Reports* of the Labour Party for 1940-1945.

Filmography

The following filmography lists in alphabetical order the films produced by the various film groups mentioned in this book. Ideally, each entry consists of the following: title, credits, technical data, print location, date of first screening and a short description of the film's contents when these are not clear from the text or title. One or more of these elements may be lacking due to absence of data. Where known, I have listed alternative titles between brackets. Silent films could be shown at a variety of speeds, ranging from 24 to 16 frames per second. For example, a silent 35mm film of 900 feet, shown at 24 frames per second (sound speed), will last 10 minutes, but the same film shown at 16 frames per second will last 5 minutes longer. Moreover, the accurate speed may vary within one film, depending on the number of turns with which the cameraman originally cranked his camera. Even with sound films, the running time as given in catalogues or advertisements could vary considerably. Thus *Peace and Plenty* is listed as a film running 25 or even 30 minutes, but the surviving print runs only for 18 (at 24 frames per second). Therefore I have listed, if possible, the length of the films in feet, based on surviving prints, this being the only accurate measure.

I am aware that deficiencies and inconsistencies may be discovered in the filmography. I have, for example, not included any advertising films of the Co-operative Wholesale Society or travel films of the Workers' Travel Association, as I consider them outside the scope of this book. Of the foreign films made available for distribution in Great Britain by the film groups mentioned in this book, I have only listed those which were substantially altered or recut by their British distributors. Thus I have excluded *Hunger in Waldenburg* (recut for British distribution by its author Piel Jutzi) or *Turksib* (English titling done by John Grierson), while I have included *Free Thaelmann!*, which was recut by members of the Progressive Film Institute in such a way that it became a different film from the American original. Like retitling, I do not consider the change of soundtrack a sufficiently decisive interference with a film to warrant a listing in this filmography. Thus Spanish Republican propaganda films, like *Non-Intervention* (1937), with an English-language soundtrack made by the Progressive Film Institute, are not included.

I hope this filmography will function as a companion to the one compiled by Trevor Ryan and published (unfortunately not as completely as Ryan had wished) in Don Macpherson (ed.), in collaboration with Paul Willemen, *Traditions of Independence: British Cinema in the Thirties*, London 1979, pp.208-224, which includes not only films produced by the film groups mentioned, but also those distributed or exhibited by them.

Abbreviations

asst.	– assistant
b/w	– black and white
d.	– director
d.c.	– distribution company
ed.	– editor
ETV	– Educational and Television Films
FPL	– Film and Photo League
m.	– music
NFA	– National Film Archive
p.	– producer
p.c.	– production company
PFI	– Progressive Film Institute
ph.	– photographer/cameramen
sc.	– scriptwriter
SFC	– Socialist Film Council
sp.	– sponsor
WFA	– Workers' Film Association

ADVANCE, DEMOCRACY (1938)
pc. Realist Film Unit, in association with Basil Wright, for the Four London Co-operative Societies; d., sc. Ralph Bond; ph. Gerald Gibbs; asst.d. Gerald Keen and A.E. Jeakins; m. Benjamin Britten, performed by the Norbury Co-operative Choral Society and R.F. Ransom; cast Fred Baker, Kathleen Gibbons; d.c. Workers' Film Association
35mm b/w, sound, 1600 ft.
print location: NFA, ETV
first screening: October 1938

AGAINST IMPERIALIST WAR – MAY DAY 1932 (alt. title WORKERS' TOPICAL NEWS No.4) (1932)
asst. Ivan Seruya
16mm, b/w, silent, 316 ft.
print location: NFA

THE AWAKENING OF MR COLE (1938)
p.c. Pelly & Healy; d. John Ferguson; sc. Richard J. Wilson; supervised by Frank H.W. Cox for the Political Committee of the London Co-operative Society; d.c. Workers' Film Association

BEHIND THE SPANISH LINES (1938)
p.c. Progressive Film Institute; d. Sidney Cole; ph. Arthur Graham, Alan Lawson; asst. Philip Leacock, Ray Pitt; supervised by Ivor Montagu; d.c. PFI, Kino (for 16mm version)
35mm, b/w, sound, 1797 ft.
print location: NFA, ETV
first screening: 26 June 1938, London

BIRMINGHAM MAY DAY PROCESSION (1936)
p.c., d.c. Birmingham People's Film Service.
16mm

BLOW, BUGLES, BLOW (1934)
p.c. Socialist Film Council; d. Rudolph Messel; sc. Raymond Postgate; ph. Leon Isaac; continuity Daisy Postgate; cast John Arnold, Terence Greenidge, George Hicks and others; d.c. SFC, from 1936 Progressive Film Institute, from 1938 Independent Labour Party

35mm, b/w, sound, 6721 ft.
print location: NFA
first screening: October 1934

BREAD (1934)
p.c. Kino; d. Sidney Moir; cast Sam Serter and others; d.c.
Kino
16mm, b/w, silent, 287 ft.
print location: NFA
first screening: May 1934

BRITAIN EXPECTS (1938)
p.c. Progressive Film Institute; d. Ivor Montagu; ed. Bill
Megarry; d.c. PFI, Kino (for 16mm version)
35mm, b/w, sound
first screening: December 1938

THE BUILDERS (1939)
p.c. Workers' Film Association for the Amalgamated Union of
Building Trade Workers
Note – this film may not have been completed.

BUILDING THE PEOPLE'S FRONT IN ENGLAND (1937)
p.c. Film and Photo League
16mm, b/w, silent
Note – this film was never completed.

BUSMEN'S HOLIDAY (1937)
p.c. Kino (?)
16mm, b/w and colour, silent
print location: NFA, ETV
Note – this film may not have been released.

CAMBERWELL IS PREPARED (1939)
p.c. Workers' Film Association for the Camberwell Borough
Council; d. Joseph Reeves; d.c. WFA
16mm, b/w, sound
first screening: June 1939

CHALLENGE OF YOUTH (alt. title YOUTH MARCHES ON) (1937)
p.c. Film and Photo League for the Socialist Youth Camp; d.c. FPL
16mm, b/w, silent
first screening: December 1937

CHALLENGE TO FASCISM (alt. title GLASGOW'S MAY DAY) (1938)
p.c. Glasgow Kino Film Group for the Glasgow Trades Council and Burgh Labour Party; d. Helen Biggar; d.c. Glasgow Kino
16mm, b/w, silent, 605 ft.
print location: NFA
first screening: July 1938

THE CHILDREN'S REPUBLIC (1939)
p.c. Workers' Film Association for the Woodcraft Folk; ph. Tom Barnes; d.c. WFA
16mm, b/w, silent

CONSTRUCTION (1935)
p.c. Film and Photo League; ph. Alf Garrard; asst. Hugh Campbell, Alf Pizer; ed. Bill Megarry; d.c. Kino, from 1937 FPL
16mm, b/w, silent, 269 ft.
print location: NFA
first screening: December 1935

CORONATION MAY DAY (alt. title THE MERRY MONTH OF MAY) (1937)
p.c., d.c. Film and Photo League
16mm, b/w and colour, silent, 419 ft.
print location: NFA (incomplete)

CRIME AGAINST MADRID (1937)
p.c. Progressive Film Institute; d.c. Kino
16mm, b/w, sound, [30 mins.]
first screening: July 1937

DAILY WORKER FILM (1937)
p.c., d.c. Kino

16mm, b/w, silent, 72 ft.
print location: NFA
first screening: December 1937

DEFENCE OF BRITAIN (1935)
p.c. Film and Photo League; members of production group
Frank Jackson, John Maltby, Paul Bradshaw, Jean Ross; d.c.
Kino
16mm, b/w, silent, [10 mins.]

DEFENCE OF MADRID (1936)
p.c. Progressive Film Institute; d. Ivor Montagu; ph. Norman
McLaren, Ivor Montagu; ed. Bill Megarry; d.c. Kino
16mm, b/w [and colour], silent, 1210 ft.
print location: NFA, ETV
first screening: 28 December 1936, London

DOCKWORKERS (1937)
p.c. Film and Photo League; d. Herbert A. Green; d.c. FPL
16mm, b/w, silent, 320 ft.
print location: NFA

ESPERANTO – THE WORKERS' WEAPON (alt. title THE RISING STAR) (1936)
p.c. Manchester Film and Photo League for the Esperanto
Club, Manchester

XVTH CONGRESS FILM (1938)
p.c. Progressive Film Institute; d. Ivor Montagu; d.c. Kino
16mm, b/w, silent, 318 ft.
print location: NFA, ETV
first screening: October 1938

FIGHT (alt. title STRIFE) (1935)
p.c. Workers' Film and Photo League; members of production
group R. Burke, Hetty Vorhaus, Frank Cox, N. Boddington,
Sam Serter; d.c. from 1937 FPL
16mm, b/w, silent, 618 ft.
print location: NFA
Note – this film came under considerable criticism and was not
released until 1937, under a new title: STRIFE.

FREE THAELMANN! (1935)
p.c. Progressive Film Institute for the Relief Committee for the Victims of German Fascism: d. Ivor Montagu; d.c. PFI, Kino (for 16mm version)
35mm, b/w, silent, 1670 ft.
print location: NFA, ETV
first screening: 26 July 1935, London

Note – this film is a re-edited, shortened version of *Ernst Thaelmann – Fighter against Fascism* (USA 1934 – p.c. Garrison Film Distributors Inc. for the Thaelmann Liberation Committee; ed. George Moscov; supervised by Tom Brandon); no prints of this version are known to have survived.

GENEROUS SOIL (1937)
p.c. Film and Photo League
16mm, b/w, silent

GLIMPSES OF MODERN RUSSIA (1930)
p.c. Atlas Film Co. for the Federation of Workers' Film Societies; ed. Ralph Bond; d.c. Atlas Film Co.
35mm, b/w silent, 1025 ft.
print location: NFA
first screening: 26 October 1930, London

HELL UNLTD. (1936)
d. Helen Biggar, Norman McLaren; ph. William J. MacLean; cast Ian Fleming, teachers and students of the Glasgow School of Arts; d.c. Glasgow Kino, Kino
16mm, b/w, silent, 520 ft.
print location: NFA
first screening: June 1936, Glasgow

HELP SPAIN (1938)
p.c. Kino for the National Joint Committee for Spanish Relief; d., ph. James Calvert; d.c. Kino
16mm, b/w [and colour], [40 mins.]

A HOLIDAY FROM UNEMPLOYMENT (1935)
p.c. O & S for the South Wales Miners' Holiday Camp, 1935; members of production group E. Stich, John Turner, Sam

Handel, Herbert Green, Alf Pizer, Phil Leacock, P. Rhodes; d.c. Kino
16mm, b/w, silent, [15 mins.]
first screening: September 1935

HUNGER MARCH (1934)
p.c. Kino; ph. Sidney Moir and others; d.c. Kino
16mm, b/w, silent, 400 ft.
print location: NFA
first screening: March 1934

INTERNATIONAL BRIGADE (alt. title INTERNATIONAL COLUMN) (1937)
p.c. Progressive Film Institute; d., ph. Vera Elkan; d.c. Kino
16mm, b/w, silent, 450 ft.
print location: NFA, ETV
first screening: April 1937

INTERNATIONAL BRIGADE EMPRESS HALL RALLY (1939)
p.c. Association of Cine-Technicians
35mm, b/w, silent, 576 ft.
print location: NFA
Note – this film was never completed.

JUBILEE (1935)
p.c. North London Film Society, Workers' Film and Photo League; d., ph. Herbert A. Green, R. Green; ed. Herbert A. Green, Sam Handel, Alf Pizer; d.c. Kino (for 16mm version), from 1937 FPL
35mm, b/w, silent, 586 ft.; 16mm, b/w, silent, 250 ft.
print location: NFA, ETV
first screening: September 1935
Note – this film was originally shot on 35mm; a re-edited 16mm version with additional footage was made by the Workers' Film and Photo League.

KINO NEWS REVIEW (1937)
p.c., d.c. Kino
16mm, b/w, silent, [30 mins.]

LIVERPOOL – GATEWAY OF EMPIRE (1933)
p.c. Merseyside Workers' Film Society; ph. John Maltby
16mm, b/w, silent
print location: NFA

MARTYRED TOWNS (1938)
p.c. International Peace Campaign; d.c. Kino
16mm, b/w, sound
first screening: September 1938

MARCH AGAINST STARVATION (1936)
p.c. Film and Photo League; members of production group
Helen Biggar, Michael Burke, Sam Feld, H. Kay, H. Ludlow,
Rudolph Messel, W. Richardson, Ivan Seruya, Sime Seruya,
E.D. Stich; d.c. FPL
16mm, b/w, silent, 845 ft.
print location: NFA
first screening: April 1937
Note – a shortened version of this film was also released by the
FPL.

MAY DAY 1933 (1933)
16mm, b/w, silent, 275 ft.

MAY DAY, 1938 (1938)
p.c., d.c. Kino
16mm

MAY DAY, GLASGOW 1937 (1937)
p.c. Clarion Film Society
first screening: November 1937

MAY THE FIRST 1937 (alt. title THE SPIRIT OF MAY DAY)
(1937)
p.c., d.c. Film and Photo League
16mm, b/w, silent, 350 ft.
print location: NFA

MODERN ORPHANS OF THE STORM (1937)
p.c. Victor Saville Productions and Realist Film Unit for the
National Joint Committee for Spanish Relief; d.c. Kino (for
16mm version)
35mm, b/w, sound, 972 ft.
print location: NFA

MR ATTLEE IN SPAIN (1938)
p.c. Progressive Film Institute; d.c. PFI, Kino (for 16mm version)
35mm, b/w, silent, 459 ft.
print location: NFA

NATSOPA'S JUBILEE (1939)
p.c. Workers' Film Association for the National Society of Operative Printers and Assistants
16mm, sound
Note – this film may not have been completed.

NEWS FROM SPAIN (1937)
p.c. Progressive Film Institute; d. Herbert Marshall; commentary spoken by Isabel Brown; d.c. PFI, Kino (for 16mm version)
35mm, b/w, sound, 3320 ft.
print location: NFA, ETV
first screening: 14 April 1937, London

1931 – THE CHARTER FILM (1931)
p.c. Atlas Film Co. for the Federation of Workers' Film Societies; ed. Ralph Bond; d.c. Atlas Film Co.
35mm, b/w, silent, [2000 ft.]
first screening: 3 May 1931, London

PEACE AND PLENTY (1939)
p.c. Progressive Film Institute for the Communist Party of Great Britain; d. Ivor Montagu; ph. Arthur Graham and others; ed. Bill Megarry; m. Van Phillips; puppet of Neville Chamberlain made by Mrs Lanchester; d.c. Kino
16mm, b/w [and colour], sound, 620 ft.
print location: NFA, ETV
first screening: April 1939

THE PEACE PARADE (1937)
p.c. Pelly & Healy; supervised by Frank H.W. Cox for the Political Committee of the London Co-operative Society
16mm, b/w
first screening: October 1937

A PENNY TO SPEND (1937)
p.c. Film and Photo League
16mm, b/w, silent
Note – this film may not have been completed.

PEOPLE'S SCRAPBOOK 1938 (1938)
p.c. People's Newsreels for the Sussex District of the CPGB; d. Ernie Trory; ph. Norman Trearson; asst. Ralph Sydenham; d.c. People's Newsreels
9.5mm, b/w, silent, [5 mins.]
print location: NFA, ETV (16mm blow-up)

PEOPLE WITH A PURPOSE (1939)
p.c. Realist Film Unit for the Workers' Film Association; d. Ralph Bond; sp. Royal Arsenal Co-operative Society; d.c. WFA
35mm, b/w, sound
print location: ETV (16mm print)
first screening: September 1939

THE PEOPLE WHO COUNT (1937)
p.c. Pelly & Healy; d. Geoffrey Collyer; asst. John Ferguson; commentary by A.V. Alexander; supervised by Frank H.W. Cox for the Political Committee of the London Co-operative Society
16mm, b/w, sound, 698 ft.
print location: NFA
first screening: October 1937

PRISONERS PROVE INTERVENTION IN SPAIN (1938)
p.c. Progressive Film Institute; d. Ivor Montagu; d.c. PFI
35mm, b/w, sound, 417 ft
print location: NFA
first screening: April 1938

RED, RIGHT AND BLOO (1937)
p.c., d.c. Film and Photo League
16mm, b/w, silent, 851 ft.
print location: NFA
first screening: October 1937

REVOLT OF THE FISHERMEN (1935)
p.c. Film and Photo League; d., ph. Michael Burke, Adrianne Hanné; d.c. from 1937 FPL
16mm, b/w, silent, 324 ft.
print location: NFA

RHONDDA (1935)
d. Donald Alexander, Judy Birchwood, B. Balfour
sp. Film and Photo League
16mm, b/w, silent, [10 mins.]
print location: NFA, ETV (incomplete)
first screening: January 1936

THE ROAD TO HELL (1933)
p.c. Socialist Film Council; d., ph. Rudolph Messel; cast: Naomi Mitchison, Terence Greenidge, Raymond Postgate, Ian Fox, Daisy Postgate; d.c. SFC
16mm, b/w, silent, 903 ft.
print location: NFA (incomplete)
first screening: July 1933

RUSSIA, 1936 (1936)
d., ph. G.R. Strauss, MP; d.c. Kino
16mm, b/w, silent, [10 mins.]

RUSSIAN JOURNEY (1937)
p.c. Film and Photo League
9.5mm, b/w, silent
Note – this film may not have been completed.

SCOTLAND SPEAKS (1938)
p.c., d.c. Scottish People's Association
9.5mm, b/w, silent
first screening: August 1938

SPAIN 1936-1937 (1937)
p.c. Film and Photo League; ph. Ivan Seruya and others
16mm, b/w and colour, silent
Note – this film may not have been completed.

SPAIN TO-DAY (1938)
d., ph. G.R. Strauss, MP; d.c. Kino
16mm, b/w, silent, [10 mins.]

SPANISH ABC (1938)
p.c. Progressive Film Institute; d. Thorold Dickinson; ph. Arthur Graham, Alan Lawson; asst. Philip Leacock, Ray Pitt; supervised by Ivor Montagu; d.c. PFI, Kino (for 16mm version)
35mm, b/w, sound, 1725 ft.
print location: NFA, ETV
first screening: 26 June 1938

SPANISH TRAVAIL (alt. title THE SPANISH DANCE) (1938)
p.c., d.c. Film and Photo League
16mm, colour, silent
first screening: January 1938
film on Spain, cut to the sound of the mass recitation of Jack Lindsay's 'On Guard for Spain' (Unity Records).

THE SPIRIT OF MAY DAY (1937)
p.c., d.c. Film and Photo League
9.5mm, b/w, silent
print location: NFA
first screening: June 1937

SPORT (1939)
p.c. Workers' Film Association for the British Workers' Sports Association; ph. Tom Barnes; d.c. WFA
16mm, b/w, silent

SUSSEX 1939 (alt. title PEOPLE'S SCRAPBOOK 1939) (1939)
p.c. People's Newsreels for the Sussex District of the CPGB; d. Ernie Trory; ph. Norman Trearson; asst. Ralph Sydenham; d.c. People's Newsreels
9.5mm, b/w, silent, [12 mins.]
print location: NFA ETV (16mm blow-up)

TENANTS IN REVOLT (1939)
p.c. British Film Unit; d.c. Kino
16mm

TESTIMONY OF NON-INTERVENTION (1938)
p.c. Progressive Film Institute; d. Ivor Montagu; d.c. PFI
35mm, b/w, sound, 2984 ft.
print location: NFA
first screening: July 1938

TOM MANN'S 80th BIRTHDAY (1936)
d., ph. J.E. Richardson
16mm, b/w, silent, 327 ft.
print location: ETV, NFA

TOMORROW, TOMORROW (1936)
p.c. Vanguard Film Association; d. N.C. Stoneham
Note – this film may not have been completed.

TOUCH WOOD (1936)
p.c. Kino; d. Frank Jackson; cast Tom Davies
16mm
Note – this film may not have been completed.

TRANSPORT (1935)
p.c. Workers' Film and Photo League; members of production
group Frank Jackson, Pete Davis; d.c. Kino
16mm, b/w, silent, [15 mins.]
first screening: May 1935

A TRIP TO RUSSIA (1934)
p.c., d.c. Kino
16mm, b/w, silent, [25 mins.]

?UTOPIA (1938)
d. Frank A.W. Cox
16mm, b/w, sound
first screening: March 1938

THE VOICE OF THE PEOPLE (1939)
p.c. Realist Film Unit for the Workers' Film Association; p.
Ralph Bond; d. Frank Sainsbury; sc. Ritchie Calder; ph. A.E.
Jeakins; comm. Ted Willis, Lewis Casson; sd. H.G. Halstead;
m. Lennox Berkeley, played by members of the East Ham
Co-op. Orchestra and sung by the New Malden and West Ham

Co-op. Choral Societies; sp. Five London Co-operative Societies; d.c. WFA
16mm, b/w, sound, 635 ft.
print location: NFA, ETV
first screening: September 1939

WE ARE THE ENGLISH (1936)
p.c., d.c. Kino
16mm, b/w, silent, 293 ft.
print location: NFA
first screening: October 1936

WEMBLEY PAGEANT (1937)
p.c. London Co-operative Society
16mm, b/w, sound, 1521 ft.
print location: NFA

WFA NEWSREEL (1939)
p.c., d.c. Workers' Film Association
16mm, colour, silent

WHAT THE NEWSREEL DOES NOT SHOW (1933)
p.c. Socialist Film Council; ph. Rudolph Messel and others; d.c. SFC
16mm, b/w, silent
print location: Metropolis Pictures Ltd. (incomplete)
first screening: July 1933

WINTER (1936)
p.c. Film and Photo League; members of production group Ralph Bond, Irene Nicholson, Jack Goldman, Pete Davis, Alf Pizer, Sam Handel, Frank Jackson, Richard NcNaughton; d.c. Kino, from 1937 FPL
16mm, b/w, silent, 318 ft.
print location: NFA

WORKERS AT THEIR SUMMER SCHOOL (1934)
p.c., d.c. Kino
16mm, b/w, silent
first screening: 28 September 1934, London

WORKERS' EDUCATION (1937)
p.c., d.c. Royal Arsenal Co-operative Society
b/w, sound

WORKERS' NEWSREEL No.1 (1934)
p.c., d.c. Kino
16mm, b/w, silent, 236 ft.
print location: NFA (incomplete)
first screening: August 1934
Note – the original version also included an item on the
Blackshirt meeting at Olympia and the counter-
demonstrations.

WORKERS' NEWSREEL No.2 (1934)
p.c. Kino; ph. John Turner and others; asst. Charlie Mann;
d.c. Kino
16mm, b/w, silent, 377 ft.
print location: NFA
first screening: October 1934

WORKERS' NEWSREEL No.3 (alt. titles MASS UNITED
ACTION BEAT THE UAB, THE UAB FILM) (1935)
p.c. Workers' Film and Photo League; members of production
group John Maltby, Frank Cox, Pete Davis, John Turner, Alf
Pizer; d.c. Kino
16mm, b/w, silent, 282 ft.
print location: NFA, ETV
first screening: March 1935
Note – a recut version of this newsreel was distributed under the
title UAB FILM by the Film and Photo League from 1937.

WORKERS' NEWSREEL No.4 (1935)
p.c. Workers' Film and Photo League; members of production
group J. Harris, John Maltby, John Turner, Alf Pizer; d.c.
Kino
16mm, b/w, silent, [approx. 15 mins.]
print location: NFA, ETV (incomplete)
Note – some episodes, shot on 35mm, have been preserved.

WORKERS' TOPICAL NEWS No.1 (1930)
p.c. Atlas Film Co. for the Federation of Workers' Film

Societies; ph. W. Mumford, ed. Ralph Bond; d.c. Atlas Film Co.
35mm, b/w, silent, 305 ft.
print location: NFA
first screening: 9 March 1930

WORKERS' TOPICAL NEWS No.2 (1930)
p.c. Atlas Film Co. for the Federation of Workers' Film Societies; ed. Ralph Bond; d.c. Atlas Film Co.
35mm, b/w, silent, 738 ft.
print location: NFA
first screening: 4 May 1930, London

WORKERS' TOPICAL NEWS No.3 (1931)
p.c. Atlas Film Co. for the Federation of Workers' Film Societies; ph. Jack Brewin and others; ed. Ralph Bond; d.c. Atlas Film Co.
35mm, b/w, silent
first screening: 1 March 1931.

YOUTH PEACE PILGRIMAGE (1939)
16mm, b/w, silent, 400 ft.
print location: NFA, ETV
Note – this film may not have been released.

Bibliography

Note – This bibliography only lists recent English-language literature. A wide range of original texts from the 1930s has been reprinted in Don Macpherson (ed.), in collaboration with Paul Willemen, *Traditions of Independence: British Cinema in the Thirties*, London 1980. Literature on the left theatre, literature, arts, etc. of the 1930s is so abundant that its inclusion would have stretched this bibliography far beyond its limits.

Douglas Allen, 'Workers' Films: Scotland's Hidden Film Culture' in Colin McArthur (ed.), *Scotch Reels: Scotland in Cinema and Television*, London 1982, pp.93-9.

Ralph Bond, 'Workers' Films: Past and Future', *Labour Monthly*, Vol.58 No.1, January 1976, pp.27-30.

Ralph Bond, 'Cinema in the Thirties: Documentary Film and the Labour Movement' in Jon Clark, Margot Heinemann, David Margolies, Carole Snee (eds.), *Culture and Crisis in Britain in the Thirties*, London 1979, pp.241-56.

Terry Dennett, 'England: The (Workers') Film & Photo League' in *Photography/Politics: One*, London 1979, pp.100-17.

Bert Hogenkamp, 'Film and the Workers' Movement in Britain, 1929-39', *Sight and Sound*, Vol.45 No.2, Spring 1976, pp.68-76.

Bert Hogenkamp, 'Workers' Newsreels in the 1920's and 1930's', *Our History* No.68, [Autumn 1977].

Bert Hogenkamp, 'Making Films with a Purpose: Film-making and the Working Class' in Jon Clark et al., op.cit., pp.257-69.

Bert Hogenkamp, 'The Workers' Film Movement in Britain, 1929-39' in Nicholas Pronay, D.W. Spring (eds), *Propaganda, Politics and Film, 1918-45*, London 1982, pp.144-56.

Jonathan Lewis, 'Before Hindsight', Sight and Sound, Vol.46 No.2, Spring 1977, pp.68-73.

Rachael Low, *The History of the British Film, 1929-1939: Films of Comment and Persuasion of the 1930s,* London 1979.

Don Macpherson, 'Constructions of Reality', *Framework,* No.9, Winter 1978/79, pp.27-29.

Paul Marris, 'Politics and "Independent" Film in the Decade of Defeat' in Don Macpherson (ed.), op.cit., pp.70-95.

Trevor Ryan, 'Film and Political Organisations in Britain 1929-39' in Don Macpherson (ed.), op.cit., pp.51-69.

Trevor Ryan, ' "The New Road To Progress": the Use and Production of Films by the Labour Movement, 1929-39' in James Curran, Vincent Porter (eds), *British Cinema History,* London 1983, pp.113-28.

Anna Shepherd, 'Helen Biggar and Norman McLaren. Based on a MS "Helen Unlimited" ', *New Edinburgh Review,* No.40, February 1978, pp.25-6.

Victoria Wegg-Prosser, 'The Archive of the Film and Photo League' *Sight and Sound,* Vol.46 No.4, Autumn 1977, pp.245-7.

Victoria Wegg-Prosser, 'England: The Hugh Cuthbertson Collection' in *Photography/Politics: One,* op.cit., pp.119-20.

Index